Creative Morality

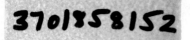

Creative Morality

Creative Morality

Don MacNiven

London and New York

First published 1993
by Routledge
11 New Fetter Lane, London EC4P 4EE

Simultaneously published in the USA and Canada
by Routledge
29 West 35th Street, New York, NY 10001

© 1993 Don MacNiven

Typeset in Baskerville by
Megaron, Cardiff, Wales
Printed in Great Britain by
T. J. Press(Padstow) Ltd, Padstow, Cornwall

British Library Cataloguing in Publication Data
MacNiven, Don
  Creative Morality
  I. Title
  170

Library of Congress Cataloging in Publication Data
MacNiven, Don
  Creative Morality / Don MacNiven.
    p. cm.
  1. Ethics. I. Title.
BJ1012.M3285   1993
171--dc20 92-30808

ISBN 0-415-00029-7 (hbk)
ISBN 0-415-00030-0 (pbk)

Contents

Preface

This book grew, in part, out of a radio series on practical ethics, entitled 'Making a Moral Choice', which I developed for Margaret Norquay, who was then the director of the Open College at Ryerson Polytechnical Institute in Toronto. The series, which consisted of twelve one-hour programmes, was broadcast by Open College/CJRT FM, from 10 February to 30 April 1985. The series was part of a wider investigation I was conducting into the relations between ethical theory and practical ethics, which led me beyond the confines of the academy into the living world of everyday morality. Besides teaching my regular courses on ethical theory, the history of ethics and practical ethics at York University, Toronto, I became involved in several public projects. My assumption was that no progress could be made with contemporary moral issues without some first-hand experience of them. I participated in TV Ontario's project 'The Moral Question' from 1979 to 1980, producing a text on ethical theory for it. I was a member of the 'Moral Values Advisory Committee' of the Board of Education for the city of North York, Ontario, from 1981 to 1984. I was on the board of directors of the 'Ontario Patient's Right's Association' from 1981 to 1985, and was chair of the Canadian Society for the Study of Practical Ethics from 1987 to 1990. I conducted seminars on practical ethics for business and health care professionals. With my colleague Harold Bassford, I organized a series of seminars at York University on professional ethics, which were later published in 1990 by Routledge under the title *Moral Expertise*.

All these activities have contributed in diverse ways to the making of this book. Although the book is essentially a work in theoretical ethics, it has its soul in the lived experiences of ordinary people who grapple with moral problems on a daily basis. Without their concern and insight, ethical theory would be empty.

Parts of the book have appeared in print before in slightly different forms: *The Moral Question: Ethical Theory*, TV Ontario, Toronto, 1982; 'Towards a Unified Theory of Ethics', in Douglas Odegard (ed.), *Ethics and Justification*, Academic Printing & Publishing, Edmonton, Alberta, 1987; 'The Idea of a Moral Expert', in my *Moral Expertise*, Routledge, London, 1990; 'Business Ethics in the Global Village', in Douglas Odegard and Carole Stewart (eds), *Perspectives on Moral Relativism*, Agathon Books, Toronto, 1991. I thank the editors and publishers of these works for allowing me to integrate some of this material into this book.

I would also like to thank Margaret Norquay for her help and insight in producing the radio series 'Making a Moral Choice' on which this book is partly based; the Department of Philosophy at the University of Leeds, especially Jennifer and Christopher Jackson, for their useful comments on the parts of the book which I read to them at Leeds in November 1990; the members of the Department of Health and Society at the Tema Research Institute, Linköping University, Linköping, Sweden, especially Professor Lennart Nordenfelt, who was my host when I lectured on my book there in 1990. I found their responses to my work extremely insightful and valuable. I would like to thank my research assistants, Mary Takacs and Deanne Rexe for helping with the footnotes and Lori Tureski for her help with the text. The index was produced with the aid of a grant from the Faculty of Arts, York University, Toronto, Canada.

I would also like to thank my daughter Maia and her husband Gordon Baird for their computer wizardry. Finally I owe a special debt to my wife Elina for her patience. She is a writer who understands better than most of us how to establish the proper balance of attachment and detachment to one's creative work.

Don MacNiven
York University
Toronto
June 1992

Introduction

'Making a Moral Choice', the 1985 Ryerson Open College radio series out of which this book developed, was essentially a philosophical study of moral dilemmas. Each programme, prepared with the help of Margaret Norquay, who was the director of Open College at the time, featured a pre-taped discussion of a specific moral dilemma, a critical philosophical commentary by myself, and selected comments from participants and listeners, read and discussed by Margaret and myself. The pre-taped discussions were unrehearsed and unsupervised. As Margaret explained in the introductory programme:

> We gathered together various groups of friends and neighbours and acquaintances, and met in someone's living room and taped a discussion of each dilemma. No one knew what he or she was going to talk about until their arrival. There was no moderator, no expert, no celebrity – just folks. We had the kind of discussion you might well have in your own family or at work when someone has read something in the paper or heard something over the air and wondered was that the morally right thing to do?[1]

Once broadcast, the dilemmas were discussed with groups of students supervised by Margaret, myself and others from the Open College/Ryerson Polytechnical Institute and York University, Toronto. Some of the participants were enrolled in the course for a university credit, others were taking it out of interest as a non-credit course, and some were listeners who just tuned in. The purpose of the series was to heighten the awareness of the ethical systems most of us use to make our moral decisions, and to provide an opportunity for people to discuss critically some important contemporary moral issues. In my commentaries I always offered solutions to the dilemmas from two different philosophical perspectives. I tried to establish first that the answers we give to our moral dilemmas are theory-dependent, and that in western cultures like Canada we tend to rely on two basic ethical traditions to solve our moral problems. I called these traditions 'utilitarian' and 'Kantian', because the names were associated with the most sophisticated ethical theories which had been developed by contemporary moral philosophers.

In the series I made no attempt to provide definitive answers to the dilemmas. I assumed that it was not the job of a practical ethicist to dictate answers to the audience. As I said in the introductory programme:

> It's not the job of the moral philosopher to tell anyone else what they ought to do. It's important to distinguish between the moralist and the moral philosopher. A moralist is someone who's trying to convert others to his moral principles. And this may sometimes be the appropriate thing to do. Being a moralist is not intrinsically bad. But in this project that we're doing preaching has no place.[2]

I accepted the principle of freedom of thought and conscience as a necessary presupposition of any project in practical ethics. As I remarked in the discussion guide which I prepared, with Margaret's help, for the series:

> Unless moral philosophers address their audiences as if they were rational moral agents who are capable of making up their own minds about right and wrong, any project in practical ethics is bound to fail. To do otherwise is to try to persuade others to accept values that are not their own and to deny the autonomy which makes rational discussion of moral questions possible.[3]

I assumed that ultimately everyone has to decide for themselves what is right or wrong, to act in accordance with their decisions and to accept the consequences of their conduct. The primacy of moral autonomy was a moral absolute for the project, and indeed ought to be for any valid form of moral education.

Many of the dilemmas used in the series were ones I had employed for some time in my lectures in moral philosophy at York University. Others were developed specifically for the series. Because of the success of the series, I continued to use that set of dilemmas in my lectures in practical ethics and ethical theory at York University, from then till now. During that time the dilemmas evolved, in dialogue with my classes and colleagues, until they reached the form in which they are discussed in this book. Some changed more than others; some barely at all. Many of the changes were related to making the contrast between the Kantian and utilitarian perspectives more distinct. Others were changed to bring them closer to the real situations on which they were based or to the real experiences of the students who attended my lectures. In most cases the dilemma grew in size and changed from the curt description of an abstract logical puzzle into something more like a concrete detailed parable.

One of the things I discovered in working with moral dilemmas is that they have both an objective and subjective side. What appeared to be a dilemma for one person or group did not appear to be a dilemma to other persons or groups. Logically, a moral dilemma is a situation in which moral principles yield conflicting prescriptions. This is the objective side of the dilemma. In the introductory programme I defined a moral dilemma as follows:

> The simplest definition of a moral dilemma is that it is a conflict between two moral principles to which we feel equally committed. You know we often find ourselves in situations where we have to choose between two alternative courses of action, each of which is morally questionable.[4]

In order for a dilemma to be real for a particular individual he or she had to accept both of the conflicting values. If both alternatives did not have an equally strong claim for someone, he or she would not see the situation as a moral dilemma. Often there was an emotive component to an individual's response which strongly affected the way a dilemma was perceived and resolved. This is the subjective side of the dilemma.

As one would expect, there was no consensus on any of the dilemmas, either in the classroom or among the radio audiences. In some cases the majority of the participants looked at the dilemma in similar ways and reached similar conclusions. But there was always one, and usually more, who approached the dilemma from a different perspective and arrived at an opposing answer. In other cases people wanted to alter the dilemma, to add material to make the episode more realistic or more lively or more complete. In one, someone thought the problem lay not in the dilemma but in why anyone would get themselves involved in such moral perplexity in the first place. No systematic empirical study of the participants' responses to the dilemmas was done. Still it was clear that the way they responded depended heavily on the ethical systems which controlled their thinking, and the systems most often appealed to were versions of utilitarianism or Kantianism. To encourage the reader to respond personally to the dilemmas I have appended the original Open College dilemmas, and attached a set of questions which should help in their analysis, at the end of this book.[5]

The second thing I have learned from teaching practical ethics over the years is that the function of the dilemma in our moral experience and in education is more complicated than I had first supposed. The dilemma is a type of case study and hypothetical cases have always been used by philosophers to illustrate or develop ethical theories. The cases used by philosophers are often contrived and unrealistic, yet they can be valuable analytic tools. Take Nozick's example of the 'experience machine', which he uses to demonstrate the inadequacy of utilitarianism:

> Suppose there were an experience machine that would give you any experience you desired. Superduper neuropsychologists could stimulate your brain so that you would think and feel that you were writing a great novel, or making a friend, or reading an interesting book. All the time you would be floating in a tank, with electrodes attached to your brain. Should you plug into this machine for life, preprogramming your life's experiences?[6]

If we believe that happiness/enjoyment is the sole intrinsic good, as the utilitarians do, then it would seem that we ought to hook ourselves up to the experience machine for life. Intuitively, however, we sense that there is something wrong with doing this. If we had the opportunity to do so, most of us would not hook up to the machine for life, although many might want to try it out for a brief period for kicks. We do not want to exchange reality for contentment, because we would no longer be able to tell when our desires were irrational. Real fears and phobias would be indistinguishable. Also we want to live active and not simply passive existences, and the machine prevents us from doing this. The machine also limits our experience by cutting us off from other human beings. If we stayed on it for life we would soon lose our personal identity because of our lack of interaction with others. Since there are no 'experience machines', as they are the stuff of science fiction, not science, this doesn't prove a great deal. However, if the argument does not refute utilitarianism it shows that theory is out of touch with our ordinary moral values, many of which are clearly non-utilitarian. Even if unrealistic hypothetical examples cannot be used to test or validate a theory, they could, as Jonathan Glover suggests, help us to discover what our deep values, the things we really cherish, are. Glover's philosophical thought experiments enlighten but they cannot prove:

On the conventional view, nothing is more damning than the criticism that some issue being discussed is based on assumptions that are 'unrealistic'. On this view, the way to think about issues like behaviour control is to avoid far out science fiction cases, and confine our thinking to the developments that, from the present perspective, seem likely. I hold the opposite view. In thinking about the desirability of various developments, it is often best deliberately to confront the most extreme possibility. Why is this? Thinking about the desirability of different futures cannot be separated from thinking about present values. And our values often become clearer when we consider imaginary cases where conflicts can be made sharp.[7]

In practical ethics, case studies have been put to a different use. There they are often employed to further a moral argument. Suppose, to use one of Glover's thought experiments, that we possessed a machine which could read minds. Wouldn't such a thought machine pose so serious a threat to human privacy that it ought to be banned?[8] This is an interesting question, but what relevance does it have for our ordinary lives as we are not likely to produce such a machine in the foreseeable future? An artificial example like this might illuminate our moral experience, but how could it test the validity of a moral judgement when there is such a lack of correspondence between the hypothetical and the real situation? As John T. Noonan Jr has pointed out:

> One way to reach the nub of a moral issue is to construct a hypothetical situation endowed with precisely the characteristics you believe are crucial in the real issue you are seeking to resolve. Isolated from the clutter of detail in the real situation, these characteristics point to the proper solution. The risk is that features you believe crucial you will enlarge to the point of creating a caricature. The pedagogy of your illustration will be blunted by the uneasiness caused by the lack of correspondence between the fantasized situation and the real situation to be judged.[9]

Noonan uses Michael Tooley's arguments justifying abortion to illustrate the problem with artificial cases. Tooley had argued that the foetus cannot be given a right to life simply because it will develop into an adult human being who will have a right to life, thus abortion is morally permissible. He uses the following hypothetical example to establish his thesis that potentiality for rational adulthood is not sufficient to support a right-to-life claim.[10] Suppose a chemical could be injected into a kitten which would enable it to develop into a cat possessed of the brain and the psychological capabilities of an adult human being. Would it be wrong to kill a kitten which had been so injected, when to do so would be to prevent the development of a rational adult? Tooley argues again that, intuitively, as it would not be wrong to kill the kitten, thus neither would it be wrong to abort a foetus. But as Noonan points out, the analogy is questionable because we do not have the experience to tell us how we would decide if we were actually faced by the hypothetical kitten.

Whether or not Noonan has fairly described Tooley's analogy, his main point is worth attention. Real moral dilemmas cannot be properly captured by lifeless abstractions, no matter how ingenious. If moral dilemmas are to be fruitful in practical ethics they must at least reflect reality. The element of realism must always be there whether we are trying to verify a substantive moral claim, validate an ethical theory or clarify our moral experience. This is why all the hypothetical dilemmas I use are always based on real experiences. We must have at least one foot in reality when doing moral philosophy.

The third thing I learned from teaching practical ethics is the need to develop a unified theory of ethics.[11] Since there is no agreement among philosophers or the general public as to which ethical system is best, philosophy has no real contribution to make in solving contemporary moral problems. Everyone approaches moral dilemmas from different and seemingly incommensurable theoretical perspectives, making public consensus not merely difficult but logically impossible. To be fruitful, practical ethics clearly requires the development of a unified theory of ethics. This still seems to me to be the central project which modern moral philosophy should direct its energies towards, but I now think that this can only be achieved if we shift our attention from prescriptive to descriptive ethical theories. Prescriptive ethical theories are designed, like prescriptive logic, to tell us exactly how to arrive at correct and indisputable answers to our logical or moral problems. Descriptive ethical theories are designed, like descriptive logic, to help us explain and understand our intellectual and moral worlds.

For example, moral dilemmas have been used by philosophers like F.H. Bradley to help us understand the dynamics of moral development.[12] Genuine moral dilemmas always contain a theoretical as well as a practical contradiction at their core. They all have, as I discovered, an objective as well as a subjective side. These inherent inconsistencies naturally disconcert the moral agent and the public, and a desire to resolve the dilemma, to return harmony to the soul and the community, naturally arises. It is the moral dilemma, and similar problems, which fuel moral development at both the personal and social levels. As we shall see in what follows, understanding the dynamics of moral growth will certainly help us in our search for solutions to moral problems. Theoretical ethics does have important contributions to make to practical ethics, but only if it is developed descriptively. Moral progress requires that we try to understand the moral world we inhabit. Our moral experience can be used to test as well as to clarify theoretical ethics. Theoretical and practical ethics are mutually dependent. Moral philosophy is an invitation to explore our moral universe with the same kind of theoretical creativity and intellectual objectivity which science uses to explore the natural universe.

Chapter 1

Private spaces

In our lives we often encounter moral dilemmas. We find ourselves in situations where we have to choose between two alternative courses of action, both of which we find morally questionable. Suppose someone believes in a moral system which respects privacy and recognizes the right to confidentiality. Then the person becomes involved in a situation where the public good appears to require invasions of privacy and breaches of confidentiality. Consider the following hypothetical example, which is based on a real life situation. The Royal Canadian Mounted Police (RCMP) have been trying for a long time to identify and locate the mastermind behind a criminal ring that recruits teenagers into drug peddling and prostitution. The criminal has adopted an assumed identity and as a result is extremely difficult to locate and so more dangerous. The RCMP finally have one lead. They learn from an undercover police agent that the drug king-pin sprained his ankle sometime in August 1977 and had it attended to in a small town Ontario hospital. They go to the appropriate Ontario Health Insurance Plan (OHIP) official and ask to see the patient treatment records for the month of August. Since only a few people will have had sprained ankles attended to during this period, the police think they might be able to get a name or names they can investigate. They plan to photo-copy the information and use it in follow-up investigations. They inform the OHIP official of the urgency and seriousness of their request. The records actually show that 82 people were treated for sprained ankles at the right time and places. This seems a lot, but since one of these must be the criminal the RCMP drug squad is after it gives them something solid to work on. Although the official knows it is standard practice for OHIP to release confidential information to the police in the course of carrying out their legitimate duties, he refuses to release the records to the RCMP. He recognizes that the RCMP are acting in the public interest, but still thinks that releasing information to them would be wrong because it violates patients' privacy and their right to confidentiality of medical information. To do so would be a breach of the general legal obligation of confidentiality which is imposed on all OHIP employees. The police cannot persuade the official to help them and they are unable to pursue their only lead. The drug king-pin continues to elude the police and carries on his vicious trade. Did the OHIP official do the morally right thing?

The OHIP official faces a classic moral dilemma, a problem which puts us into a no-win situation. Whatever the OHIP official does he seems to be doing something wrong. If he refuses to help the police investigation, as he does, then he allows an evil criminal organization to continue to flourish. If he caves in to the police pressure to release the information, he would violate his obligation to protect the privacy and the right to confidentiality of the medical patients who use OHIP. The hypothetical example is based on a real life situation. In the real case the RCMP were actually looking for a deep cover agent of a foreign power, not the leader of a narcotics drug ring.[1] The case was changed from spying to drug dealing because the original case, in which the OHIP official actually released the confidential information to the RCMP, wasn't always regarded as a dilemma. Most thought intuitively that it would be wrong to release the information to the police to catch a spy, but releasing confidential medical records to catch a drug dealer endangering innocent children might be morally acceptable. The spy case seemed to me to be a real dilemma, as it did to many of my students with whom I discussed it. What is a moral dilemma for one person is not always a dilemma for another person. To have a real dilemma requires an equally serious commitment to the conflicting values.

The presence of moral dilemmas in our lives indicates that the moral systems controlling our thought and conduct have broken down and are no longer capable of guiding us. Unless we have an adequate way of resolving dilemmas, our moral systems will remain incoherent and will continue to fail us. Sometimes we resolve conflicts between obligations by ranking them in priority order. If we decide, as the OHIP official did, that protecting patients' rights is morally more important than protecting the public good, then we will refuse to release the confidential medical records to the RCMP. At other times we appeal to more general obligations. Suppose I assent to the principle of social utility, and believe that the most moral act is the one which produces the greatest amount of happiness for the greatest number. I could perhaps justify releasing the information to the police because this appears to produce the most happiness and the least harm.

Both these methods of resolving moral dilemmas depend on making appeals to developed ethical theories. This is obvious in the latter case because of the reference to the principle of social utility. But ranking obligations also presupposes an appeal to theory because there must be some standard against which the obligations are compared and weighed, otherwise the ranking would be arbitrary. In any case, rational answers to moral dilemmas appear to be theory-dependent; they all have an intellectual frame of reference, in terms of which they make sense.

The way in which a moral dilemma is resolved then often depends on the ethical theory which is directly or tacitly appealed to. Generally in western cultures we appeal to one of two main ethical traditions, which I call the conservative Kantian and the liberal utilitarian traditions. These traditions differ from each other in many significant ways, and because they do they often, although not always, arrive at conflicting answers to the same moral problems. These theories have been developed in different ways in western philosophical thought and recent moral philosophy, but there is no agreement among professional philosophers as to which form of either theory is the best. To discuss this dilemma I will develop the theories in ways which emphasize their differences rather than their similarities.[2]

The theories differ from each other both epistemologically and morally. Some epistemological differences first. For example, the methods the two systems use to justify moral judgements are basically different. The utilitarian holds that the rightness or wrongness of actions is determined by the actual consequences. Kantians, on the other hand, hold that the rightness or wrongness of actions is determined by the motive of duty or conscientiousness. They are non-consequentialists, who hold that an action is right if it conforms to a rationally acceptable moral rule. The actual consequences are irrelevant. It is the intent of the moral agent which is important. A moral rule is shown to be acceptable if it can be made into a universal natural law, valid for all rational agents.

The theories also view the function of rules in moral reasoning quite differently. The utilitarians are particularists, who believe that the rightness or wrongness of an action depends on the context or situation. For the utilitarian, particular experience always takes epistemological priority over moral rules. A well-established particular case always overrides a useful moral rule, hence all moral rules are likely to have exceptions. If a breach of confidentiality in a specific set of circumstances would produce a greater amount of happiness on the whole, then it would be morally right to break a confidence. For the Kantian, however, moral rules always take epistemological priority over particular experience. If an action is inconsistent with a universal law valid for all rational agents, then it is morally wrong. The Kantians are universalists, who hold that moral rules apply equally to everyone. The rightness or wrongness of an action does not depend on the context or situation. A true universal moral rule can have no exceptions. Respect for confidentiality is one such rule, hence it is always wrong to break a confidence. This analysis holds in spite of the fact that modern ethical theorists have developed elegant forms of rule-utilitarianism and act-deontologism, and theories which combine elements of act and rule systems.[3]

Utilitarian and Kantian moral principles also differ radically from each other. The first principle of utilitarian morality is the principle of utility: you ought to do that action which will produce the greatest happiness for the greatest number or maximize happiness/minimize suffering. The morality of an action is determined by its social utility. The first principle of Kantian morality is the principle of respect for persons: always treat persons, including oneself, as ends in themselves and never merely as a means. Social utility can never be an overriding consideration, because we cannot use anyone merely as a means to someone else's well-being. Another significant moral difference between the traditions is that for the utilitarian a good end always justifies the means, provided it does not produce more harm than good, while for the Kantian ends, however good, cannot justify means which violate the principle of respect for persons. The utilitarian subscribes to the principle of expediency, while the Kantian subscribes to the Pauline principle that you cannot do evil in order to do good. 'Why not indeed "do evil that good may come", as some libellously report me as saying'?[4]

The systems differ from each other in many other significant ways, and they will be developed more fully in the next chapter.[5] The differences already noted will be sufficient to illustrate the way ethical systems often control the resolution of moral dilemmas. To see this more clearly, let's apply these two traditions to the dilemma faced by the OHIP official.

The question raised in the dilemma is whether confidential medical information ought to be released to help a legitimate police investigation. If the OHIP official relied on the utilitarian tradition, which adopts the principle of social utility as the first principle of ethics, he would be likely to release the information to the police. If he relied on the Kantian tradition, which adopts the principle of respect for persons as the first principle of ethics, he would not be likely to release the information to the police.

Let us look at a utilitarian response to the dilemma first. In this tradition the rightness or wrongness of an action is determined by whether it maximizes happiness and minimizes suffering. The utilitarian would support releasing the confidential medical information because doing so would be the most socially useful thing to do. The police are trying to nab the head of a nasty crime organization which recruits innocent teenagers into drug peddling and prostitution. Stopping the leader's criminal activities would clearly benefit society as a whole and would pose little threat to others whose records would be released to the police. There is, of course, the possibility of incriminating innocent people. The utilitarian would argue that the probability of innocent people being harmed in this instance is quite remote, so the risk is acceptable. In the actual case there was some risk because 82 health claims were photo-copied and so far as anyone can determine still remain in the possession of the RCMP in Ottawa, where they pose a potential threat to 81 innocent people. If they are filed in the Canadian Police Information Centre data banks, then the risk is real because many government departments, agencies and crown corporations have access to this information.[6] However, if this criminal is allowed to roam at large, great harm will be done to many adolescents and their families. The utilitarian would point out that OHIP officials routinely released confidential health information to the police, and that it was OHIP policy to co-operate fully with law enforcement agencies performing their legitimate duties.

The utilitarian would also have to consider the long range effects releasing the information would have on our general practice of respecting individual privacy. Wouldn't releasing the information undermine the trust citizens have that the government will protect their privacy? However, this undesirable side-effect will only happen if the release is made public. In this case there is no reason to think that anyone except the two investigating officers and the OHIP official would know about it, so no harm would be done to the practice. Besides, releasing this type of information to the police has done no harm in the past, and would not be likely to do any in this instance.

Even if this consequence is unavoidable, and the practice is threatened, utilitarians might still argue that releasing the information is morally acceptable because privacy itself is not essential to our well-being. They could argue that a world without privacy would be better than the secretive world in which we now live.[7] Why do we need privacy anyway? To protect us from our enemies and our competitors, perhaps. But imagine what it would be like to live in a world without privacy, a world in which we did not keep secrets from or lie to each other. Wouldn't a totally open society eliminate crime, spying and dishonest business practices? To achieve this we would have to produce a more co-operative and less competitive society than we presently have, in the west at least, but would this be such a bad thing? There are perhaps some secrets we would like to keep, even in an open society. We might not want to tell someone that we think the latest painting he or she has acquired is wanting in taste. Perfect honesty can hurt the feelings of others. And of course we may have skeletons in our closets which we dare not share even with those we are closest to, far less with strangers. However, both these problems could be overcome if we learn to give and receive criticism in constructive ways.

We certainly could use more openness and co-operation in our society, but it is not clear that creatures like ourselves could survive the pure sunlight of totally honest human relationships. During an examination of a middle-aged patient who wanted a check-up before going on a rare two-week vacation, a doctor discovers the patient has terminal cancer. The patient has at best six months to live. Should the doctor tell the patient or not? If the patient asks him directly, should he lie? Clearly to tell the truth would cause considerable unnecessary pain and destroy what little happiness the patient has left. In some cases ignorance is bliss. So why not lie and let the patient enjoy his holiday? Being totally honest isn't always in people's best interests. What is more, we live in a world in which we cannot always trust our neighbours to be concerned about our well-being; even if they are, they would be less likely to understand what our best interests are than we would ourselves. This is even more certain when we consider the state, whose capacity for the invasion of privacy is so great and so ominous, especially when coupled with bureaucratic indifference to the individual and with advances in computer technology which so greatly increase its capacity to collect, retain and access information about its citizens. In the computer age, privacy is at risk and needs more than ever to be jealously guarded.[8] Privacy, it would seem, is also an essential ingredient of a democratic state. To fail to protect individual privacy is to take the first step down the road that leads to a totalitarian police state. Since utilitarians believe democracy is more likely than a police state to produce the greatest happiness of the greatest number, they are committed to protecting individual privacy.[9]

The utilitarians would also have to consider the effect on the health care system of releasing confidential medical information. Doctors need the truth from patients in order to cure them. But patients will not freely tell their doctors or their psychiatrists the truth unless confidentiality is guaranteed. This is especially so if the truth embarrasses patients or leaves them vulnerable. If patients believe health care professionals won't guarantee confidentiality they will be less open about their past history than good medical practice requires. It follows that health care professionals should not release confidential medical information without the patient's consent.

However, having provided a standard utilitarian defence of privacy does not imply that releasing confidential information without a patient's consent is always wrong. Utilitarians would point out that in practice confidentiality is not absolute. We already make exceptions to the rule and our health care system is still functioning well enough. In fact, absolute confidentiality would hamper good medical practice. For example, medical information needs to be released to all the health care professionals who are participating in a patient's care. It would be impractical, even dangerous, to consult with patients every time their cases were being discussed with other professionals. In some countries doctors are legally required to report gunshot and stab wounds to the police, and they do not need a patient's permission to do so. If the police are going to control violent crime, they need access to information which criminals would be loath to release, so their right to confidentiality cannot always be respected.[10]

In some countries health care professionals are required to report a contagious disease which is a threat to public health. Surely no one would object to a doctor reporting venereal disease even if the patient wanted it to be kept secret. Moreover, in some societies health care professionals are also required to report cases of child abuse. To ask permission would merely alert the child abusers to the fact that the doctor is on to them.[11] Some health care officials think that they should be allowed to inform others, especially spouses and sexual partners, when a patient has AIDS, even when the patient refuses to give consent.[12] Again, it is argued that the public good overrides the patient's right to confidentiality in these unusual circumstances, and this is reflected in current legal practice. To quote Gilbert Sharpe, an expert on medical law in Canada:

Physicians and other health care professionals must remember that, except where there are clear legal duties to report, they are not required to volunteer information about their patients, even to the police. In fact, in most circumstances and jurisdictions there is an obligation to maintain secrecy under provincial confidentiality laws. A decision to volunteer information to the police should only be made in the very rare, exceptional circumstances, that cannot safely be handled in any other way (e.g., a hostage taking, espionage, terrorism); the minimal amount of essential information should then be disclosed; and only after an assurance of confidentiality has been given by a fairly high ranking police officer.[13]

There are other exceptions to the rule of confidentiality relating to apprehending criminals and to public safety for which strong cases can be made. A couple of examples will explain the utilitarian's point. Most will remember the American case of Richard Speck, the mass murderer, who killed eight nurses in Chicago in the mid-1960s.[14] The police had set up a nationwide search for Speck because they knew he was extremely dangerous and would likely kill again. Speck went to a doctor to cure a minor medical problem. The doctor recognized him from a police 'wanted' poster in the hospital and reported the visit. The utilitarian would argue that the doctor did the right thing in breaking his patient's confidence and reporting the visit to the police, because Speck was apprehended, tried, convicted of first-degree murder, sent to jail for life, and the lives of other nurses were certainly saved, for Speck had planned to kill again. The actual consequences justified the breach of confidentiality. Most will also remember another American case – that of Charles Whitman, the man who slaughtered 15 people with sniper fire from a university tower in Austin, Texas, in the late 1960s.[15] Apparently, before he committed this horrendous crime, he had informed his psychiatrist of his intention to do so. He even mentioned a tower and his desire to kill people with sniper fire. The psychiatrist, however, did not warn the police because he felt he should always keep a patient's revelations confidential. The utilitarian would argue that what he did was morally wrong, because keeping the confidence produced more harm than good for everyone affected. The actual consequences did not justify keeping the confidence.

The utilitarian also believes that health care professionals have a duty to warn others if a patient is a real danger to him or herself. A patient tells her psychiatrist that she is so despondent that she intends to kill herself. The utilitarian would argue that the psychiatrist ought to inform both the police and perhaps the patient's relatives if there is real danger that the patient will attempt suicide, causing great harm to herself and unhappiness to others.

Utilitarians would point out that we have made many exceptions to the rule of confidentiality without destroying our health care system. Releasing confidential medical information would be similar in the OHIP case, since no harm would be done. The utilitarians could correctly point out that democracy would not be damaged nor the doctor–patient relationship undermined, so long as the breach of confidentiality were not made public or officially legitimized. In this case, there should be no reason why anyone except the OHIP official and the police should be aware of what happened. So on balance, the desirable consequences would outweigh the undesirable ones and the confidential medical information should be released.

That's a utilitarian response to the dilemma. Now let us look at a Kantian response. The Kantian would think it is morally wrong to release confidential medical information, because it is inconsistent with the principles of respect for persons and respect for human rights. The Kantian sees the doctor–patient relationship as one between two autonomous persons who are centres of value. Because it is an interpersonal relationship, it presupposes the principle of respect for persons. Respect for persons entails respect by the health care professionals for the moral and legitimate legal rights of patients. In Canada, for example, these legal rights include the right to refuse treatment, the right to informed consent and, most important for the OHIP case, the rights to confidentiality and to personal privacy.[16] Although it was standard practice for OHIP to release confidential health information to law enforcement agencies, doing so violated section 44 of the 1972 Ontario Health Insurance Act, which places a general obligation of confidentiality on all OHIP employees. To give the information to the RCMP would be to break the law.[17]

The Kantians value privacy because it protects the dignity and the moral integrity of the person, and not simply because it protects them from harm, which is the utilitarian argument. Rational moral agents require not only physical but moral privacy if they are to function as conscientious creatures who must take responsibility for their conduct. For the Kantian, a person's privacy has been breached as soon as anyone becomes privy to information about him or her without consent or without the protection of confidentiality. The Peeping Tom still violates privacy even if he is undetected. It is not just a matter of whether the information is accurate or dangerous to the person, but that his or her personal autonomy is weakened, and self-control is diminished. The Kantian would argue that to release confidential medical information without the consent of the patient is to violate these very important rights, to fail to respect the personhood of the patient.

The Kantians think that utilitarians misunderstand the doctor–patient relationship, because utilitarians see human relationships merely as exercises in mutual self-interest. For utilitarians, all human relationships are essentially instrumental. People use each other merely as a means to their own ends and not as ends in themselves, as moral agents. The patient is seen as a consumer of medical services, the health professional as the seller. The patient wants to be cured, the doctor wants to make a profit. We might call this the commercial view of human relationships. The market model of human relationships has become all-pervasive in the modern world, gradually replacing moral with economic and power relationships based on self-interest. Some human relationships are essentially commercial, but to look on all human relationships in this way is morally unacceptable for the Kantian. The relationships between lovers or friends cannot be interpreted this way, nor can the relationships between teachers and students or doctors and patients. They can all contain commercial elements, and certainly this is an important aspect of a doctor–patient relationship, but it is not its essence. The market model may be advantageous for our business activities, but not for everything we do. Social change is not always progress. For the Kantian, even commercial relations must be based on respect for persons; hence it would be morally wrong for merchants and customers to cheat each other. The market model would allow for indirect obligations to customers. Honesty is good for business, but these obligations can always be overridden for commercial gain. For the Kantian, it is morality rather than profit which is the bottom line. Interpersonal relationships are essentially moral for the Kantian.

According to Kantians, a doctor–patient relationship based entirely on the commercial model would be morally self-defeating. Patients pay for services and they expect to get their money's worth. If they don't get top quality, they are likely to take legal action against the health care professional. The doctor–patient relationship would become adversarial rather than co-operative. Purely commercial relationships encourage people to treat each other as mere means to their own ends, rather than as ends in themselves. Manipulation of others becomes the paradigm for human relationships.

The commercial model also makes it too easy to justify exceptions to confidentiality. Kantians are absolutist when it comes to moral rules. To be consistent, any Kantian system appears to require exceptions to moral rules in order to avoid conflicts. Surely the Kantians must recognize the public welfare as well as individual rights? Surely they must recognize that even if a breach of confidence is immoral it cannot always be immoral, especially when it serves the public good? We have a conflict here between keeping a confidence and the public good, but the Kantian would argue that the conflict is apparent rather than real. The OHIP official's refusal to breach confidentiality would be properly described as an act of honesty and not a betrayal of public trust.[18] Allowing exceptions to rules makes breaking them and violating human rights too easy. Confidentiality is likely to be breached whenever it is expedient to do so. If the police or health care professionals assume it is in the public interest, they will breach it. If health care professionals think it's in their patients' interests, they will breach confidentiality. According to the Kantians, this excuse for breaches of confidentiality is very dangerous because it develops quickly into a vicious form of medical paternalism, which ignores the right of the patient to be an equal partner in his or her health care.

The Kantian would not even be sympathetic to releasing medical information in the case of Speck, the nurse murderer. The Kantian would argue that the health care system should never be used as an arm of the law. Police 'wanted' posters should not have been circulated to health care professionals in the first place. This may be acceptable in a police state but not in a democracy. The Soviet Union's use of the health care system to control political dissidence, at least before the advent of glasnost and the collapse of the Eastern bloc, could be cited as an example of this kind of abuse of a health care system. People who disagreed with those in power were treated as if they were mentally ill and confined to psychiatric institutions.

Even though it might have prevented the tragic killings, the Kantians would argue that Whitman's psychiatrist did the right thing in refusing to release information to the authorities. The deaths were the unintended consequence of a morally right action, i.e. keeping a patient's confidences. It was the Texas sniper's actions, not those of the psychiatrist, which were evil. The psychiatrist did nothing wrong. We cannot be held responsible for the bad unintended consequences of right conduct. For the Kantian, we cannot do evil in order to do good.

The Kantian would conclude that the doctor–patient relationship needs very strong protection, so strict confidentiality must always be maintained. The Kantian would also argue that the purpose of a democratic state is not simply to provide for the greatest good for the greatest number, but to protect human rights. The Kantian would point out that the conduct of the police in the OHIP case raises the question of what their proper function is in a democratic society. Is the prime goal of the police to catch criminals or to protect the rights of citizens? Although Kantians recognize that one of the objectives of the police force is the maintaining of law and order, they believe that this goal should always be subordinate to due legal process. According to Kantians the police should never be above the law. Protecting human rights must always take precedence over catching criminals. The utilitarians are of course also interested in protecting human rights. After all they are democrats too. Still, the Kantian would argue that the principle of social utility implies that rights are always subordinate to the public good and hence can always be overridden. For the Kantian, human rights are paramount so there can be no compromise. Confidential information must never be released without the consent of the patient.

The Kantian would be unhappy with the present laws governing confidentiality of medical information in Canada, for example. In Canada a patient's medical records are legally the property of the doctor. In fact, it is very difficult for Canadian patients to get access to their own medical records, for personal or legal reasons. The Kantian believes that patients should have free access to their medical records and wants the law changed to reflect this right.[19] The Kantian then would argue that the OHIP official did the morally right thing in not releasing confidential medical information to the police.

That was a Kantian response to the dilemma. Now let us sum up. This dilemma involved a conflict between the Kantian principles of respect for persons and respect for human rights, and the utilitarian principles of social utility and expediency, i.e. a good end justifies the means. The two systems do not always produce conflicting answers to moral dilemmas, but in this situation our analysis suggests that they would. In the real dilemma on which this hypothetical problem was based, the protagonists actually appealed to many of these utilitarian arguments to justify the release of the confidential medical information, and to many of the Kantian arguments to justify not releasing the information. Those using utilitarian arguments tended to believe that it is morally permissible to release confidential medical information to the police if it will help them apprehend dangerous criminals, since this appears to benefit society more than not releasing the information. So they would conclude that the OHIP official ought to have released the information to the police. On the other hand, people who relied on Kantian arguments tended to believe that it was morally wrong to release confidential medical information without the consent of the patient.[20] So we are dealing here with real dilemmas and real arguments which give expression to these two systems in our common moral experience. Of course we could be dealing with protagonists who are using the theories inadequately. Perhaps, if properly applied, the two theories might yield the same conclusion. For the argument in this book, it is less important that the utilitarian and Kantian protagonists in this story have the right utilitarian or Kantian answers, than understanding that in some cases we have the right utilitarian and Kantian answers, and that these are incommensurate. What is important is to recognize that the way we answer moral questions does depend on the frame of reference which is implicit in the ethical theory appealed to. Different theories appear to give different answers to the same moral problems. If they did not, why should ethical theorists ever bother to adopt one theory rather than another, and defend them so vigorously, as they do? If the answers the theories produced were all one and the same, why bother defending them at all? If this is the case, then how do we choose between the competing theories? At present that choice appears to be arbitrary because there is no higher unified theory to appeal to, hence ethical theorists cannot fully justify their answers to moral problems.

This is an unhappy situation for moral philosophy, both practically and theoretically, because it ceases to be fully relevant for practical ethics and it cannot account for a fundamental aspect of our moral lives, our experience of moral dilemmas. I have argued elsewhere that what is required to solve practical moral problems is a unified system of ethics.[21] I want to suggest that the current impasse in ethical theory can be overcome if we see moral reasoning as an organic, creative process rather than a mechanistic predictable one. Mechanistic models assume that we can develop a hierarchical system of principles, secondary moral rules and inference procedures which, when properly applied, will allow us to predict correct moral conclusions for all conceivable moral dilemmas. But in practice this is never the case, as our ordinary moral experience shows us. The infinite complexity of particular moral experiences will always defeat a mechanistic casuistry because it cannot capture the uniqueness of growing individuals or developing social institutions.

This observation holds whether the systems are developed deductively, as the Kantians tend to do, or inductively, as the utilitarians tend
to do. Applying the systems with great intellectual ingenuity, as these
systems often require, does not alter the situation. Even if there is no
automatic decision-making procedure produced by these systems,
nothing changes because it is still a matter of applying rules to solve
cases, of applying fixed theory to mutable practice. Since particular
experience instantiates principles and rules, and principles and rules
structure and give meaning to particular experience, any form of linear
thinking, whether 'up' from particulars to rules, or 'down' from rules to
particulars, will fail to express properly the reality of individual moral
experience. Because the individual moral agent is creative and
essentially unpredictable in both thought and action, linear thinking
will be unable to capture the unique process of an individual's or a
society's moral development.

If we adopt an organic model of moral reasoning, the problem of
unpredictability is solved because organic casuistry can account for
and help us to understand patterns of moral development. According
to organic casuistry, when obligations conflict this indicates that the
moral system which is controlling our thought and conduct has
become incoherent. We are in a state of intellectual, emotional and
moral disequilibrium, and we will remain so until the conflict is
resolved. If we try to rid ourselves of the unease by mechanistic or
linear methods of reasoning we will fail to solve our dilemmas, as we
have seen. Moral dilemmas are the death knells of mechanistic
casuistry but not of organic casuistry. To solve a moral dilemma we
have to change or modify our system of morality. But we do not know
what to change: our system of rules, or our conduct. Do we, for
example, hold to our rule protecting individual confidentiality or do
we make an exception for the public good? There is, I would suggest, a
dialectical relation holding between rules and particular moral
experience which is never adequately captured by mechanistic models
of moral reasoning. It is the circle, not the straight line, which is the
proper metaphor for moral thought.

For the utilitarian, particular experiences will always take epistemological precedence over rules, while rules will always take precedence
over particular experience for the Kantian. In practice this means, for
both systems, that a value which is and ought to be respected will fail to
find adequate expression in our social systems and/or our personal
lives. In the OHIP dilemma, the utilitarians abandon the principle of
respect for persons as it is expressed in the principles of respect for

privacy and confidentiality, while the Kantians abandon the principle of social utility as it is expressed in terms of the principle of non-maleficence, in protecting others from harm. The solutions they present are both deficient in significant ways. In each case values are sacrificed and each solution results in a state of affairs which is less morally rich than we would desire.

However, if we understand morality as a process of growth or development, as organic casuistry does, then it follows that to resolve a moral dilemma we need to grow at either the personal or the social level, and often both. Moral dilemmas represent critical moments in the moral development of persons and/or societies. When we confront our moral dilemmas and honestly try to resolve them we will be driven to reach more highly integrated states of affairs both personally and socially. When a moral dilemma has been properly resolved, when we have restructured our personal and social affairs in such a way that we express the conflicting values properly, we and our community will have grown morally. For organic casuistry, moral dilemmas represent opportunities for moral growth rather than situations which always involve making hard choices in which something of great value is usually lost.

Moral growth occurs when we have reached richer and more highly integrated states of affairs, personally or socially. Richness and integration then are the two objective criteria of moral growth. To reach richer and more highly integrated states of affairs requires creative moral thought. Creative thought is an essential characteristic of organic systems of reasoning but not of mechanistic systems of reasoning. Solving moral dilemmas requires more than merely the mechanistic application of rules to particular cases or their simple modification by appeal to particular cases. Moral thought can usefully be compared to scientific thought. As the great nineteenth-century philosopher of science, William Whewell, noted, scientific thought is a process of discovery as well as proof. A mechanistic logic may be devised for proving hypotheses but not for searching for fruitful hypotheses to test. You may produce a set of Cartesian rules for the precise direction of the mind to test hypotheses, but not for discovering them. The process of discovery is essentially a creative process; the process of proof is not, even if it is not automatic.[22] Moral thought is more like the process of discovery than that of proof. The creative challenge for ethical thought is to try to restructure our experience into richer moral wholes. Self-realization is essentially a creative process.

In creative thought the relationship between rules and particular cases is dialectical rather than linear, hence for organic casuistry rules do not automatically take epistemological priority over particular cases or vice versa. In fact we cannot separate rules and particular experience in this absolute way. They are just different aspects of a unified moral experience, which involves interpreting rules for individual cases, or understanding rules in terms of individual cases. There are no particular experiences which are uninterpreted by rules and principles. And rules and principles are only instantiated in particular experience. Universal and particular judgements are internally rather than externally related, as mechanistic theories maintain. For the organicists they are mutually dependent epistemologically. The one would not be what it is without the other. Hence you cannot understand one without understanding its relation to the other. It follows that act and rule theories are also mutually dependent.

If we approach the OHIP dilemma from this idealist perspective we need to apply a principle of coherence which roughly stated says: any state of affairs X is morally better than any state of affairs Y, if X is morally richer, more highly integrated and/or more fecund than Y, where fecund means 'facilitates richness and integration'.[23] This principle of coherence provides us with objective criteria which can guide our attempts to solve complex moral dilemmas and to grow morally. Although we cannot derive answers from them directly, we at least know what we are looking for, what we want to avoid, what an inadequate answer would look like and what an adequate one would be like if we ever found one. What we should be looking for are more complex personal and social structures which would give adequate expression to the conflicting values. It is a principle which facilitates self-realization or self-development.

In the OHIP dilemma, the utilitarian solution appears to deal inadequately with respect for persons as it expresses itself in terms of privacy and confidentiality, while the Kantian solution deals inadequately with the principle of social utility as it expresses itself here in terms of concern for the public good, in trying to protect others from harm. For organic casuistry the problem becomes that of restructuring this situation so we can protect patients' rights and still help a legitimate and urgent police investigation. This requires us to look at the dilemma from different perspectives, because there is no one direction in which we ought to look. There is nothing in the criteria which points us directly to a solution. We have to look at it in as many fecund ways as possible. We could, for example, look at the doctor–patient relationship again.

One psychiatrist suggested the following solution to Whitman's case, the sniper at the University of Texas. He argued that this was a tragic case but also a rare one. He noted that many mental patients frequently express their hostility towards others to their therapists, but this does not normally mean they will act on these threats. They are frequently expressing fantasies and not their real intentions. So these cases are not black and white. A judgement is required by the psychiatrist or therapist. They have to decide whether their patients are real threats to others or themselves, or not. This does not excuse the psychiatrist in the Whitman case, for he may have made a serious professional error and should be held accountable for that, but it does give us a deeper insight into the therapist's dilemma. It locates the problem as one in professional ethics. Clearly professional therapists need to recognize that the claims of the public good are valid and that perhaps they need to develop better techniques than they presently have to make judgements like these, and to deal adequately with their patients when they recognize their threats as real. Justice Krever in his report acknowledged the validity of the public interest in these situations, although he maintained that the OHIP official in the real case was wrong in releasing the information, because this involved breaking the law. Justice Krever declined to recommend that health professionals or OHIP officials be required by law to release confidential medical information, even to report gunshot or stab wounds. He thought the public interest would be better served by giving health professionals the discretion to do so if they thought this was for the public's safety.[24] This acknowledgement might require considerable modification to the code of ethics which governs the practice of Canadian health care professionals.

The OHIP case could be seen as a problem of police ethics as well as a problem in medical ethics. In some societies, the police need to be reminded that although their function is to catch criminals this must always be done with due respect to the rights of individuals. The police cannot be above the law. In his report Justice Krever remarked: 'In a democratic society, no police force, no matter how generally well respected, should be allowed to be a law unto itself.'[25] In the hypothetical dilemma, the idealist would argue that the OHIP official was right not to release the information in the first instance, but he could also have tried to think of other less sensitive information which could help the investigating officers get a warrant which would have allowed them legal access to specific information they required for their investigation. He could have made better use of his moral imagination. His response was incomplete rather than completely wrong, but given the present threat to our right to privacy he should still be commended. If, however, this sort of information is not sufficient and there is no way of obtaining the information they believe they require without crude violations of a patient's right to privacy and confidentiality, then the police will just have to find some other way to nab the crook. They must become more imaginative in their police work.

For different reasons both utilitarians and Kantians recognize, as we saw, that privacy is an important value that needs to be jealously guarded. It is certainly a value which the Enlightenment discovered, but it is not necessarily tied to the idea of radical individualism, as some scholars suggest:

> Thus, the claim to privacy, as we know it, is eminently a phenomenon of the industrial and post-industrial age, in which the exigencies of urban life have led to an atomic concept of society in place of the earlier or organic model.[26]

The alienation of the individual from the community may be a hallmark of post-medieval society, but the idea of the individual as something distinct from the community is not alien to organic theories of the individual or social institutions. An idealist theory of ethics requires an adequate theory of individual rights, because freedom from the coercive power of the state is necessary for the healthy and full development of a person.[27] Privacy is required not only to protect ourselves from others, as the utilitarians maintain, and to sustain the integrity of the moral agent, as the Kantians maintain, but to allow individuals to grow morally and to realize themselves fully.

In any case the solutions discussed in this chapter are only hypothetical solutions to a hypothetical dilemma, which is presented from a certain perspective in an incomplete way. Real solutions can only be discovered in real life where the story occurs in its full complexity.

Chapter 2

Western moral traditions

Rational answers to moral dilemmas appear to be theory-dependent. They make sense only within a specific intellectual frame of reference, hence the way in which a moral problem is resolved will depend on the ethical theory which is explicitly or implicitly appealed to. Generally, in western cultures, we appeal to one of two main ethical traditions, the liberal utilitarian and the conservative Kantian traditions, to solve moral problems. The selection of these two traditions as central to modern moral discussion is not ad hoc, because they constantly appear in contemporary moral arguments and are frequently crucial to those disputes. They also play different roles in the dynamics of social change in our culture.

Both systems have deep roots in western culture. Kantianism represents an older, conservative tradition which is related to both secular and religious humanism. It also contains elements of the classical natural law tradition. I derive its name from Immanuel Kant, the eighteenth-century German philosopher who presented the theory in one of its strongest modern forms. Utilitarianism represents a newer, liberal tradition which is associated with the rise of modern science. I derive its name from a short treatise written by the nineteenth-century English philosopher John Stuart Mill, in which he presented the theory in one of its strongest and most enduring forms. The liberal utilitarian tradition tends to be one of moral reform, working on the edge of moral progress, while the conservative Kantian tradition tends to be one of traditional morality, defending and reshaping the moral status quo.

These systems have taken many different forms in western philosophical thought. It's important to stress again that there is no agreement among moral philosophers as to which form is best. The two systems as presented in this book are not strictly faithful to either Kant or Mill, or to any other particular philosopher. Rather they are outlines of each system expressed in the most extreme forms. They are developed, both philosophically and morally, in ways which emphasize their differences rather than their similarities. Alasdair MacIntyre in his brilliant book *After Virtue* develops these traditions in ways which emphasize their similarities rather than their differences. He sees both traditions as expressions of the breakdown of the moral order which the western world is now experiencing. This moral order informed western culture from classical Greece to the Enlightenment. What the traditions share, MacIntyre suggests is, first, common roots in Northern European, Protestant, Christian cultures. Second, each in its own way is trying to create a scientific morality. They are foundationalists seeking a rational basis for morality which is logically independent of any cultural or social context. Third, they believe in radical individualism, i.e. individuals are ontologically and morally independent of the social groups and institutions to which they belong. Fourth, they assent to the principle of individual liberty and support a system of universal natural human rights. Fifth, they each contribute to the rise of general moral scepticism which renders modern moral philosophy morally impotent and helps to sow the seeds of moral anarchy. In all of these observations MacIntyre is certainly correct, but the differences between the traditions are of equal importance for our understanding and resolution of contemporary moral dilemmas and for studying the dynamics of moral change.[1]

Although there is no direct correspondence between the descriptions of the traditions I provide and historical reality, nevertheless they will help us to understand that reality. Our ideas do not have to mirror reality in order to help us discover truth. The pictures I present of these rival traditions will not be exhaustive, but they express what I see as their essential spirit which is manifest in the recent history of western culture. They are not to be interpreted as fully developed formal logical systems, in which basic non-moral presuppositions are thought to entail substantive moral propositions. This would involve an illicit logical move from fact to value, to commit the 'naturalistic fallacy' or to breach Hume's 'No ought from is' law. That law can be formulated as follows: no set of non-moral premises can entail a moral conclusion.

Nor should we think of them as fully developed empirical systems which derive substantive moral claims inductively from non-moral presuppositions. What we might call the narrow formulation of the law suggests that the naturalistic fallacy is a mistake in deductive logic. This leaves open the possibility that substantive moral propositions could be inductively derived from non-moral presuppositions. A wider formulation of the law would rule this out. This formulation would read as follows: no moral conclusion can be derived from a set of non-moral premises. In fact we should not picture these systems in terms of either deductive or inductive logic, rather we should look at them as star systems which grow by intellectual gravity into galaxies and galactic clusters of thought throughout the course of their history.[2]

I see these traditions as heterogeneous and containing more than one type of ethical theory which contemporary philosophers would classify as distinct theories. For example, the Kantian tradition, as I describe it, contains forms of religious ethics – such as the divine command theory, where 'X is right' means, 'God commands X' and 'X is wrong' means 'God forbids X' – which are not strictly based on the doctrine of natural law, although we can understand how the natural law theory developed out of it.[3] The utilitarian tradition, as I describe it, contains an element of contract theory, like that developed by Thomas Hobbes, which is now thought by modern contract theorists like John Rawls to be quite distinct from traditional utilitarianism and even to possess Kantian elements.[4] Still, contract theory and utilitarianism have more in common with each other than they do with the Kantian or natural law tradition, and this is true in spite of claims to the contrary by many modern contract theorists. The divine command theory and the Kantian or natural law tradition have more in common with each other than they do with utilitarianism. None of this should surprise anyone, because traditions are complex historical movements which grow in myriad ways. New theories develop out of older ones, much as new languages grow out of older ones, and both rarely escape their origins entirely. Children frequently reject the outlook of their parents vehemently simply because they must if they are to mature. Perhaps this is why the new generation of contract theorists so strongly rejects the utilitarian tradition which gave birth to them. They are ashamed of the mistakes of their forebears and want to distance themselves from them so that they can be independent, as Protestant Christians distanced themselves from Catholic Christians, Christians distance themselves from Jews and modern philosophers from medieval philosophers. Nevertheless we remain the children of our parents and we mirror them in important and unexpected ways. We understand ourselves better when we understand our origins. We also understand ourselves better intellectually when we recognize the traditions from which our ideas have developed. Ethics without a tradition is like a contradiction in terms.

Explicitly or implicitly we are all working within historical traditions, and to deny this is to obscure the intellectual frame of reference which guides our thought. Let us look at some general philosophical differences between the traditions first, then at some of their substantial moral differences.

PHILOSOPHICAL DIFFERENCES

First, the methods the two systems use to justify moral judgements are basically different. This is because each system is developed from different philosophical assumptions about the nature of knowledge. Utilitarians are empiricists, who believe that all knowledge is based on experience. Utilitarians use scientific method, which depends on observation and experiment in acquiring knowledge, as their paradigm of proper reasoning. Their goal from Bacon onwards has been to create a scientific ethics. Science has radically altered the way we think and respond to the natural world, so we should expect the same fruitful results if the methods of natural science are applied to the moral world. Scientific methodology revolutionized technological progress and was to revolutionize moral and social progress. It is not surprising then to find that utilitarians hold that the morality of an act depends upon the consequences it produces, rather than the motives from which it is performed. The actual consequences of acts are observable while motives are not, and this makes them amenable to the scientific method.

The Kantians, on the other hand, are rationalists. They think that all knowledge is ultimately based on reason. They use mathematics and formal logic as their paradigms of reasoning, and a method that is scientific. In this model conclusions are reached by deduction from self-evident propositions. A self-evident proposition in mathematics might be: a straight line is the shortest distance between two points. A self-evident proposition in morality might be: the good deserve to be rewarded and the bad to be punished. The Kantians reject the idea that ethics can be reduced to an empirical science and are sceptical about moral progress. They reject consequentialism. They are non-consequentialists who hold that the morality of an act depends upon the motive and intentions behind it and not merely on the actual consequences.[5] Hence giving money to charity to gain a tax write-off might be morally acceptable to a utilitarian because the actual consequences are beneficial: the poor get the help they need. But this is not so for a Kantian, because the motive was bad. The giving was selfish and showed no concern for the poor. Starting from different epistemological assumptions leads each theory to stress different aspects of an act as relevant for assessing its rightness or wrongness. Utilitarians starting from empiricism become consequentialists. Kantians starting from rationalism become non-consequentialists.

Although both traditions work within the general framework of reference theories of meaning and correspondence theories of truth, they differ as to what moral judgements refer to.[6] The utilitarians tend to interpret moral judgements as descriptions of states of affairs, which can be shown to be true or false by reference to experience. If it is true that stealing food will enable someone to feed his or her family, then it would be morally permissible to steal food. For the utilitarian, moral judgements are hypothetical imperatives, which rely on true predictions. If you want X, then you ought to do Y. Kantians, on the other hand, see moral judgements as prescriptions or commands. For them, moral judgements are more like recommendations to make something the case than descriptions of what actually is the case, or predictions of what will be the case. They are categorical imperatives. Sincere assent to a moral judgement means acting in accordance with it and not merely giving intellectual assent to it. If people sincerely assent to the rule that stealing is morally wrong, then they simply shouldn't steal. If they do, they can no longer claim that they sincerely assent to the rule.[7]

Utilitarians base their moral judgements on the actual consequences of acts, rather than on the motives of the agent. Hence utilitarians might do something which a Kantian would think is wrong. But they would justify it on the basis of the consequences. Whatever maximizes happiness and minimizes suffering is morally right. If a lie would produce the greatest amount of happiness and the least amount of unhappiness, then it would be morally right to lie. Kantians would disagree, because lying always involves a conscious intent to deceive, to use others as a means to ends without their consent. Kantians hold that lying in any circumstances is wrong. Moral rules like 'telling the truth' and 'no lying' are universal and apply equally to all moral agents in all circumstances. The Kantians are universalists who hold that moral rules apply equally to everyone, while the utilitarians are particularists who hold that the rightness or wrongness of an act depends upon the circumstances. A lie in one context will likely produce different consequences to a lie in another context. What is right for one person is not necessarily right for another person. Because people and situations are never exactly the same, absolute moral rules cannot be generated from particular experiences.

The empiricist background of the utilitarians leads them to downgrade the role of moral rules in ethical thinking. Rules for them are generalizations or inductions from experience and not universal moral absolutes. The utilitarians are particularists, contextualists or situationalists, who believe that the rightness or wrongness of an action depends upon the context or situation. For them, particular acts are epistemologically prior to rules. A well-established particular judgement will always override a useful moral rule. All moral rules will likely have exceptions. Any moral rule can be disregarded if a particular act will produce the greatest happiness and the least unhappiness. Surely the Dutch family who hid Anne Frank were right to lie to the Nazis when they were searching their house for Jews? For the Kantian, coming from a rationalist perspective, moral rules always take epistemological priority over particular acts. As universalists, the Kantians hold that moral rules apply equally to everyone. If an act is inconsistent with a universal moral law then the act is morally wrong. An act is shown to be morally acceptable if it can be consistently generalized into a universal rule which applies equally to all rational agents. For the Kantian, the rightness or wrongness of an action does not depend on the context or situation. A true universal moral rule cannot have exceptions. There are moral absolutes. Murder is murder wherever one finds it and it is always wrong. So is lying. Everyone has a right not to be deceived and everyone has an unconditional duty to tell the truth. The right to truth, like all human rights, is valid for all persons in all circumstances. It's morally better to say nothing and accept the consequences rather than lie. If any harm is done to the self or others it is done unintentionally, and we have wronged no one. The right thing to do in the Anne Frank situation is to be silent even if this puts one in harm's way. If the Nazis discover Anne Frank, as they eventually did, and murder her, her protector is not to blame. It is the Nazis who are evil, not the honest person.[8]

To be consistent, any Kantian system appears to require exceptions to moral rules to avoid conflicts. Intuitively most people do not think that the Dutch family which aided Anne Frank by lying to her Nazi pursuers acted immorally. Kantians are divided on the solution to the problem. Kant did not provide a clear answer. Sometimes he appeared to allow for exceptions to moral rules, but at other times he preferred to redescribe the actions referred to in the rules so that the conflict disappeared. For example, so called heroic suicides would not be classified as genuine suicides, because the basic intention of the agent was not to take his or her life but to do good to others. Heroic suicides are acts of altruism. Similarly, in the example of Anne Frank keeping silent would be an act of honesty, not one of malevolence or indifference.[9] Redescription is an alternative way of achieving consistency in a Kantian system. Many modern Kantians prefer to allow for exceptions to rules to give the theory the flexibility which the complexity of our moral lives requires.[10] In this book, I will use the method of redescription rather than exceptions to develop a consistent Kantian ethics, because this represents the typical way the theory appears in modern ethical debates. It treats the Pauline principle of never doing evil to bring about good as a moral absolute, and so never appeals to the principle of the lesser evil to resolve moral dilemmas as the utilitarians do. It preserves the general doctrine of moral absolutes, something which is passionately rejected by all liberal utilitarians and which serves to distinguish them clearly from conservative Kantians.

Kantians are also strict objectivists, or realists, who hold that the rightness or wrongness of an action is independent of the person making the judgement. They don't believe that the rightness or wrongness of actions depends on the views of the person making the judgement. They are realists who hold that moral judgements refer to some aspect of the real world. A belief that the world is flat does not make it flat. A belief that lying is morally acceptable doesn't make it acceptable. The utilitarians, on the other hand, are not strict objectivists. A subjectivist element is always involved for them because moral judgements are relative to the individual agent's perspective and preferences. There is nothing for moral judgements to refer to except the agent's subjective state. In this they differ from scientific judgements, which do refer to data which are independent of the judge. This observation holds true in spite of the fact that utilitarians have developed interesting objectivist forms of the theory.[11] The fact that there are no subjective forms of Kantianism, as there are of utilitarianism, indicates that the debate between subjectivity and objectivity in ethics is internal to the utilitarian tradition, but not to the Kantian tradition. The utilitarians have to demonstrate that their theory can be objective; the Kantians do not because objectivity is implicit in the theory.

Because it has more affinities with subjectivism, utilitarianism tends to be more tolerant of diverse moral opinions than Kantianism is. On the other hand, scepticism which denies the possibility of moral knowledge has always been the natural companion of utilitarianism but not of Kantianism, although the latter, like the former, is equally an answer to the problems raised by general moral scepticism. The general sceptic holds that there is no objective method for establishing the truth or falsity of moral claims, as there is for scientific ones. Whether lying is morally right or wrong is a matter of opinion or feeling, not knowledge. Both traditions assume that an adequate moral epistemology must provide an answer to the general moral sceptic. If it does not, it will not be able to provide the expertise required to solve moral problems. They have in common the search for an abstract rational foundation for morality. Alasdair MacIntyre has shown this was the major project that modern moral philosophy undertook, after the intellectual hegemony of the Christian Middle Ages collapsed with the development of Protestantism and modern science.[12]

Descartes (1596–1650) is considered the father of modern philosophy and foundationalism, because he invented the method of doubt.[13] Descartes set out systematically to question every belief he thought was true. He discarded every belief he could not be absolutely certain was true. He doubted the truth of his common sense beliefs about the existence of material objects like tables and chairs and other minds, as well as his most sophisticated and complex scientific beliefs, until he arrived at his famous 'cogito': I think therefore I am. This proposition was, he thought, one which could not be doubted without self-contradiction. This was the absolutely certain truth from which he thought he could reconstruct the house of knowledge his method of doubt had destroyed. As it turned out, he was wrong about its absolute certainty, as empiricists like Locke, Berkeley and Hume were to demonstrate. They showed that even our knowledge of the self was insecure. The empiricists, however, did not abandon foundationalism, the search for absolute certainty on which to build knowledge. In fact they thought that they had discovered it in simple judgements of perception, like 'I see this red patch of colour.' These were propositions which could not be doubted and which possessed the character of absolute certainty on which we could base both our common sense and scientific knowledge.[14] In foundationalist epistemology, the problem of general scepticism is central. Only the absolute certainty of logical necessity or infallible sensation can defeat the general sceptic. MacIntyre argues that the foundationalist project in ethics failed when both rationalists and empiricists discovered that, given the assumptions of absolute certainty, there was no valid way to get from fact to value.[15] Their dream of a scientific ethic vanished and was replaced with the current practical and theoretical anarchy in morals.

Hume's law, which gives formal expression to this unbridgeable gap between fact and value, is a sign of the bankruptcy of foundationalism rather than the crowning achievement of modern moral philosophy. The failure of modern philosophy to provide a rational foundation for ethics ultimately led to the triumph of general scepticism, and the collapse of ethics into various forms of irrationalism. The utilitarian tradition collapses into emotivism and the Kantian tradition into existentialism. MacIntyre's analysis is, for the most part, surely right. Still, general moral scepticism remains an internal problem for the utilitarian rather than an external one as it is with the Kantians.

Another major difference between the systems is that the utilitarians are primarily concerned with right and wrong conduct, while the Kantians are primarily concerned with the development of moral virtue in the individual. The utilitarians emphasize judgements about the rightness or wrongness of particular acts, the effects they have on others, the amount of happiness or unhappiness they produce for others. The Kantians, however, are basically interested in judgements about the goodness or badness of persons. Hence the utilitarians would not be bothered by the fact that someone gave money to a charity to get a tax write-off in the way a Kantian would. For the utilitarian it is the conduct which matters, especially in the way it affects others. After all, the poor get the money and that's what is important. For the Kantian it is the character of the agent which matters, and not just the charitable conduct. Acting from selfish motives indicates a deficiency in the moral character of the agent, and this is intrinsically bad. Utilitarians would be concerned about the tendencies of certain personal dispositions to produce good or bad consequences on the whole, but this concern is secondary to direct consequences.[16]

This difference in emphasis points to another fundamental opposition between the two perspectives. The utilitarians tend to view morality as essentially social and alien to the individual, while the Kantians tend to view morality as essentially private and natural to the individual. This is why the utilitarians hold that morality is something created by humans to protect their interests and not a set of moral laws discovered in nature, as the Kantians do. Morality is a matter of contract or agreement. It is conventional rather than natural. Many utilitarians do hold that some sort of innate moral sense or psychological mechanism, like sympathy or empathy, is necessary to bridge the gap between self-interest and concern for others, and this suggests that at least benevolence, if not justice, is more natural than artificial.[17] For utilitarians, there are no duties to the self; only duties to others.

Hence they draw a radical distinction between the public and private spheres of human life, and morality falls within the public not the private sphere. They distinguish sharply between prudence and morality. Private acts which don't affect others are beyond the scope of morality. A drunk who's not harming anyone else is not acting immorally as far as the utilitarians are concerned. He may be acting imprudently, that is harming himself, but that's his business and not society's. The Kantian, however, believes that there are duties to the self and these duties are central.[18] Self-regarding duties, properly understood as forms of self-respect, are fundamental for the Kantian. Drunkenness is a moral vice because it shows disrespect for the self as a rational agent. The Kantians are deontologists who believe that morality is an end in itself. For them, adhering to a system of duties and obligations is intrinsically valuable. The utilitarians, however, are teleologists who hold that morality is not an end in itself. It possesses only instrumental value. For them, adhering to a system of duties and obligations makes sense only if it is a means to happiness.

These antithetical sets of philosophical assumptions about the nature of human knowledge, moral reasoning and morality are related to other opposing sets of psychological, sociological, theological and metaphysical beliefs. Many of these assumptions were formulated by Kant, Hegel and idealists like F.H. Bradley.[19] Others were identified by modern philosophers like Alan Donagan.[20] Hobbes and Mill had also isolated many of them.[21] I shall deal only with those which I consider to be the most conceptually important and relevant for this study of moral perplexity in the modern world.

First, the systems presuppose radically different psychologies. Utilitarianism develops against a background of empirical association psychology, the precursor of modern behaviourism, which holds that all our ideas, scientific or moral, are acquired rather than innate. Conscience and moral character are products of a developmental process and are not natural givens. Kantianism, on the other hand, develops against a background of rational psychology, the descendant of vitalism, which holds that our fundamental ideas are innate rather than acquired. For the Kantians, conscience is a natural given and moral character is simply the attempt of the will to act in conformity to it. In order to act on rational moral principles the conscientious person must have desire under control. For the Kantian, reason always takes precedence over desire as a guide to conduct. For the utilitarian, however, desire and the pursuit of pleasure or happiness take precedence over reason. Reason for the utilitarian is always, as Hume argued, the slave of the passions.[22]

Because of their radically different views of human nature, they develop radically different theories of virtue. For the Kantian, virtue becomes a trait of character which facilitates the conduct of a moral agent and relationships between moral agents. Vice becomes a trait of character which inhibits or retards the capacity of a moral agent to act or interact with others. Since we need courage to act morally in the face of strong fears, courage is a virtue and cowardice a vice. For the utilitarian, a virtue becomes a disposition which benefits the self or others. A vice becomes a disposition which harms the self or others. Since a benevolent disposition tends to promote the general happiness, while a malevolent disposition tends to promote unhappiness, benevolence would be a virtue and malevolence a vice.[23]

The utilitarians are also determinists, who hold that all human conduct can be explained in terms of efficient causality, by the same general laws which explain why one billiard ball moves another when they collide. This should not surprise us, since they hold that reason is subordinate to desire and hence they tend to reduce will to desire. Desire has causal force, while reason by itself is impotent. The Kantians on the other hand are non-determinists or libertarians, who believe in agent causality. Human conduct for them can be explained by reason intervening directly in the course of nature. The will cannot be reduced to desire.[24]

The systems also presuppose different sociologies as well as different psychologies. For the utilitarian, morality is, as we saw, essentially alien to human nature. It is something imposed on the individual by society. Evil, like good, has its origin in society, not in people. We may be naturally selfish but we are not naturally malevolent. As Hobbes observed, if we harm one another we do so to benefit ourselves.[25] Humankind is no more naturally evil than naturally good. A moral sense might be needed to make moral education work but evil, like good, is a product of society – not the moral agent. Society is ultimately responsible for both moral good and evil, not the individual. For the Kantian, on the other hand, morality is natural to people. It is not something artificially imposed by society. Society with its governments and systems of criminal justice is a natural expression of the fact that evil people abound and require punishment. Evil, like good, has its roots in the human soul. The individual is responsible for moral evil, not society. For people there are no excuses, except perhaps weakness of will. Both theories, of course, subscribe to radical individualism in one way or another and hold that social groups are ontologically dependent on the individuals which compose them. This is confirmed by the fact that both Kantian and utilitarian theories of virtue are developed independently of people's social roles. The good person is universally the same wherever found.

The systems' relations with religion are also basically opposed. Utilitarianism is essentially secular. Natural science developed fully only when it cut its ties with religion. A dogmatic science is self-contradictory. Similarly, a morality modelled on the epistemological ideals of natural science is not likely to flourish unless it too becomes theologically neutral. Utilitarianism is not necessarily incompatible with a religious point of view. John Stuart Mill noted that utilitarianism and Christian ethics shared a concern for the well-being of mankind. One modern Protestant theologian, Joseph Fletcher, holds that a certain form of utilitarianism contains the essence of Christian morality.[26] In spite of this, utilitarianism has less in common with that morality than Kantianism has. Moral reform has been more closely allied with secular morality than with religious morality. The latter, not surprisingly, tends to represent the moral status quo. Kantianism, on the other hand, is directly rooted in complex ways in the Hebrew–Christian ethical tradition of western culture.[27] That tradition is essentially non-consequentialist, prescriptive and universalist. The good person obeys God's commands no matter what the consequences. God's moral laws are concrete, objective and universal, and possess the force of natural laws. Human beings are autonomous moral agents who are free to obey or disobey the moral law. They are responsible for their conduct and accountable to God for it, hence they believe in the doctrine of the immortality of the soul and the day of judgement. The Kantians tend to see morality as an integral part of a universe created by God. At the metaphysical level they tend towards spiritualism, seeing mind as ontologically superior to matter. The utilitarians, by contrast, tend to be materialists, who see matter as ontologically superior to the mind.[28]

MORAL DIFFERENCES

The substantive moral outlooks the two systems adopt differ as radically as their general philosophical positions. The two systems adhere to fundamentally different values. The first and primary moral principle of utilitarianism is the principle of social utility. That is, the most moral act is the one which produces the greatest happiness (pleasure) for the greatest number. The main goal of the utilitarian is to maximize human happiness (pleasure) and minimize human suffering (pain). However, the first and primary principle of Kantianism is the principle of respect for persons. That is, always treat persons, including oneself, as ends in themselves and never merely as means. The main goal of the Kantians is the pursuit of virtue and the avoidance of vice. Both systems develop a set of secondary principles or rules which control the application of these basic values to concrete moral experience. The goal for each theory is to produce a consistent set of precepts which will guide conduct rationally, solve moral problems and resolve moral dilemmas.[29] A review of some of these secondary precepts will yield a richer picture of these complex and opposing systems of value.

For the utilitarian, happiness (pleasure) is the sole intrinsic good; unhappiness (pain) the sole intrinsic evil. For the Kantian, moral virtue is the sole intrinsic good; moral vice the sole intrinsic evil. One system generates a morality of happiness, the other a morality of respect. For the Kantian, suicide is morally wrong because it displays a lack of self-respect. It involves the denial of the intrinsic value of a person. For the utilitarian, suicide would be morally acceptable if it prevented great suffering.[30]

Because morality for utilitarians is a means to the greatest happiness, they believe that this end always justifies the means. This is the principle of expediency. For example, President Truman justified the atomic bombing of Hiroshima on utilitarian grounds. He argued that using the bomb would bring the war to a speedy end, save countless lives and cause the least suffering for both the Allies and the Japanese. Because morality for Kantians is an end in itself, they hold that the end, no matter how good, never justifies the means. This is the principle of conscientiousness. One must do one's duty for duty's sake and not because of some end which is external to it. Honesty, truthfulness and sincerity have intrinsic rather than extrinsic value. You cannot do evil in order to do good. Kantians think that the atomic bombing of Hiroshima was morally wrong, because it involved the deliberate killing of innocent people.[31] For Kantians, it is wrong to use people merely as a means to achieve the good of others. They subscribe to the Pauline principle of never doing evil in order to do good. Donagan argues that the Pauline principle should be interpreted as a logical principle of consistency, rather than as a substantive moral principle, because it functions in Kantian systems as a mechanism for resolving conflicts of rules.[32] There is certainly merit in this proposal, because the Pauline is the basic ranking principle for Kantian systems and possesses general rather than specific content. Nevertheless it is a moral prescription which is at the heart of conscientiousness, and so cannot be treated as a purely formal principle.

Another moral difference which emerges is that the utilitarians believe life is valuable only when it possesses an acceptable balance of happiness over unhappiness, while the Kantian believes that life is valuable no matter what its quality. The Kantians assent to the principle of sanctity of human life, the utilitarians to the principle of quality of life. The utilitarian would accept euthanasia because it is a beneficent act. The Kantians would reject it. They would say euthanasia was wrong no matter how poor the quality of life might be. Everyone has a right to life because life is intrinsically valuable, hence everything possible must be done to preserve it.

Attitudes towards social morality are also essentially different. Utilitarians want to create a benevolent or caring society; Kantians want to create a just society based on respect for human rights. Many utilitarians hold that a just society is a necessary condition of a benevolent society, but attempts to reduce justice to forms of utility have proved difficult if not impossible. Since principles of justice are non-consequentialist, they provide few problems for the Kantian. It is the consequentialist principles of beneficence and non-maleficence which pose problems for the Kantian – but not for the utilitarian. Kant even went so far as to claim that an action performed from benevolence had no moral worth. Kant did hold that we have both duties of non-maleficence and benevolence to others, but these imperfect duties took second place to the perfect duties of justice towards others.[33] For the utilitarian, goods should be distributed according to need, even if this involves preferential treatment for some. For the Kantian, goods should be distributed fairly. This is the principle of egalitarianism or equality. The utilitarians think we ought to help the poor even if they have no right to our goods. The Kantians think that helping the poor is a matter of charity, not of moral obligation. In adopting this caring attitude towards the needy and helpless the utilitarian can be said to express a feminine approach to ethics. In western society, at least, women appear to be encouraged to be nurturing and dependent and to put the needs of others before themselves, while men are encouraged to be aggressive, self-reliant, and to deal with others on the basis of fair competition. Kantian morality appears to be fundamentally masculine.[34]

The attitudes of the two systems towards the morality of punishment are also basically opposed. Kantians believe in retributive justice. For them, wrongdoers ought to be punished. For utilitarians, however, punishment is justified only if it deters further wrongdoing or benefits the offender. Because they think that society rather than the individual causes social deviance, they have a more compassionate attitude towards the deviant than the Kantian does.[35]

Although the two traditions share an interest in human freedom, they express this interest in different ways. If foundationalism can be designated the great epistemological project of modern moral philosophy, then the discovery and development of the principle of individual liberty can be cited as its great moral project. The relationship between foundationalism, the doctrine of radical individualism and the principle of individual liberty is philosophically complex. MacIntyre conceives them as so tightly logically interrelated that the failure of the first two doctrines would entail abandoning the principle of individual liberty. It is not clear, however, that the principle cannot find a home within non-foundationalist systems which reject the principle of radical individualism. Individualism in some form is, I think, essential to capture the autonomy of moral agents at the highest level of their development, and hence is necessary for any adequate ethical theory. The traditions recognize this, but their moral attitudes towards human freedom are again quite different. Because they see morality as something imposed on the individual by society, the utilitarians believe that we ought to able to do as we please so long as we don't harm others. This is the utilitarian form of the principle of individual liberty. The Kantians, however, because they believe that morality is inherent in human nature, hold that we are never free to do as we please. We must always act morally. We are autonomous moral agents whose rationality limits us. We must respect the freedom of other moral agents. We are free to act within the limits that a rational morality imposes on us, but cannot be allowed to limit the freedom of other moral agents. This is the Kantian form of the principle of individual liberty, which we can call the principle of autonomy to distinguish it from its utilitarian counterpart.[36]

Finally, the two systems have radically different moral attitudes towards animals and nature. The Kantians believe that humans are the only beings in nature that have intrinsic value. Non-human animals do not. Their position is homo-centric. The utilitarians, however, believe humans are not the only beings in nature that have intrinsic value. Any species that can feel pleasure and pain has value. Their position is zoo-centric. For the utilitarian, the moral universe includes the whole of sentient creation, hence they hold that we have a duty to maximize the welfare of animals and if necessary give them legal rights.[37] The Kantians would reject the idea that animals have rights, although they would not condone cruelty to animals or the wanton destruction of nature.[38]

A UNIFIED SYSTEM OF ETHICS

Ordinarily most of us are strictly neither utilitarians or Kantians. Our moralities are a mix of utilitarian consequentialist and Kantian non-consequentialist principles. Even the most systematic of us tend to incorporate important elements of the opposing standpoint into our moral practice. Frequently the most difficult dilemmas we face, at both the personal and social levels, occur when the two traditions come into conflict. MacIntyre has noted that it is this type of conflict which underlies the apparently incommensurable moral dilemmas of our time (e.g. abortion, capital punishment and economic justice), and which explains why it is impossible in our culture to reach moral agreement on these divisive issues.[39] MacIntyre has also suggested that within idealist systems, because they are functional, facts do entail moral conclusions. Hume's law is not a timeless moral truth which is relevant to every moral system, as most modern moral philosophers assume. In fact its scope is very limited. It applies only to foundationalist systems, like utilitarianism and Kantianism. In idealist systems of ethics our duties, rights, liberties and responsibilities are defined by social roles, by the functions we perform within a social entity. Modern moral philosophers have simply ignored the many counter-examples in our moral language, in which facts entail values. Take the following cases from MacIntyre's *After Virtue*. He is a sea-captain. Therefore, he ought to do whatever a sea-captain ought to do. This watch is grossly inadequate, irregular in its time keeping, and too heavy to carry about comfortably. Therefore, this is a bad watch. This farmer gets a better yield for his crop per acre than any other farmer in the district. He has the most effective programme of soil renewal anywhere. His dairy herd wins all the first prizes at the agricultural show. Therefore, he is a good farmer.[40] The concepts of 'sea-captain', 'watch' and 'farmer' are all functional concepts which only make sense in terms of the purpose or functions they are characteristically expected to serve, hence reasoning in terms of them makes it possible for facts to entail moral conclusions. All of MacIntyre's examples bear a striking resemblance to one used by John Searle in his famous article, 'How to Derive an "Ought" from an "Is" '. Searle's example was:

'Jones promised to pay Smith 5 dollars. Therefore; Jones ought to pay Smith 5 dollars.'[41] Searle argues that promising is by definition an act of placing oneself under an obligation. The moral rule 'One ought to keep promises' is a constituent of the practice. The practice could not be what it is without the rule. This can be shown by noting that its inverse, 'One ought not keep promises', appears self-contradictory. The rule defining the practice is a necessary truth. Hence a moral conclusion about what someone ought to do is entailed in the fact that a promise has been made. We need, according to Searle, to distinguish between brute facts, like 'Jones is six feet tall', and social facts, like 'Jones got married' or 'Jones is a sea-captain', if we are to understand how facts can entail values. It is social or institutional facts which entail moral conclusions for both MacIntyre and Searle. For them, moral concepts only make sense in terms of what Wittgenstein called 'a form of life'.[42] It is certainly correct to say that the moral principle 'Keep Promises!' is a constituent of the practice of promising, just as 'keeping good time' is the function of a watch, but it does not follow that it is a necessary moral truth. R.M. Hare has demonstrated that it is better to treat the rule as a synthetic prescription which can be sensibly contradicted, because this allows us to deal with the problem of exceptions to the rule, and allows practices as a whole to be questioned morally. Some practices, like farming, we might want only to modify – perhaps to include in it more humane treatment of animals – while others, like slavery or racism, we might want to abandon entirely.[43]

If we accept this analysis, the question which automatically arises is whether there is any sound way to resolve dilemmas which involve this kind of deep opposition. Ultimately the way we try to resolve moral dilemmas will, as we have seen, depend on the method of justification which is implicit in the system of ethics appealed to. If you are a utilitarian who holds that the rightness or wrongness of an action depends on its actual consequences you will likely, although not always, come to a different solution from the Kantian who holds that the motives behind the action determine its rightness or wrongness, irrespective of the actual consequences. If the theories, when properly applied, always arrived at the same answers there would be no reason to remain either a utilitarian or a Kantian, as their passionate contemporary advocates wish to do, because the two theories would be commensurate. The assumption I make in this book is that the two theories in their present forms are not commensurate and so do in fact produce different results in certain cases when applied to the same dilemma. Once we accept this assumption then the fundamental question becomes: how do we decide which theory of justification is the best? At present there is no agreement among professional moral philosophers as to which theory or which form of the theories is best, hence any choice between them will be arbitrary. The situation in ethics resembles that in psychology, where there is a plurality of competing theories. But ethical theorists are worse off than psychologists at the moment, because there is no agreement among professional philosophers as to which method or criterion would be appropriate for deciding between competing theories or for developing a unified theory of ethics. Psychologists use essentially the same scientific methodology, or so they claim. Their problem is that their science has not developed to the stage where a unified theory of psychology is a realistic goal. But it is not an intrinsically impossible goal, as appears to be the case in ethics.

Because there is no unified theory of ethics, professional ethicists cannot actually solve real moral problems or provide directions which would solve them. They can analyse moral problems from different ethical perspectives, e.g. utilitarian and Kantian approaches to police invasions of privacy, but they have not been able to show which perspective is the best, nor agree on a method which might decide the issue between them. This is an unacceptable situation, both theoretically and practically, for contemporary moral philosophy, because its theories cease to be fully relevant for our moral lives. Of course it is only unacceptable if one holds, as practical ethicists do, that moral philosophy ought to be relevant for practical moral experience. Until recently it was widely held that moral philosophy or ethical theory was an autonomous subject which was logically independent of practical ethics and ought to have no direct bearing on practical issues.[44] This has been the orthodox view in the English-speaking world since 1903, the year in which G.E. Moore published *Principia Ethica*, until now when it has been challenged by the revival of practical ethics. The autonomous or specialist view involves the rejection of the idea of moral expertise. Everyone agrees that ethical theorists can analyse moral problems from different theoretical perspectives, but what they cannot do is to say which perspective is best. That decision, it appears, will always be arbitrary. Hence the idea that there can be moral experts analogous to scientific experts is an illusion, and perhaps a dangerous delusion. Surely the moral busybodies the notion produces will be a serious threat to freedom of thought and conscience, values which are essential for any democratic society. Ethical theorists would become false philosopher kings, trying to impose their values on others, based on the ill-founded idea of moral expertise. Ethical theorists should stick to their analysis of ordinary language and leave the solutions to moral problems to the good and the wise.

In spite of its consistency with common sense, the orthodox view has serious difficulties. The main one centres on moral education. If we accept the orthodox position, then moral education in all its forms will disappear from our school systems at all levels. This is in fact what has happened in our culture and is reflected in the way we deal or fail to deal with moral values in our universities. Theoretical or analytical ethics continues to be taught by philosophers, and scientific or descriptive ethics by social scientists. Moral education gets left out in the intellectual cold and becomes the province of anyone who has a moral axe to grind, and the moral values which are implicit in theoretical and scientific ethics remain unexamined. This neglect of moral education has dire consequences for our civilization. It explains, in part, the wide gap which has developed between our technologies and our moralities. There appears to be a real decline in moral standards in western civilization. Moral scandals occur in increasing numbers in every area of our lives, in politics, in medicine, in business, in science, in sports and in religious institutions. Our civilization appears to be becoming amoral. It is not simply that we are becoming more evil, but that evil no longer concerns us. We no longer believe that our professional lives have moral dimensions. As recently as 1987 the Canadian Philosophical Association rejected the idea of adopting a code of ethics for philosophers, in spite of the fact that philosophers are becoming increasingly involved in the market place.[45] Because the orthodox position leads to the impoverishment of practical ethics and moral education, and leaves us impotent in the face of moral crisis, it must be abandoned or radically altered.

If we abandon the orthodox view which holds that theoretical and practical ethics are logically independent of each other, what do we replace it with? I would suggest an idealistic or holistic viewpoint as an alternative. On this view the three branches of ethics are seen as logically interdependent. These logical relations will be complex and will not involve entailment relations between sets of philosophical or scientific propositions and substantive moral principles. It will accept the orthodox claim that moral conclusions cannot be derived, deductively or inductively, from any set of non-moral premises. The precise nature of the logical relations between moral and non-moral claims will only become clear as the argument of this book proceeds, although we have already made some progress towards this description in Chapter 1, where we discovered the natural epistemological criteria of richness and higher integration which can give direction to our moral thought and development.[46] In this idealist view, although practical, scientific and theoretical ethics can be distinguished for the purposes of division of labour and practical necessity, they form part of a unified comprehensive system of understanding. At the higher levels of thought philosophical and scientific ethics cannot be morally neutral and practical ethics cannot be totally independent of science or moral philosophy. The moral neutrality of theoretical and descriptive ethics are working hypotheses only and not ultimate intellectual divisions.

If we do accept this idealistic vision of the human understanding, we will be committed to some form of moral education and moral expertise, and this has its own problems. The important question now becomes: are these implications so undesirable that we should abandon holism and scamper for the security blanket of the autonomous view? The answer is a clear no. Let's take moral education first. To begin with there are no morally neutral systems of education. Canadian schools, for example, teach the historic values of liberal democracies, i.e. respect for freedom of thought, religion, human rights and moral tolerance. A resource guide for teaching values in Ontario public schools, published in 1983, says in a section titled 'Values for Which the School Stands':

> In general Canadians consider some values to be essential to the well-being of their society. These values reinforce the democratic rights and responsibilities of individuals and are based on the belief of the fundamental worth of all persons regardless of race, creed, colour, sex, or background.[47]

Examples can be multiplied ad infinitum. Moral neutrality in schools is simply a myth. Nor is moral education, as I have argued elsewhere, inconsistent with democratic values.[48] If we clearly distinguish between moral indoctrination and moral education, as the idealist view suggests we ought to, then moral education presents no insoluble problems for a democracy. Since indoctrination denies that the learner is an autonomous moral agent it defeats the primary purpose of an idealist-based system of moral education, which is to produce mature moral agents. It may be difficult to achieve this goal, but there is no logical reason why moral education cannot promote respect for freedom of thought and conscience as the Ontario school system suggests it ought to. Indeed to ignore moral education in our schools at any level is self-defeating, because what we do not do explicitly we will do implicitly. By supporting moral education, as holism recommends, we have at least a chance to deal with the modern crisis in morality. Because idealism commits us to a form of moral education is a reason for adopting holism, not rejecting it. But what of the idea of 'moral expertise', which it also commits us to?

If holism commits us to the ludicrous idea of a moral expert, shouldn't this be sufficient grounds for rejecting it? Again, I think this does not constitute good grounds for rejecting a holistic approach to moral philosophy and practical ethics. The moral expert who emerges from our two main traditions of utilitarianism and Kantianism is the scientific specialist. These specialists arrive with their well-formed ethical theories, and their good intentions to address the moral problems of the age, to help others in moral distress and to provide intellectual clarity in order to solve particular moral dilemmas in medical, business, environmental or professional ethics. They are bound to be autocratic and paternalistic, because their theories are designed to produce correct answers which follow once intellectual error has been routed. This is not moral conceit but the professional excellence of the specialist. Other professionals which the moral expert deals with in practical contexts – doctors, nurses, lawyers, research scientists, business people – expect the expert to act with the same professional competence they require of themselves. Tell us the answer so we can get on with our jobs. This is not to deny that professional ethicists have made and continue to make genuine contributions to our moral world. They do, but more often they do so in spite of their well-developed ethical theories rather than because of them. The ethicists doing field work in hospitals and government departments understand this failure best.[49] They realize they are doing something they ought not to be doing. They are not like other experts at all. They are fakes and they know it. Ethicists clearly need a new concept of moral expertise if they are to maintain their professional capability. But what sort of expert, if any, is appropriate? We recognize many different types of moral experts. There are saints, moral heroes, great moral philosophers, pastors, religious teachers and wise friends.[50] Which model, if any, is relevant?

Traditional prescriptive ethical theories fail to account for a fundamental aspect of our moral lives, our experience of moral dilemmas. The major project for contemporary moral philosophy then must be the development of a unified system of ethics, and the goal of this book is to lay the foundation for such a unified system. Clearly, from what we established in Chapter 1, that system cannot be a formal axiomatic system, in which a body of theorems is rigorously deduced from a small set of self-evident or unproven assumptions. Nor can it be an informal deductive system, like that suggested by Alan Donagan in his recent book, *The Theory of Morality*, even if the system is flexible and its principal concepts only fully understood in their applications.[51] Both are mechanical systems which prove inadequate for resolving moral dilemmas. Indeed, foundationalism of any kind would be a mistaken enterprise, at least in ethics. This suggests that current attempts to base ethics on sophisticated forms of contract and game theory are fundamentally flawed and should be abandoned because they represent just another form of mechanical casuistry, which does not help us to understand patterns of moral development or genuinely to resolve moral dilemmas.[52]

There are three possible strategies for achieving a unified theory of ethics. First, elect to be a utilitarian of some sort but build Kantian elements into the system at either the philosophical or the principled level or both. If an incommensurable conflict between utilitarian and Kantian considerations appears at either the theoretical or practical level, the utilitarian considerations would be given priority. Utilitarians have, for example, argued that motives are relevant for deciding the goodness or badness of persons but not for testing the rightness or wrongness of actions.[53] Others have presented essentially utilitarian defences of Kantian values.[54] Still others have presented essentially Kantian defences of utilitarian values.[55] Mill himself built a theory of rights based on egalitarian principles into his system of utilitarianism.[56] In fact any utilitarian thinker who has gained respect among professional moral philosophers has recognized and tried to account for the Kantian features of our moral experience.

Second, elect to be a Kantian of some sort but build utilitarian elements into the system at either the philosophical or the principled level or both. Again, with hard choices Kantian considerations would take priority over utilitarian ones. Kantians, including Kant himself, have, for example, generally recognized the validity of the principle of beneficence and integrated it into their systems.[57] It is also the case that any Kantian thinker who has gained respect among professional moral philosophers has recognized and tried to account for the utilitarian aspects of our moral experience.

Third, adopt a generally idealistic approach to the problem and develop a coherent system of morality which integrates what is true and valuable in both the utilitarian and Kantian systems, at both the

philosophical and moral levels. This is the approach developed by
F.H. Bradley,[58] and it will be the approach favoured in this book. It is
an approach which, because of the eclipse of idealism in twentieth-
century English thought, has been unduly neglected by English-
speaking moral philosophers until very recently.[59] Adopting an idealist
approach to the problem means substituting a descriptive for a
prescriptive ethical theory. Prescriptive ethical theories such as
utilitarianism and Kantianism are designed, like prescriptive logic, to
tell exactly how to arrive at correct indisputable answers to our logical
or moral problems. Descriptive ethical theories such as idealism are
designed, like descriptive logic and epistemologies, to explain and help
understand our intellectual and moral universes. The justification for
adopting idealism in preference to the others will only become clear as
the argument of this book develops. However, it should already be
clear that the prescriptive solutions offered by the first and second
methods will prove inadequate. If, in hard cases, we always choose
utilitarian values over Kantian ones, then the Kantian values will not
find proper expression in our value system. If, in hard cases, we always
choose Kantian values over utilitarian values, then utilitarian values
will not be given proper expression in our value system. In both cases
values which we want to see prosper would be diminished, and perhaps
lost.

The argument in defence of idealism will not proceed in a linear
fashion but will develop by taking up a series of dilemmas which reflect
contemporary moral problems, allowing fundamental theoretical and
practical issues to surface from the analysis. It will circle the dilemmas,
illuminating them from different perspectives, letting the context
decide what is theoretically and practically important. Some themes
developed in one chapter will of necessity be repeated in other
chapters. This is unavoidable for holistic methodologies. It will look at
the dilemmas first from utilitarian and Kantian perspectives, then
from idealist ones. Always we shall be looking for ways to create richer
and more highly integrated intellectual and practical unities. We shall
not, however, be concerned with telling people what they ought or
ought not to do.

The moral philosopher is not a moralist who tries to indoctrinate a
set of values in others. Pontification has no place in the project. Since
the concerns of this book are practical as well as theoretical, a new
profile of the ethicist or moral expert will be required.[60] The idea that
there can be experts in morals as there are in medicine, law and
engineering strikes us at first sight as absurd. Moral questions are

surely different from technical or scientific ones. With the latter, we can legitimately appeal to an expert in the appropriate field for the best answer. With the former, this is clearly not the case. Moral decisions are very personal matters. They belong to unique individuals acting in unique circumstances and it is our values which help define our uniqueness. Part of these circumstances will be the institutional morality which originally defines our values for us and which will always be an essential part of our moral lives. Nevertheless each one of us must, in the end, make up our own minds for ourselves about what we ought or ought not to do. Neither the ethicist nor anyone else can do this for us. Unless moral philosophers approach their audiences as if they are rational agents who are capable of making up their own minds about right and wrong, any project in practical ethics is bound to fail. To do otherwise is to try to persuade others to accept values which are not their own and to deny the autonomy which makes intellectual exploration of moral problems possible. The moral expert who emerges from organic casuistry is the moral educator who facilitates the creativity of moral agents.

In order to facilitate the comparison of the two traditional systems, liberal utilitarianism and conservative Kantianism, when they are applied to the dilemmas, I have listed them, somewhat artificially, in two parallel columns below. I have included the psychological, sociological, theological and metaphysical assumptions under the heading of 'philosophical assumptions' because they normally belong to the reflective rather than the dynamic side of the systems. I have listed the liberal utilitarian tradition first, in the left hand column, and the conservative Kantian tradition second, in the right hand column. This captures again in an artificial way the dialectical interaction between suggested liberal reforms and orthodox conservative responses.

LIBERAL/UTILITARIAN AND CONSERVATIVE/KANTIAN ETHICS

LIBERAL UTILITARIANISM PHILOSOPHICAL ASSUMPTIONS	CONSERVATIVE KANTIANISM PHILOSOPHICAL ASSUMPTIONS
1 Empiricism: All knowledge comes from experience.	1 Rationalism: All knowledge comes from reason.
2 Consequentialism: Rightness/wrongness depends on the actual consequences of acts.	2 Non-consequentialism: Rightness/wrongness determined by motive of duty – by conformity to a rationally acceptable moral rule. Actual consequences are irrelevant.
3 Descriptivism: Moral judgements are based on the prediction of what will happen as the result of an act: if you must steal bread to feed your family, then you ought to.	3 Prescriptivism: Moral judgements command acts. If someone sincerely assents to a moral rule, he or she must act in accordance with it. If you assent to a moral rule that says stealing is wrong, then you ought never steal.
4 Particularism: Rightness/wrongness of an act depends upon the context.	4 Universality: Context is irrelevant. Rules apply equally to everyone.
5 Acts: Acts are logically prior to rules. A moral rule can be broken if greater happiness will result. Rules are generalizations from experience.	5 Rules: Rules are logically prior to acts. If an act is inconsistent with an acceptable moral rule then the act is morally wrong. The morality of an act is deduced from rules.
6 Subjectivism: The morality of an act is relative to the perspective of the agent. Lying may be right for one person but not for another.	6 Objectivism: The morality of an act is independent of the perspective of the agent. A belief that lying is right does not make it so.
7 Conduct: Utilitarians are concerned primarily about acts. Morality is concerned with right and wrong conduct – not with the motives of the agent. Giving to charity for a tax break is morally OK.	7 Virtue: Morality is primarily concerned with moral judgements about agents rather than acts. Giving to charity for a tax break is morally wrong. Motives are important.

8   Public morality:
Concerned with public conduct. Private actions which affect no one but the agent are excluded from moral judgement. There are duties to others but no duties to the self; e.g. a drunk who is not harming anyone else is not acting immorally.

8   Private morality:
Concerned not only with public morality but primarily with private morality. There are duties to the self. Drunkenness is a moral vice because it shows disrespect for the self.

9   Teleology:
For the utilitarian, adhering to a system of duties and obligations is a means to happiness.

9   Deontology:
For the Kantian, adhering to a system of duties and obligations is an end in itself.

10   Empirical psychology:
Conscience is innate. Reason is the slave of desire. A virtue is a disposition to produce happiness.

10   Rational psychology:
Conscience is acquired. Reason is independent of passion. A virtue is a character trait which aids conduct.

11   Determinism:
All behaviour can be explained by efficient causes (motives). The will is reduced to desire.

11   Non-determinism:
Man is free. Conduct is explained by agent causality. The will cannot be reduced to desire.

12   Convention:
Morality is created by contract or agreement. Good and evil have their origin in society.

12   Nature:
Morality is natural to people. It is discovered not created. Good and evil have their origin in humankind.

13   Secularism:
Morality and religion are unrelated.

13   Theologism:
Morality and religion are inherently related.

14   Materialism:
Matter is ontologically superior to mind.

14   Spiritualism:
Mind is ontologically superior to matter.

LIBERAL UTILITARIANISM MORAL PRINCIPLES AND PRECEPTS

CONSERVATIVE KANTIANISM MORAL PRECEPTS

1   Social utility:
Maximize happiness and pleasure; minimize human pain and suffering.

1   Respect for persons:
Always treat persons as ends in themselves; never merely as a means.

2   Hedonism:
Pleasure (happiness) is the sole intrinsic good; pain (suffering) the sole intrinsic evil.

2   Self-perfection:
Moral virtue is the sole intrinsic good; moral vice the sole intrinsic evil.

3   Expediency:
A good end always justifies the means. If dishonesty, lying or insincerity advance one's interests and do little harm to others, then they are acceptable.

4   Quality of life:
Life is only valuable when it possesses an acceptable balance of pleasure/happiness over pain/suffering.
Euthanasia is morally acceptable.

5   Beneficence:
Help others in need. Good should be distributed according to need. General good takes precedence over individual rights.

6   Femininity:
Be caring, partial and nurturing.

7   Deterrence and reform:
Punishment is justified only if it deters further wrongdoings or benefits the offender.

8   Individual liberty:
Do as you please as long as you don't harm others.
Be tolerant of others.

9   Zoo-centrism:
Humans are not the only beings in nature that have value; any species that can feel pleasure/happiness, or which suffers, has intrinsic value. Animal welfare: maximize the welfare of animals; animals ought to have legal rights.

3   Conscientiousness:
Do your duty for duty's sake. Honesty: always keep promises and contracts. Truthfulness: always tell the truth, never lie. Pauline principle: never do evil in order to do good.

4   Sanctity of human life:
Life is sacred and an end in itself; it is valuable no matter what its quality.

Euthanasia is morally wrong.

5   Justice:
Always treat people equally. Respect human rights. Rights take precedence over charity.

6   Masculinity:
Be impartial, fair and self-reliant.

7   Retributive justice:
Only the guilty should be punished.

8   Autonomy:
Act morally but don't interfere with the moral freedom of others.
Evil cannot be tolerated.

9   Homo-centrism:
Only persons possess intrinsic value. Nature (plants and animals) does not. Animals have no rights, but there should be no wanton cruelty towards them or wanton destruction of nature.

Chapter 3

Academic honesty

A brilliant high-school student in Grade 13, who has consistently headed his class every year, has to hand in a final essay to complete his year. He is in line for an important scholarship which he urgently needs if he is to go on to the high-profile university of his choice. If he does not do well in the essay he will not get the scholarship. At the time the boy's single mother is critically ill. Since he is the oldest of the children, he has to assume the responsibility of looking after his two younger sisters. Under these circumstances it's impossible for him to do his usual scholarly job in preparing his essay. He considers buying an essay from a commercial service which prepares essays for university students he knows, and which has been used by other students in his high school. The cost is reasonable and this will ensure that he will do well enough to secure the scholarship. There is little or no chance that he will get caught. If this student does not get the scholarship it will not be awarded to anyone else because no other student could qualify for it. He consults a few close friends and most think that there is nothing wrong with what he is thinking of doing. Is it morally right for the student to plagiarize his essay?

The problem raised by this dilemma is whether students are ever justified in cheating to get high grades. The way we resolve the dilemma will, as we have seen, depend on the general ethical tradition we rely on to provide us with answers. The ethical systems western cultures normally adhere to can, I have argued, be roughly divided into two main camps which I have named liberal utilitarianism and conservative Kantianism.[1]

Both systems, as noted, have deep roots in our culture. Kantianism represents an older conservative tradition which is related to both secular and theological humanism. Utilitarianism represents a newer reformist tradition which is associated with the rise of modern science.

In Chapter 2, I developed these traditions in ways which emphasized their differences rather than their similarities. Some differences between these primitive forms of utilitarianism and Kantianism are philosophical or theoretical, others are practical or substantial moral differences. One major philosophical difference concerns the methods they use to justify moral judgements. The utilitarians are consequentialists who hold that the rightness or wrongness of actions are determined by the actual consequences. Kantians, however, are non-consequentialists who hold that the rightness or wrongness of an action is determined by the motive behind it and not by its actual consequences. Acting dutifully or conscientiously is what is important for the Kantian. We must be principled and act in conformity to acceptable universal rules which are valid for all moral agents.

Another significant philosophical difference is that Kantians are strict objectivists or realists, who hold that the rightness or wrongness of an action is independent of the person making the judgement, while the utilitarians tend to be subjectivists, who hold that moral judgements are relative to the individual's perspective. To say that cheating is wrong is to express our emotional disapproval of cheating, not to make some sort of factual claim, as the Kantians would have it.[2]

Further philosophical difference relates to the function of rules in moral reasoning. The utilitarians are particularists, contextualists or situationalists, who believe that the rightness or wrongness of an action depends upon the context or situation. All moral rules are likely to have exceptions. If cheating in a specific set of circumstances would maximize happiness/minimize suffering, then it would be morally permissible to cheat. The Kantians, on the other hand, are universalists who believe in moral absolutes. A true universal moral rule can have no exceptions. Cheating is cheating wherever you find it and it is always wrong.[3]

The systems, as indicated before, also have major moral differences. The first principle of liberal utilitarianism is the principle of social utility: you ought to do that act which will maximize happiness/minimize suffering. The morality of an action is determined by its social utility. The first principle of conservative Kantianism is the principle of respect for persons: always treat persons as ends in themselves and never merely as a means. Social utility can never be an overriding consideration because we cannot use anyone merely as a means to someone else's well-being. Another significant moral difference between the traditions is that for the utilitarian a good end always justifies the means, while for the Kantian ends, however good, cannot justify means which violate the principle of respect for persons. The utilitarians believe in expediency and trying to bring about the best result for everyone in every situation. The Kantians accept the Pauline principle of never doing evil in order to achieve good. They believe in fairness and impartiality. Principles like honesty and truthfulness express fundamental obligations for the Kantian which cannot be waived simply for convenience. These philosophical and moral differences, among others, are crucial for deciding the way the student's dilemma will be resolved. Let's look at a utilitarian response to the dilemma first, then go on to a Kantian response.

Utilitarians hold that the rightness or wrongness of an action depends on the balance of happiness over suffering it produces, hence they would argue that the student should plagiarize his essay. There are extenuating circumstances. The student's mother was critically ill at the time the essay was being prepared and this explains his poor showing. The student had always done well on previous essays. He was clearly the best student in the class and was expected to win the scholarship anyway. No other student could receive the scholarship because no other qualified. If the student didn't get the scholarship he wouldn't be able to go to university. A promising career would be ruined. Society would lose the benefit of a new talent. A sick mother would be less well cared for. So more harm than good would be done if the essay was not plagiarized. Even his friends, who were morally uncomfortable with the idea of cheating at school, agreed to this. Nothing is gained by adhering strictly to the rules against cheating on examinations or plagiarizing essays or by sticking blindly to the rules laid down for academic competitions.

The utilitarian holds that moral rules are expendable because no two situations are alike. To tell a lie in one context might bring about disastrous consequences but in another context telling a lie might bring about good consequences. Whether it is right or wrong to lie will depend on the actual circumstances. Utilitarianism is a form of situation ethics which holds that the context in part determines the moral character of an action. For utilitarians, the particular case always takes epistemological precedence over a moral rule. There are no absolute moral rules. Lying is not intrinsically bad. Just observe our normal moral practice. We lie to protect ourselves, our friends and the innocent from harm. We lie to protect our privacy. Doctors lie to protect their patients' interests. Politicians lie to protect the national interest. More importantly, teachers and professors plagiarize to get ahead in the academic world. So the utilitarian would say that in some situations the student should cheat; in others he should not.[4] A student should stick to the rules of academic honesty in some situations, but not in others. It depends upon the circumstances. Of course, the student has to consider the long range as well as the short range consequences of plagiarizing the essay.

He should also recognize that cheating could undermine the faith other students have in fair competitions. If he is not honest and fair, then why should he expect other students to be honest and fair? Students are always being told not to cheat in examinations, not to copy their essays verbatim from books, not to get another person to write their essays or their exams for them. If you are caught cheating or plagiarizing, you are severely punished by the school authorities for it. Play fair! Be honest! These are the rules for all students. If academic dishonesty becomes widespread this would undermine an educational system which has treated the student well so far and in which he wants to remain. In this case, however, the student runs little risk of being caught, so these undesirable effects are not likely to come about because he cheated this once. More immediately, he would have to consider the effect his action would have on his friends, especially those who disagreed with what he was considering doing. In the actual case these students respected his right to do what he thought best, even though some wouldn't consider doing it themselves.

Plagiarizing the essay might also have a bad long range effect on the scholarship student himself. He would always wonder whether he could have won the scholarship without plagiarizing and what his peers and teachers would think of him if they knew he had cheated. In the long run he will be just cheating himself. The utilitarian would argue that in this particular case it's not likely that cheating would undermine the student's confidence in himself, because this particular student had expected to win anyway. In any case academic dishonesty was widespread in the upper-middle-class school he attended. Cheating was simply part of what was involved in living in a highly competitive school environment. It was even widespread among the teachers and professors who imposed the rules on students.[5] What he was doing was simply a trial run for surviving in the dog-eat-dog society he would enter when he finally left school. What he was doing was not that different from the normal university practice of paying graduate students to do research for busy professors. He was simply delegating work when circumstances made it impossible to do the work for himself: surely a sensible business procedure. Nor is it likely that his teachers would detect the plagiarism, as they trusted the student completely. Rules do not place us under strict obligations. For the utilitarian, moral rules can always be waived in order to produce happiness. For them, moral rules are not absolutes which can't be broken but are guidelines which are only useful up to a point. They are not moral laws but generalizations from experience. We know from experience that in most cases telling the truth will bring about the best consequences; as we say: honesty is the best policy. But we also know from experience that there are situations where acting honestly will bring about the worst consequences. For the utilitarian, the gains of each deception must be weighed against the danger that we may undermine the socially useful practice of telling the truth. In this situation, the balance of happiness over suffering is most likely to be produced by the student plagiarizing his essay so he can get the scholarship.

In any case who is to say what is right or wrong? All this talk about academic honesty and dishonesty, rightness and wrongness, goodness and badness, presupposes that we have some objective way of determining what is right and wrong, in the same way we can determine truth and falsity in science. But is this really the case? Surely moral disagreements are often more emotional than rational; this explains why it is so difficult, if not impossible, to resolve moral disputes rationally. The current debates over abortion, capital punishment and euthanasia clearly substantiate this. Moral claims cannot be proved to be true or false by appeal to objective evidence, because they are emotional expressions of individual preference.[6] They are logically like judgements of taste. If John says that he likes coffee and Jane says that she likes tea, they are expressing their preferences for different drinks. There is no factual dispute between them. They are simply expressing different individual tastes. Similarly, when John says that academic dishonesty is morally acceptable, while Jane says it is morally unacceptable, they are merely expressing their individual preferences for or against a certain type of conduct. Their judgements do not refer to any objective fact, hence disputes about them are not amenable to rational solutions as factual or scientific disputes are. If John says it is raining outside and Jane says it is not, the dispute can be settled by looking outside to see if it is the case or not. But what is there for moral judgements to refer to, other than the emotions and the opinions of the person making the moral judgement, if they refer to anything at all?

Moral judgements are, at best, matters of opinion only and not matters of fact. Everyone is entitled to his or her own moral opinions, and shouldn't we treat everyone's opinions with equal respect?

Teachers or peers have no right to impose their values on others. This is why moral education is out of place in any school system. As long as the student is comfortable with his moral judgement then that is all there is to it. If anything matters morally it is our own preferences and approvals, not those of others. After all, circumstances vary from person to person and different individuals have different wants and goals. What is right for one individual may not be right for another. Getting married and raising a family may be the right thing for June to do, but having a career and being a single mother may be the right thing for Jane to do, and who is to say that June's life-style is morally better than Jane's? A life of scrupulous honesty may be right for some people but not for others. The interest of the individual is best left to the individual to decide. Each of us is most likely to be the best judge of what is good for us, and each of us is most likely to be truly concerned about our own well-being. Others are more likely to be concerned about themselves first and about us second, if they are concerned about us at all. Morality is essentially subjective, not objective, a matter of individual preference rather than fact. What is important is that we should feel comfortable with our moral decisions, whatever they are, and not whether they conform to a mythical set of objective standards. It is the actor not the observer who has to live with the decision. There is nothing intrinsically wrong with academic dishonesty. It is all a matter of circumstances. In morality it is better to leave the final say to the individual.

We live in a free democratic society which teaches us to be tolerant of people who have different moral viewpoints and to treat their moral opinions with a respect we would not grant their scientific opinions. Because moral judgements are merely expressions of individual preference, then it follows that all moral judgements are equally valid and all ought to be equally tolerated. Understanding this both explains and justifies the principles of tolerance, freedom of thought and conscience, and freedom of choice, which are fundamental values in a democratic society. These are surely values which we want to protect. Intolerance has no place in a democracy. Moral education has no place in a democratic society. So long, then, as the student is comfortable with his decision to cheat, as he appeared to be, then it would be morally permissible for him to do so.[7]

That was a utilitarian response to the dilemma, now let's look at the Kantian response. If the student had relied on the Kantian tradition, which adopts respect for persons as the first principle of ethics, he would not have plagiarized his essay. In the first place plagiarizing is unfair to the honest students he is competing against. Most students want to get good grades in school and to do well in academic competitions. So why should someone who is dishonest, who cheats to get better marks, be allowed to do better than the honest students, who study hard, play by the rules and don't cheat? For the Kantian, morality is not just about the distribution of benefits and harms, but adhering to the rules of honesty and fair play. These rules apply equally to everyone, even in situations where none gets hurt. What if the situation were reversed and this student had lost his scholarship to another cheater? Would he be willing to grant an exception in this case? Not likely! Exceptions based on individual self-interest are unfair. Students who do not earn the appropriate grades should not get scholarships.

Kantians believe the principles of honesty and fairness express fundamental human values. The rules they generate, like no cheating in school, are an inherent part of morality. They are objective moral truths and should be scrupulously adhered to. This is why university authorities and the general Canadian public were outraged by revelations of serious cases of academic dishonesty which occurred in 1989 at York University in Toronto. This scandal even involved police raids on a Toronto business establishment, Custom Essay Services, which had supplied plagiarized essays to York students. As Shirley Katz, the Associate Dean of Arts at York University, remarked:

> Of all the offenses I have seen involving dishonest practices, the submission of essays for academic credit not written by the proposed author is, in my view, a particularly pernicious offense. It undermines the very essence of a university and it is virtually undetectable.[8]

Both society in general and the vast majority of university students expect university authorities to see that the academic system is honest and that the rules of fair competition are adhered to. These expectations justified the university's dramatic attempts to clamp down on plagiarizing, cheating on examinations and other forms of academic dishonesty. From the perspective of the teacher, academic dishonesty is always wrong. Surely all teachers have a moral obligation to create a learning environment which is free from academic dishonesty. This is not a matter of individual taste, as if it were alright for some teachers to morally approve of cheating and others to disapprove. Teachers who fail to teach and enforce these values are remiss in their duties. Even worse are teachers who plagiarize to enhance their academic careers. They are moral hypocrites who are bad role models for the students they teach. Moral judgements are not merely matters of subjective preference but expressions of universal objective moral laws which are valid for all rational agents. They apply to teacher and student alike.

A fundamental moral disagreement exists between the teacher and the potential plagiarizer. To suggest as the subjectivists do that none exists is an extremely odd way to interpret our moral experience. Subjectivism implies that there can be no real disagreement between any two individuals.[9] If a teacher asserts that plagiarism is wrong, and a student that it is morally acceptable, then the teacher is really saying nothing more than, 'I disapprove of plagiarism' and the student nothing more than, 'I approve of plagiarism.' According to the subjectivist there is no moral disagreement between them, because their judgements do not refer to the same thing, if they refer to anything at all. At most, the teacher is talking about his or her personal attitude towards plagiarism, and the student is talking about his or hers. If both are sincere then both judgements would be true. But in our ordinary moral universe people do actually disagree, and this has important implications about the way we live our lives and for the way we organize our institutions. We cannot simply agree to disagree about the morality of plagiarism in the school environment, any more than we could with respect to cheating in Olympic athletic competitions. The Canadian public was as shocked by the discovery that some of our leading Olympic athletes were using anabolic steroids to enhance their performances as it was by university scandals, and here also a definitive moral answer was required. We simply could not ignore the moral issue involved.

In cases like these we must make up our minds as to which moral viewpoint is acceptable, but subjectivism leaves us no way to do this. Plagiarism is wrong because it violates the rules of fair academic competition, just as steroid use violates the rules of fair athletic competition, hence to plagiarize in this or any other circumstance would be wrong. Nor can we simply define what we are doing in any way we please. Plagiarizing is not a form of delegating work any more than using steroids is a way of body building. It is true that we live in a democratic society which rightly respects the principles of moral tolerance, freedom of thought and freedom of conscience. But if we accept moral tolerance must we accept general moral scepticism? Clearly not. We are not required to tolerate evil. Subjectivism implies absolute moral tolerance and this is clearly unacceptable. All moral viewpoints are not equally valid and so cannot be equally tolerated. Moral education based on objective moral values does have a place in a democratic society.[10] All moral opinions surely ought to be treated with respect, because they represent the views of rational moral agents, but this is different from allowing them full practical expression. Freedom of thought and freedom of conscience are not co-extensive with freedom of conduct.

Then there is the question of self-respect. Even if no harm came to the student because of the plagiarizing, he would still be achieving his valid goals by immoral means and this would be inconsistent with respecting himself as a rational moral agent. For the Kantian, you are not allowed to do evil in order to do good, so it would always be wrong to succeed by cheating.[11]

This dilemma involved a conflict between the utilitarian principles of social utility and individual freedom, and the Kantian principles of honesty, fairness and self-respect. The two traditions, as noted, do not always arrive at opposing answers to moral dilemmas but frequently they do. In this case they appear to do so. The dilemma is based on a real situation which actually occurred in a Canadian high school. The friends and relatives whom the protagonist consulted for advice arrived at opposing answers because some approached the dilemma with a utilitarian bias while others approached it with a Kantian bias. Those who relied on the utilitarian tradition tended to argue that it would be alright for the student to plagiarize his essay. Those who relied on the Kantian tradition tended to argue that the student should not plagiarize the essay.

The utilitarians argued that the student ought to go ahead and plagiarize his essay to ensure he would get the scholarship. Cheating in this particular situation would produce more good than harm on the whole for everyone affected by the action. Freedom of conscience is a basic democratic value and our school systems should respect this, hence moral decisions are best left up to the individual. In any case moral decisions are ultimately subjective and are not open to verification in the same way as scientific judgements. There is no objective moral truth. Moral judgements are expressions of individual preference, not matters of fact.

The Kantians, on the other hand, held that the student ought not to plagiarize his essay, even if this cost him the scholarship. To do so would be inconsistent with the principles of honesty, fairness and self-respect. We cannot break moral rules, like fairness in academic competitions, whenever it is convenient to do so. Principles of justice are universal, objective and valid for all rational moral agents. Certainly we have an obligation to ourselves to develop our talents as much as possible, but we must do this only through legitimate moral means. For the Kantian, we must not do evil in order to do good. We cannot sacrifice self-respect for success.

Because personal or subjective factors are normally involved in the utilitarian approach, it tends, in practice, to decline into scepticism and self-serving rationalism. Because the Kantian approach strives for strict objectivity, in practice it tends to decline into a rigid and inflexible rationalism, into what R.M. Hare called a 'hide-bound morality'.[12] As a result the utilitarian solution abandons the principle of respect for persons, as it expresses itself in honesty, fairness and self-respect, while the Kantian solution abandons the principle of utility, as it expresses itself in prudence, in avoiding harm to the self. The solutions presented are once more deficient in significant ways, and both theories produce states of affairs which are less morally adequate than we would want. If we hope to make any progress with the problem in our universities, we need to alter our current moral perspectives on academic dishonesty. We need to look for ways in which the opposing values of honesty and social utility can be given fuller and harmonious expression within the learning environment. One way to do this is to determine why we as a community value academic honesty and reject academic dishonesty.

Why do we believe that plagiarizing is morally wrong?[13] To answer this question we need to understand what plagiarism is. At York University plagiarism is defined as follows:

> Plagiarism is the representation of another person's ideas or writing as one's own. The most obvious form of this kind of academic dishonesty is the presentation of all or part of another person's published work as something one has written. However, paraphrasing another person's writing without proper acknowledgement may also be considered plagiarism.[14]

Plagiarism then is the unacknowledged presentation of someone else's academic work as one's own. This definition is adequate because the phrase 'as one's own' distinguishes it from legitimate unacknowledged presentation of other people's academic work. One can make use of another scholar's work without plagiarizing it. In fact all students and academics must build on the work of their predecessors. Scholarship has a social as well as an individual dimension. Indeed most of our knowledge is derived from the cultures which rear us. Very few of us ever make truly original contributions to knowledge. Our world views, like our moralities, are largely products of our societies rather than ourselves. We cannot make explicit reference to everything we have learned from others. If we did almost everything we wrote would be footnoted.

We now know what we mean by plagiarism, and it is clear that the scholarship student in the dilemma was plagiarizing in this sense, although at one point he tried to describe what he did as simply delegating work. Clearly he was not doing this. His main intention was to deceive, not delegate. He knew that this was a false description of what he was doing. Plagiarizers, like others who do wrong, often try to disguise what they are doing from others and frequently from themselves. What is it then that we find unsavoury in this kind of activity? There are two standard arguments which academic communities use against plagiarism. First, plagiarism is unfair to the honest students, those who do not cheat; and second, plagiarism has no educational value. Let's look at the argument based on fairness first.

Everyone wants to get ahead in school, so why should someone who cheats to get better marks be allowed to do better than the honest student who respects the rules and doesn't cheat? This appears to be such a clear breach of fundamental principles of justice and fairness that there is no question of its immorality. To quote *Teaching and Learning at York* again:

> Within this shared enterprise, instructors have another, rather heavy, responsibility, that of making certain students can function in an atmosphere free of academic dishonesty. Students need to know that if they work honestly, they will not suffer because of those who do not.[15]

The academic community tends to give this clearly Kantian argument precedence over utilitarian ones, although it recognizes that it is utilitarian considerations which often create the stresses which lead students to plagiarize:

> University education includes demands that might tempt some to violate standards of academic honesty. There are pressures on students to achieve high grades, obtain financial support, meet research or publication deadlines, gain recognition from the scholarly community, and secure employment.[16]

Recognizing these pressures and others, e.g. heavy work loads, extra-curricular concerns like sports and outside jobs, plus the personal and parental problems facing the student in the dilemma, may help us to understand why students plagiarize, and may even arouse our sympathies towards them, but they do not make cheating morally acceptable for us. Utilitarian considerations may explain academic dishonesty, even excuse it, but they can never justify it.[17]

Utilitarian considerations also suggest that the problem of academic honesty has deeper roots, because all these pressures are really side-effects of the students' involvement in an educational system which is organized around competition. After all it is grades, not learning, which determine who gets into the professional schools and graduate programmes. It is the appearance of learning which counts for success, not learning itself. The appeal to fairness thus presupposes a competitive learning system. But is competition really good for education? There are arguments on both sides. Competition, we think, brings out the best in people. When people compete they are forced to produce their best. Look at the way free-market economies work. Of course they only produce continued economic growth if the competition remains fair, thus fairness seems to be a requirement of free-market systems. Still, it's not clear that all our social institutions should be modelled on the free-market system. Perhaps a co-operative or more individuated system would work better for our institutions of learning. One advantage the co-operative systems have is that plagiarism would be eliminated, because knowledge is not seen in these systems as a kind of private property belonging to some individual. Truth in some sense is thought of as belonging to society as a whole and not to the individual. In the Middle Ages, which created the university in the first place, only Aristotle was footnoted. Copyright is a modern invention.[18] There is some merit in the claim that knowledge is public property. Co-operative projects are not considered plagiarism at York University, provided permission has been granted by the course director.[19]

However, we cannot entirely deny the importance of the individual in the pursuit of truth. Knowledge may be a social project but it has no ontological existence apart from individual knowers. If we attempt to create a better balance between competitive and co-operative forms of education in our school systems, we are more likely to reduce the stresses on students which fuel academic dishonesty. But as long as we retain competitive forms of education, the argument based on fairness will stand and academic dishonesty will remain morally unacceptable for our institutions of learning.

Although the argument based on fairness presupposes a competitive system of education, the second argument, based on plagiarism's learning value, appears to apply to all educational systems. Plagiarism has no educational value because it involves no relevant learning process. Yes, the plagiarizer learns how to cheat, but what one learns by using an essay service is hardly what the teacher intended the student to learn. The student was expected to learn some physics, or economics or English or philosophy, and not dishonesty. Plagiarism is inconsistent with the central purpose of a university, which is the pursuit and dissemination of truth. There is no place for academic dishonesty in a university because honest and open enquiry are inherent values in a learning institution. You cannot have a university community which does not comprise a group of scholars and students pursuing truth. Imagine a university dedicated to the pursuit of ignorance, intellectual error and sloppy academic standards! Universities, like all social institutions, embody a set of values which define their function and codes of conduct which ought to govern their members. We can conclude then that academic honesty is an intrinsic value for a university. To quote *Teaching and Learning at York* again: 'A clear sense of academic honesty and responsibility is fundamental to good scholarship.'[20]

Learning and acquiring knowledge, understanding and wisdom are essential to the learning process, hence they are intrinsic values for any educational system. Here we come face to face with the medieval value of learning for its own sake. Acquiring a university degree, especially a liberal arts degree, in order to get into the professions for social success or material gain are extrinsic to the learning process, hence learning possesses only instrumental value. What the student wants is the power which accreditization of knowledge brings, not knowledge for its own sake. He wants the appearance of scholarship, not scholarship itself. Here we are face to face with the modern Hobbesian value of applying learning to practical problems, whether individual or social. For Hobbes knowledge was power:

> The passions that most of all cause the differences of wit, are principally, the more or less desire of power, of riches, of knowledge, and of honour. All of which may be reduced to the first, that is desire for power. For riches, knowledge and honour are but several sorts of power.[21]

The fundamental question we are faced with is how to harmonize values which are intrinsic to the academy and those which are extrinsic. As MacIntyre has correctly pointed out, the idealist distinction between values which are intrinsic to a social institution and those which are extrinsic to it, is important for understanding our moral problems. But he appears to be pessimistic about the possibility of harmonizing intrinsic and instrumental values when they conflict. If the choice is an absolute either/or then he would certainly be right to choose the values inherent in our institutions, but this is not always the case. Must we reject these extrinsic values entirely, as MacIntyre appears to suggest?[22] I think not. Both values represent valid functions of a modern university, but the intrinsic value of relevant learning must be taken as basic for the institution.

You cannot train good professionals if they are not skilled and knowledgeable. Professional incompetence cannot be the goal of professional education any more than ignorance can be the goal of a liberal education. We have seen that universities embody a set of intrinsic values which define their function and which determine, in part, codes of conduct which ought to define the conduct of their members. The rules which give expression to these intrinsic values, like 'Pursue Truth', 'No Plagiarism' and 'No Sexual Harassment', should not be thought of as necessary moral truths which cannot be logically contradicted. Social practices and the values they enshrine can be criticized. Practices grow and develop. They can be modified or abandoned in the light of our moral experience.[23] This holds for every profession and not just for institutions of learning. All professions have public as well as private goals. They all serve the public interest in some way and this interest in part defines the values of the profession. It is essential for our school systems, and certainly our universities, to teach professional ethics as well as technical competence. All education, both liberal and professional, must always possess a moral dimension. Once it is understood that our professional as well our school life is part of a complex moral universe, it will be easier to understand why academic dishonesty is ethically unacceptable even for budding professionals. It is the intrinsic values of these institutions which establishes the objective core against which moral education in the schools must develop. That objective core cannot be established, in the first instance, by appeal to abstract ethical theories, like utilitarianism and Kantianism, which try to circumvent the concrete morality which is embedded in our social institutions.

It is one thing to establish that plagiarism is immoral within the context of a university, but this does not necessarily justify institutional regulations against plagiarism. It does not automatically follow that because something is immoral that it ought to be controlled by social regulations. Because the social enforcement of morality is always a threat to individual liberty, a separate argument is needed to justify it. This suggests that the doctrine of absolute moral tolerance, which is implicit in subjectivism, makes no sense in an educational institution. Since morality presupposes the existence of moral agents, creatures who are capable of making up their own minds about right and wrong, acting on their moral beliefs, and taking responsibility for their conduct, restricting moral freedom should always be done with care. This also suggests that the doctrine of absolute intolerance, which is implicit in some forms of objectivism, also makes no sense in educational institutions. The problem is rather, as an idealist approach suggests, what can and what cannot be tolerated within a community of scholars.[24]

The university regulations at York University are justified because they are designed to protect the fundamental values of the university. These strict regulations, which can involve severe academic punishments, including suspension from the university, show academics and non-academics that we, as a scholarly community, take the values of fairness and the pursuit of truth seriously. We must be committed to creating a learning environment which is free from academic dishonesty, as we are to creating an environment which is free from sexual harassment, and which maximizes intellectual freedom.[25]

University regulations of this severity would only be justified if due respect was also given to the individual rights of students. These rights must be seen as an inherent part of institutions of learning. No educational process, moral or non-moral, can be effective if students are not recognized as rational agents who are capable of intellectual development. Any form of education which denies the learner is an autonomous rational agent will fail because it defeats the primary purpose of education, which is to produce mature intellects. Any student accused of academic dishonesty has the right to be informed of the charges and be given an opportunity to reply to them. He or she should also have a right to appeal against any penalties to the appropriate institutional bodies. Our approach to the problem of academic dishonesty should not be only punitive and legalistic. We need to approach the plagiarizer with compassion as well as justice.

Plagiarism often has its source in personality dysfunctions. Chronic plagiarizers often lack a secure sense of personal identity and are afflicted with low self-esteem. They feel horrible and stupid about what they do, but are compulsively drawn to this form of self-defeating conduct. This suggests that the plagiarizer is faced with a serious problem in personal growth and probably needs counselling to outgrow the problem. This should not surprise us, because morality is not simply an arid intellectual exercise of applying rules to cases, but a process of personal growth which varies from individual to individual. MacIntyre has amply demonstrated that social practices have their inherent virtues as well as inherent moral values and rules.[26] The good scholar possesses academic honesty as the good soldier possesses courage. The plagiarizer in this dilemma was not a compulsive plagiarizer, yet he too required moral growth to cope properly with the dilemma he faced. By taking the route of academic dishonesty he failed to use his predicament as an opportunity for moral growth, and remained morally stagnant.

The idealist distinction between values which are intrinsic to social institutions and those which are extrinsic to it also provides a fundamental defence against general moral scepticism. Morality appears to be an inherent part of all social institutions. Our morality is, as F.H. Bradley argued, defined in the first instance by our social roles.[27] Our duties, rights, privileges and freedoms are defined by the stations we occupy in life. We are students, teachers, citizens, fathers, mothers, wives, husbands, sons, daughters, brothers, sisters, doctors, lawyers, ministers, Christians, Muslims, Jews and atheists. It is through our social roles that we live out a good deal of our lives and in terms of which we first learn to be moral agents, so we cannot escape morality even if we wanted to. One cannot be a true amoralist, because general moral scepticism, which denies the possibility of moral knowledge, is practically incoherent. To deny morality is, as F.H. Bradley pointed out, to assert it, because denying something has value implies that you have a standard for assessing the value of things.[28] The sceptic is someone who wants to escape from the moral world, but this is impossible. He or she wants to be an amoralist; that is, someone who either refuses to make moral judgements or who tries to ignore the moral aspect of life. But this is not practically possible. We live in a moral as well as a material universe and to deny this is simply to deceive ourselves. When we choose a set of values we are making a choice not only about the way we intend to act, but also about the kind of people we are going to be. Morality is concerned with creating the good person as well as creating good conduct. When we choose to become an amoralist we are choosing to be a person of a certain kind and this is perhaps the most basic moral decision we can make.

Since it depends on a foundationalist approach to knowledge, general moral scepticism will fare no better theoretically than general scepticism did.[29] To assert that we know nothing is to claim we know we are ignorant. The general sceptic is a mythical figure invented by the foundationalist's theory. When foundationalism vanishes so too will the general sceptic. I am not talking about specific moral scepticism, about questioning particular moral claims put forward by our societies. A healthy scepticism is as much a mark of a mature moral intelligence as it is of the mature scientific intelligence. Moral dilemmas are signs that we do not fully understand the moral universe, and they produce the desire to understand. They give us the motivation to grow intellectually and morally. But general scepticism does not. It simply provides a convenient rationalization for bad conduct and forces the moral agent, and society in general, to avoid moral dilemmas. It leads to moral paralysis and stagnation rather than growth.

Although these arguments are clearly compelling, general moral scepticism is still widespread today. Why is general moral scepticism still a problem? What are its perennial attractions? One common source of moral scepticism is the irrationality and violence which often accompany the great moral problems of our age. Issues like racism, abortion, capital punishment, war, terrorism, poverty, animal rights, environmental pollution and euthanasia generate such intense emotion that many of us are led to doubt that moral disagreements are amenable to reason. Another source of scepticism is the failure of moral philosophers to produce a unified theory of ethics that would solve the problem of rational methodology in ethics. Both these problems are more likely to be solved if we abandon our unproductive foundationalist ways and return to the exploration of our moral universe and the institutions which embody it. If we do, the true scholar – the lover of wisdom, who recognizes the obligation to create and sustain an environment which is free from academic dishonesty and sexual harassment, and which maximizes intellectual freedom – will replace the intellectual charlatan, that pale shadow of the true scholar, which too often is the dominant figure in the Academy.

Chapter 4

Experimental ethics

A Canadian social scientist wanting to study public and police attitudes towards homosexuals who have casual sexual encounters in bathhouses, disguises himself as a homosexual voyeur in order to observe and interview homosexuals. Unknown to his subjects, he also records their automobile licence plate numbers so he can do follow-up studies. Later, in the disguise of a public health official, he goes to their homes and acquires very personal information about their families, marriages, jobs, religion, children, etc. The results of the study show beyond reasonable doubt that public authorities, especially the police, hold unjustifiable negative stereotypes of the people who frequent bathhouses. The scientific community thinks the results are extremely valuable since they help to reveal the stereotypes and bias in terms of which the dominant heterosexual group perceives the gay community and which lead them to discriminate unjustly against them. Consequently, some police forces are persuaded that it is a waste of time to spend public resources in order to arrest the people involved in this victimless crime. Did the social scientist do the morally right thing by obtaining his information in this manner?[1]

The question raised in this dilemma is whether social scientists are ever morally justified in carrying out research in which deception is an essential part. Are we justified in deceiving the subjects of an investigation to secure scientific knowledge? Does a good end always justify the means? Those who defended the claim that the studies were ethical tended to rely on utilitarian arguments, while those who thought that the studies were unethical tended to rely on Kantian arguments. Utilitarianism tends to support the claim that the studies were ethical because they served good ends. They increased our understanding of homosexuality, and modified the negative attitude the general public and the police have towards the gay community. In this case a good end does justify the means. The utilitarian argues that the results of the bathhouse studies are morally acceptable because they produce more good than harm. From the utilitarian perspective it would be morally permissible to deceive the subject of a scientific investigation to gain socially useful knowledge. The moral justification of science is its social utility. The utilitarian would argue that without scientific research the great technological advances which are characteristic of the modern age would never have been achieved. The utilitarian then would place few moral restrictions on the scientific investigator, even when his or her research involved the use of human subjects. Any research would be morally permissible if it were scientifically valid and if the social benefits gained outweighed the risks to the subjects involved. The bathhouse studies appear to meet these criteria. The studies were scientifically important and the methodology used was scientifically acceptable. The researcher also tried to make the risk to the subjects minimal.

The utilitarian holds that the principle of utility – maximize happiness/minimize unhappiness – should take precedence over the principle of respect for persons, and the rights of privacy and informed consent it endorses. If we give priority to the utilitarian principle of maximizing happiness and minimizing unhappiness, then invasions of privacy can be justified in research involving human subjects, especially if the subjects observed never become aware that they are under observation, as was the case in the bathhouse studies. Invasions of privacy might be further justified if the identity of the subjects and the information about them are kept confidential, as this will help make the risk to the subjects minimal. This way no one will be harmed and we can gain valuable information about human behaviour, in this case the behaviour of homosexuals. The risk to the subjects will also be minimal if careful follow-up studies and adequate debriefing are carried out by the researcher. In the bathhouse studies follow-up studies were done both to get more data and to monitor the danger to the subjects. Debriefing was not carried out because the subjects remained totally unaware that they were involved in the research. To let them in on it at this late stage of the project would surely have done more harm than good. This is one of the advantages of field over clinical and laboratory research.

From the utilitarian perspective, if the rights of informed consent and privacy were rigorously enforced for research using human subjects, this would destroy the scientific study of people. Social science would have to be abandoned, and all the benefits it produces for humankind would be lost. The gay community would continue to be harassed by the police and useful social resources would continue to be wasted because of policies based on ignorance and prejudice. Many important research projects violate the subject's rights to privacy and informed consent, particularly when deception is necessary to prevent the subject from affecting the results. As the Canadian Medical Research Council observed, in some stress, addiction and gender studies deception is part of the experimental protocol. It is essential for the success of the research:

> The above procedures and requirements for obtaining an ethically valid required consent are of general application. However, they are not applicable to research in which it is essential that the subject be unaware of the nature of the research or even that he is the subject of research. In such cases, informed consent would in- validate the protocol. For example during the course of an experiment concerning the physiology of stress, a subject might be led to believe that something threatening to him has gone wrong with the experiment (perhaps a red dye simulating blood appears on a bandage) when in fact nothing has gone wrong at all. Again so that no one seeks alcohol elsewhere, alcoholics in an addiction study might not be told that half of the subjects in the study are receiving a placebo. As a further example to assure non-prejudiced results investigators might administer tests in order to determine gender- related responses, but tell the subjects that the tests are designed to study cognitive skills.[2]

The Milgram studies in obedience, conducted at Yale University in 1960–3, are a good example of an extremely important social science experiment which possibly should not have happened.[3] In the original experiment, as described by Milgram:

> A person comes to a psychological laboratory and is told to carry out a series of acts which come increasingly into conflict with conscience. The main question is how far the participant will comply with the experimenter's instructions before refusing to carry out the actions required of him.[4]

The object of the experiment is to see how far the subject will go in obeying an authority before refusing to continue to do things which the subject believes to be morally wrong. How susceptible are we to succumbing to authority rather than adhering to our consciences? The experiment was conducted as follows:

Two people come to the laboratory for an experiment on memory and learning. One of them is designated as a teacher, the other as a learner. The experimenter explains that the study has to do with the effects of punishment on learning. The learner is conducted into a room, seated in a chair, his arms strapped to prevent excessive movement, and an electrode attached to his wrist. He is told that he has to learn a list of word pairs; whenever he makes an error, he will receive electric shocks of increasing intensity. The real focus of the experiment is the teacher. After watching the learner being strapped into place, he is taken into the main experimental room, and seated before an impressive shock generator. Its main feature is a horizontal line of thirty switches, ranging from 15 volts to 450 volts, in 15-volt increments. There are also verbal designations which range from SLIGHT SHOCK to DANGER – SEVERE SHOCK. The teacher is told to administer the learning test to the man in the other room. When the learner responds correctly, the teacher moves on to the next item; when the other man gives an incorrect answer the teacher is to give him an electric shock. He is to start at the lowest shock level, 15 volts, and to increase the level each time the man makes an error, going through 30 volts, 45 volts, and so on.[5]

The shock machine is tested on the teacher to make sure it works, and in some variations of the experiment the learner is asked about his heart condition and if it is medically alright to proceed with the experiment. The learner proclaims that it is alright. The job of the teacher then is to ask the learner a set of questions and to administer electric shocks to the learner if he makes mistakes. The shocks are administered with increased severity until the correct answer is given. What the teacher does not know is that the learner is not a naive subject like himself, but an actor who is collaborating with the experimenter to deceive the teacher. No real shocks are ever delivered to the learner. The actor merely simulates a person receiving electric shocks. Nor does the supposed learner have any history of heart trouble. All this is unknown to the teacher throughout the experiment. What was surprising about the results of the experiment is that a large majority of the subjects, some with considerable sweating and anxiety, went on to administer what were apparently severe, and even potentially lethal, shocks to the learner at the behest of the white-coated academic authority. They did this in spite of the screams and the protests of the victim. The experiment appeared to show how susceptible an ordinary citizen of a democracy is to the pressure of authority. Milgram concluded:

The results, as seen and felt in the laboratory, are to this author disturbing. They raise the possibility that human nature, or – more specifically – the kind of character produced in American democratic society, cannot be counted on to insulate its citizens from brutality and inhumane treatment at the direction of malevolent authority. A substantial proportion of people do what they are told to do, irrespective of the content of the act and without limitations of conscience, so long as they perceive that the command comes from a legitimate authority.[6]

We had always assumed that this sort of blind obedience to authority was characteristic of totalitarian societies but not of democratic ones like the United States or the UK or Canada. It could happen in Nazi Germany, as it did during the Second World War, but not here. Indeed one of the motives for the experiment was to try to understand what makes a highly civilized, cultured and Christian society like Germany in the 1930s and 1940s carry out such an inhumane and savage social policy as the Holocaust. The moral behaviour of the Third Reich was frightening and puzzling. As Milgram noted:

Obedience as a determinant of behaviour is of particular relevance to our time. It has been reliably established that from 1933 to 1945 millions of innocent people were systematically slaughtered on command. Gas chambers were built, death camps were guarded, daily quotas of corpses were produced with the same efficiency as the manufacture of appliances. These inhumane policies may have originated in the mind of a single person, but they could only have been carried out on a massive scale if a very large number of people obeyed orders.[7]

One of the most frightening findings of Milgram's experiments was the disappearance of a sense of moral responsibility in the subjects as obedience came to supersede conscience:

The most common adjustment of thought in the obedient subject is for him to see himself as not responsible for his own actions. He divests himself of responsibility by attributing all initiative to the experimenter, a legitimate authority. He sees himself not as a person acting in a morally accountable way but as the agent of external authority.[8]

As the danger to the learner increased, those who continued tended to shift the moral responsibility from themselves to the experimenters.

The 'you're the boss' syndrome took over, much as the 'I was only following orders' syndrome took over in Nazi Germany. The studies gave us fresh insights into the psychological and sociological mechanisms which allow us to act contrary to our consciences. They warned that those of us living in democracies ought not to be smug about the problem and think that it cannot happen here.

In spite of the scientific importance of Milgram's work, his experiments involved clear breaches of the experimental subjects' rights to both informed consent and privacy. The naive subjects were lied to, and the privacy of their consciences was invaded. Initially the criticisms levelled against Milgram by some of his peers in social psychology concerned not the rights of the subjects but their well-being. They were utilitarian criticisms.[9]

Milgram was able to respond to these criticisms because he followed the standard guidelines then in practice for protecting subjects from harm during experiments which use deception. Milgram's experiment would certainly have passed the Canadian Medical Research Council's 1978 guidelines.[10] Those guidelines required that research conform to the following rules if it is to be ethical:

1 The benefits of the research must outweigh the risks to the subjects.
2 The research must be scientifically valid.
3 The risk to the subjects should always be minimized.
4 The subject's informed consent is required, except when the protocol of the experiment requires deception.
5 If deception is used the risk to the subject must be minimal and not just minimized.
6 If deception is used adequate debriefing should take place as soon as possible.
7 If deception is used proper follow-up studies are necessary.
8 Remuneration may be given so long as it does not interfere with informed consent.
9 Data collected should be treated with absolute confidentiality. Results should not be published without the subject's consent.

Milgram's research was scientifically valid, yielding important knowledge, and deception was clearly part of the experimental protocol. He saw that the risk to the subjects was minimal and not just minimized. He did underestimate the stress the experiment put on many of the subjects because neither he, nor anyone else, had anticipated that so many subjects would act contrary to conscience. This was an unintended consequence of the experiment which no one could have foreseen, but once noticed it could be minimized. He used adequate debriefing procedures, making sure that the subjects realized no harm was done to the learner and that no matter how they performed during the experiment their self-esteem was left intact. Proper follow-up studies were also carried out to see that no lasting harm was done to any of the subjects. So far as Milgram could tell none of the subjects was harmed, and some even benefited from their participation. They came to understand themselves better and many not only approved of the experiments but said they would do it again if they could. Strict confidentiality was maintained and no data were published without the subjects' informed consent.[11] Milgram's experiments were ethical given the ethical standards at the time of the research. These standards clearly presupposed a utilitarian frame of reference. The ethics of research is governed by the principle of maximizing benefits and minimizing harm. This should not surprise us, because utilitarianism grew out of the same intellectual climate that produced the scientific and technological revolution. Utilitarianism is the philosophy of progress. As John Stuart Mill rhapsodized:

> Yet no one whose opinion deserves a moment's consideration can doubt that most of the great positive evils of the world are in themselves removable, and will, if human affairs continue to improve, be in the end reduced within narrow limits. Poverty, in any sense implying suffering, may be completely extinguished by the wisdom of society combined with the good sense and providence of individuals. Even that most intractable of enemies, disease, may be indefinitely reduced in dimensions by good physical and moral education and proper control of noxious influences, while the progress of science holds out a promise for the future of still more direct conquests over this detestable foe.[12]

The long range effects of continued violation of human rights by scientific researchers need also to be considered by the utilitarian. The extensive use of the practice might undermine the trust and high respect the general public has towards science and scientists. People would become cynical about science and resources, both human and material, would be less likely to be invested in scientific research. Social science could even become a bit of a joke. As one Toronto wag put it: 'The last time the police raided the Bath Houses all the found-ins listed their occupation as social scientists.' This effect will only occur if the practice becomes public and if it is presented as ethically unjustified. If it is presented to the public along with its utilitarian and other justifications, e.g. that the research has met university and government ethical standards, then it will be publicly acceptable. It is unethical conduct by professionals that is unacceptable to the general public. The utilitarian criticisms cannot be easily made to stick against Milgram, but the arguments on human rights have more force.

If the bathhouse studies are compared to the Milgram experiments they seem to fare better ethically. Even if the bathhouse studies involved violations of privacy and informed consent, none of the subjects experienced any stress; nor were they harmed, because their identities and the specific information collected about them were kept completely confidential. These studies were at least as ethical as Milgram's experiments. The well-being of the subjects was a prime concern for the researchers in both cases. With respect to the bathhouse studies, it could be further argued that no human rights were violated.[13] These studies, unlike Milgram's, were not clinical experiments but field studies of public behaviour. Do we need to ask another person's permission to observe him or her in public places? Clearly not, hence there was no need to get the subjects' informed consent before observing them. Informed consent may be required in experimental or clinical settings, but not in field studies. Further, do we invade the privacy of others when we watch them in public places, like restaurants, parks and bathhouses? Clearly not, hence no invasion of privacy occurred. Again, experiments in clinical settings may pose a threat to privacy, but not field studies in public settings. As a result, the utilitarian could also argue that the bathhouse studies would pass the current Medical Research Council of Canada guidelines as well as those in force at the time of the Milgram studies. In the 1987 MRC guidelines there is a strong shift away from the purely utilitarian perspective of the 1978 MRC guidelines towards a Kantian perspective. The new guidelines are much more critical of deception in experimental research involving human subjects, because it violates the rights of the individual. Still, they allow it when it is essential to scientific integrity that subjects remain unaware of the nature of the research:

> Because the concept of deliberately misleading research subjects runs so much counter to the principle of respect for persons, the committee had great difficulty accepting that deception could ever be ethically justified. However if research situations should arise where it is essential to scientific integrity that the subjects remain unaware of the nature of the research, the following rules should be applied.[14]

So even if there has been a significant shift in a Kantian direction in the new 1987 MRC guidelines, the utilitarian perspective is still predominant. It is the utilitarian principle of individual liberty that is cited as the philosophical basis of the shift, rather than the Kantian principle of autonomy. The shift is interpreted by the committee as a development of utilitarian ethics rather than an attempt to adopt a more Kantian ethic.[15]

That was a utilitarian analysis of the dilemma. Now let us look at a Kantian approach to the dilemma. The Kantians would support the claim that the bathhouse studies were unethical because they would see them as inconsistent with the principle of respect for persons. If we respect persons we must never use them merely as a means to an end, no matter how worthwhile that end may be. If we accept the principle of respect for persons we must logically accept the principle of respect for human rights. Persons have moral rights because they are rational creatures capable of deciding for themselves what is good or bad, right or wrong, or how they will contribute to the happiness of humankind. Since the bathhouse studies violate the subject's right to informed consent and right to privacy, they would be unethical from the Kantian perspective.

The Kantians would not accept the argument that field studies, unlike clinical experiments, do not require informed consent, or that they do not involve invasions of privacy. Gays surely use bathhouses to obtain privacy. They clearly do not want to be observed. The investigator had to become a lookout for his subjects so he could win their confidence and observe them. The claim that the researcher was merely looking at activity which was public obscures his disingenuous behaviour. It merely masks evil. There was invasion of privacy. An invasion of privacy can occur for the Kantian even if no harm is done. Consider the following case: suppose a Peeping Tom spies on a young woman by peering through her bedroom window, and secretly takes pictures of her undressed. Further suppose that he does this without ever being detected and that he uses the photographs entirely for his own amusement, without showing them to anyone. Further imagine that this occurs on very warm days, which require the blinds to be raised to cool the room. The young woman is not an exhibitionist. Clearly a utilitarian would have to admit that the Peeping Tom does nothing wrong. For it seems clear that the only consequence of his action is an increase in his own happiness. No one else, including the young woman, is caused any unhappiness at all.[16] For the utilitarian, there is no invasion of privacy because no harm is done. For the

Kantian, on the other hand, there is an invasion of privacy, and what the Peeping Tom does is wrong. He fails to respect the woman he spies on, because he does not have her consent to do so or to use her in this fashion. The subjects of the bathhouse studies were also duped into participating in scientific research without their consent. The investigator conducted interviews with them under false pretences in their homes. There was need for informed consent here because it is quite likely that many of the subjects would have refused to participate if they had known what was going on. Again, a failure to respect someone as a person can occur even if no harm is done.

To emphasize the importance of human rights, the Kantian would point to the important place human rights have in our society. The Kantian would argue that if deception is valid in this situation it ought logically to be valid in any other similar situation. To deny this is to deny the principle of universalizability, a logical principle which is implicit in any moral system which claims to be rational. The principle can be formulated as follows: to say 'An action X is morally right' implies that any relevantly similar act is also right. When we make moral judgements we normally imply that we can produce good reasons in support of it. The rule prescribes that we must judge similar cases similarly, on pain of irrationality. Some philosophers, like R.M. Hare, have argued that universalizability is all that is required to produce a rational system of ethics. Others have argued that the principle is equivalent to or implies the principle of fairness, i.e. we ought to treat people equally or impartially, or the principle of utility, i.e. we ought to give equal consideration to the happiness of all concerned, and is not merely a formal logical principle but a substantive moral principle, which rules out certain forms of subjectivism and egoism because they cannot be consistently universalized.[17] For Kantians, moral rules are valid only if they can be made into acceptable universal rules, so they would have no trouble accepting the principle of universalizability.

This puts the utilitarian defence of deception in experiments involving human subjects in an awkward position. If they want to avoid irrationality, utilitarians must accept the principle of universalizability. But if deception, and violating human rights, are valid for the social science researcher, then they must be valid for the police, or any other government official, when collecting any information they deem to be of social value. Since these procedures are dangerous infringements of our civil liberties why make an exception for the social sciences? Do we trust scientists more than we trust the police and the tax collector? Perhaps, but there is more to it than this. It's important to establish trust between the researcher and the subject if scientific findings are to be valid. But trust is founded on respect for persons. We can't trust anyone who violates our humanity. This is so even if the scientist tries to restore trust by proper debriefing to explain why the deception was necessary, and by using follow-up studies to see that no harm has come to the deceived subjects. There appears then to be no sound moral reason, from the Kantian perspective, for allowing scientists to use deception to collect data or to test hypotheses, even if this might be socially useful.

The Kantian is willing to put greater moral restrictions on scientific research than the utilitarian. The Kantian argues that science is a two-edged sword which can produce evil as well as good. Science may have discovered antibiotics and put men on the moon, but it also raises serious moral problems for humankind. Because of its enormous potential for good, we have been slow to recognize the darker side of science. We have failed, according to the Kantian, to put the necessary time, energy and money into addressing the moral questions which science raises. As a result, moral understanding has always lagged far behind scientific knowledge and technological progress.

The dilemma of using human beings as research subjects is something which we have only recently become fully aware of. There were no such problems for Newton when he split light up into the spectrum by using prisms. Light is not a living organism. However, once human beings become the subject matter for scientific study new moral problems arise. Medical and social science research frequently involves some risk to the subject. This might be acceptable when the research is therapeutic and is performed as part of a patient's treatment, or where the experimental subject has a good chance of benefiting from it. The situation is more complicated when the research is non-therapeutic, as both the Milgram experiments and the bathhouse studies were, and is performed primarily to gain knowledge which might benefit humankind but is not immediately beneficial for the subject. Surely no such experiments should be conducted without the patient's or the subject's informed consent? In the 1978 MRC guidelines the distinction between therapeutic and non-therapeutic experiments was dropped and both types of experiment were treated as essentially the same, requiring the same strict ethical standards. The guidelines pointed out that the distinction can create harmful misconceptions because it blurs the distinction between experiments and treatment, and undermines the need for obtaining full and careful consent.[18] The Kantians would approve of this because of its concern for strict informed consent no matter what the type of experiment. They would be less happy with the revised 1987 guidelines because in them therapy and research are once again sharply separated, with the former, including experimental therapy, being largely left to the discretion of the health care professional, and the latter falling within the scope of the guidelines. Ethically, therapy must always take precedence over research because the best interest of the patient takes top priority, but the question of informed consent becomes secondary:

> An informed patient may consent to enter a research study but, if therapy is also involved, the best interest of the individual must be the highest concern of the physician responsible for care. The patient is always entitled to the best clinical judgement of the physician and research considerations must never displace this. This is true even if the patient requires innovative treatment that, while therapeutically appropriate, is also of research interest.[19]

The moral problem of using humans as subjects in experiments was dramatically bought home to us during the 1949 Nuremberg trials. The revelation of the hideous experiments conducted by German medical scientists on prisoners in Nazi concentration camps shook the western world to its core. Prisoners were forced to participate in scientific experiments in which they were maimed and killed. In a series of experiments to test the effect of high altitudes on humans, prisoners were put into pressure chambers and the air pressure quickly reduced. German scientists dressed in clean white lab smocks observed and recorded when first the ear drums and then the lungs of the subjects burst. In other experiments prisoners were infected with contagious diseases, including jaundice, typhus and malaria, in attempts to find safe inoculations. The experiments were thought to be justified because they might help the German war effort, and humankind as a whole would benefit if the research was successful.[20] According to the Kantians, the Nuremberg revelations provide a horrifying demonstration that acquiring useful scientific knowledge does not justify means which violate fundamental human rights, such as the right to informed consent, the right to refuse to participate in any experiments, the right to personal privacy and, finally, the right to life.

Some interpreters have argued that the Nazis doctors were really pseudo-scientists, and that no good scientist would have performed the concentration camp experiments. They suggest that the experiments were badly designed and produced no valuable scientific knowledge.

They argue that if an experiment is scientifically sound it will also be ethical. They claim that good science is necessarily ethical science. If this were true it would simplify the moral life of scientists, because the only moral obligation they would have is to produce good science. But can we identify good science with ethical science? In the first place it's not clear that the concentration camp experiments produced no valuable scientific knowledge. Some data and information gained in these experiments have proved useful in studies of hypothermia.[21]

Second, there are historical examples of good science which used what we would now recognize as unethical means. In 1796 Edward Jenner, the discoverer of the smallpox vaccine, used an 8-year-old orphan boy, James Phipps, as his main research subject, and the boy underwent great physical stress and suffered permanent physical damage by being injected with cowpox vaccines.[22] We cannot assume then that good science can be equated with ethical science, and current guidelines in most civilized countries have rejected this assumption. The idea that scientists should be allowed complete freedom to conduct research as they please without any social control has been abandoned in favour of, at least, voluntary ethical guidelines.[23] Besides, equating good science with ethical science merely avoids addressing the ethical questions associated with experiments with human subjects.

Further, the Kantians point out that after Nuremberg the United Nations adopted a set of principles governing the use of humans in scientific experiments, which has been called the Nuremberg code. It was a landmark in the attempt to develop and realize a universal system of human rights. The code's basic rule is no experiments on human subjects without their informed consent – a rule which expresses a Kantian, rather than a utilitarian, moral stance.[24] One of the ironies of Milgram's experiments, which appear to violate this rule, is that they were designed to help us understand why people behave in the way the Nazi doctors did. Another irony of the research is that the obedient subjects often tried to justify the experiments by appealing to their social utility.[25]

Adherence to this rule not only condemns the concentration camp experiments but raises serious moral questions about the use, under any circumstances, of captive subjects like prisoners or nursing home patients, or incompetent subjects like children, foetuses or the mentally disabled, or minority groups like homosexuals.[26] The rule clearly bans experiments on captive or incompetent subjects, because their ability to give informed consent is either greatly diminished or non-existent.

The same consideration can easily be extended to the gay community, whose members are vulnerable in a way the heterosexual community is not. The bathhouse study illustrated that the rule of informed consent is even more restrictive for social science than for natural science. To use deception to get people to participate in an experiment or to use them in research without their knowledge blatantly violates the rule of informed consent, as well as violating the subjects' right to privacy. There has been a clear movement in civilized countries away from the utilitarian laissez faire attitude to deception in research, towards a more restrictive Kantian view, and this is reflected in the 1987 MRC guidelines.[27] The changes are not sufficient for the Kantian, because they stop short of a complete ban on experiments with captive and incompetent subjects:

> By definition a legally incompetent subject is not autonomous, and cannot give a legally or ethically valid consent. However these people may suffer illnesses on which research is necessary if methods of therapy are to be improved or instigated. In some cases, the illness may cause the incompetence. Some of the needed research may be expected to benefit the research subjects, but other needed research may not.[28]

A total ban on the use of these types of subject is the only way to prevent violations of the rights of these vulnerable groups. The Kantian would say we can wrong someone even if he or she is not directly harmed. In the case of the bathhouse studies we can assume that the subjects wanted to keep their activities secret. The Kantian would argue that the search for knowledge about human sexual behaviour would not be a sufficient warrant to override the homosexual's right to privacy and informed consent. By spying on people, you have not treated them with the respect appropriate to rational moral agents.

That was a Kantian analysis of the dilemma. Now let's sum up. In this dilemma we have a conflict between the Kantian principles of respect for persons, respect for human rights and the Pauline principle that you cannot do evil in order to do good, and the utilitarian principles of social utility and expediency, i.e. a good end always justifies the means. If we always choose respect for persons and human rights over social utility, then scientific research involving deception can not be morally justified. Unless we can discover a rational way of choosing between the socially expedient and human rights, our dilemma will remain unresolved.

Before we try to answer the question, we should remind ourselves that it is not the job of the moral philosopher to tell other people what they ought to do. Moral philosophers must always remember that they are addressing moral agents, that is, people who are capable of making up their own minds about what is right and wrong and acting on their decisions. Hence moral philosophers must respect this autonomy and the freedom of conscience which comes with it. They should also remember that professionals, because they are directly involved with the ethical problems of their professions, bring a unique perspective to these problems, which often provides insights that abstract theoretical approaches would miss.

It could be argued that accepting the principles of autonomy and professional privilege could lead to forms of subjectivism and moral conservatism. Subjectivism would not necessarily follow. As we have seen, even if everyone's moral opinion is worthy of respect, this doesn't imply that everyone's moral opinions are equally valid. Some moral opinions are simply better than others. Racists, for example, are as entitled to their opinions as anyone else and it would be wrong to try to coerce them to change their minds. We can try to reason with them if this is possible, but never to coerce them or to brainwash them. But even if we must show tolerance towards a racist's moral beliefs, it doesn't follow that the racist's and non-racist's values are equally sound. Objectivism in some form is theoretically necessary, but it must be formulated in a way that does not result in moral dogmatism or moral intolerance. We must distinguish between the claim that every moral question has a right answer and the claim that we know for certain what the right answer is.

The first claim is an expression of faith that the moral universe, like the natural universe, is rational – a presupposition which seems to me necessary for a rational project like moral philosophy to proceed, and one which is implicit in the form of idealism I am defending. If it is the case that the objective criteria for morality are coherence and richness, it must be the case that there are no incommensurable dilemmas. Every dilemma must have a solution which allows the conflicting values to be simultaneously and harmoniously expressed. Otherwise our moral epistemology would be at cross purposes with reality. The second claim is a form of dogmatism which has no place in moral philosophy. We do certainly encounter dilemmas we don't know how to resolve. Even if all moral opinions are not equally valid, we can never be absolutely sure that any moral judgement is absolutely right or absolutely wrong. No one ever has possession of the complete truth and this holds for the moral philosopher as well. Moral decisions are often very personal matters. They belong to unique individuals acting in unique circumstances. We all, each one of us, have to make up our own minds about what we ought to do or ought not to do. Neither the philosopher nor anyone else can do this for us. The most the moral philosopher can contribute is to suggest strategies for solving moral problems and to explore with others the suggested solutions which emerge from applying them, to see if we can discover which is the better way.

The most important strategy for resolving moral dilemmas is to look for creative alternatives which will allow us to continue to express the conflicting values harmoniously. In the bathhouse case the conflicting values are those of socially useful knowledge and respecting human rights. We need to look at the principles and try to see what options we have for implementing them.

In this dilemma we have very little flexibility with respect to human rights. The rule – no experiments on human subjects without their informed consent – seems to be a valid response to our experience with experiments involving human subjects during, and after, the Second World War. This rule has also led us to examine more carefully our use of captive and incompetent subjects – like prisoners and children in orphanages – and other groups, like gays, which have been systematically discriminated against. It looks then like a sound moral rule that can only be tinkered with in minor ways at best. It does, however, need to be modified. To place a strict Kantian interpretation on the rule would strangle the principle of beneficence. There are, for example, good arguments for continuing to conduct experiments on captive and incompetent subjects, because a complete ban would deprive these groups of research which would benefit them. Their participation in therapeutic experiments or innovative treatment, although presenting problems, would be ethically acceptable. Their participation in non-therapeutic experiments, however, would remain moot.[29]

On the other hand, we seem to have more flexibility if we look at the way we conduct research with normal human beings. If social scientists were to stop using deception in their research would this be such a great loss to the science? The rule of informed consent, of course, doesn't affect experiments where control groups are used but the individual subjects don't know whether they are members of the control group or not. This procedure is sometimes called the 'single blind technique'. Nor does it affect experiments where neither the experimenter nor the subject know who is in the control group. This procedure is sometimes called the 'double blind technique'. So long as the subject is informed about the experimental protocol, no deception showing disrespect for the subject's human rights will occur.[30]

Naturally, the rule will seriously affect other research projects, like the Milgram experiments or the bathhouse studies. The rule certainly puts extra demands on researchers. They would have to become more inventive and resourceful in their work than they already are. They must develop new methods of research or develop older methods which have gone out of fashion.[31] Perhaps they might be led to reexamine the fundamental way they look at human beings. Scientific psychology, in its legitimate effort to transfer scientific methodology from the study of nature to the study of people, has presupposed a mechanistic conception of humans. It is assumed that human behaviour must be explained in terms of efficient causality rather than teleologically, in terms of goals and purpose. Experimental subjects are seen as natural objects rather than as living creatures. This conception of people implies determinism and determinism appears to be inconsistent with any kind of morality. If we have no choice there can be no morality. Morality presupposes that human beings are rational agents who can make up their own minds about right and wrong and take responsibility for their actions. Determinism appears to rule this out.[32]

In any case, the more creative we are the better our science should be and the more we are likely to learn about ourselves. When human rights are properly integrated into scientific research we should produce better science. There is no moral escape for scientists who conduct experiments with human beings. They must accept the facts that moral considerations will always put restrictions on the research and that they must never treat their research subjects merely as a means to an end, but always as persons. This is not easy to do and it will demand of the researcher a great amount of methodological invention. Surely creativity is something which lies close to the heart of true science. Ethical restrictions put no limits on scientific creativity, rather they are spurs to greater creativity. The Pauline principle, that we ought not to do evil in order to do good, should be interpreted as a general methodological principle directing us to restructure the situation in ways which allow full expression to the conflicting values. Its first thrust is negative. It tells us what is not a proper solution to a moral dilemma – in this dilemma, not to respect fully the research subjects' rights to privacy and informed consent. It requires us to be consistent, in this negative sense, with the values we already assent to.

This is the Kantian interpretation of the principle defended so brilliantly by Donagan.[33]

In the idealist interpretation I am suggesting, the principle has a positive thrust as well, directing us to find creative solutions to our moral problems, to produce interpersonal states of affairs which are richer and more highly integrated than the current ones responsible for the dilemma. When thus interpreted it ceases to be merely a restrictive, niggardly principle which inhibits growth, and is transformed into a principle of creativity and growth, which is essential to both science and morality. It becomes a principle which should be intellectually and morally attractive to both the liberal utilitarian and the conservative Kantian alike. If experiments must become more ethical, then ethics must become more experimental.

Chapter 5

Urban terrorists

John's best friend, Bill, is a member of an anti-nuclear organization. John is not himself a member of the group but shares similar concerns about nuclear war and the need to work for peace, and does all he can to support his friend in his peace activities. The group has become completely frustrated at the lack of progress the disarmament movement has made in Canada. Canada is still not a nuclear-free zone and the cruise missile is being tested there. Everyone in the organization agrees that the non-violent approach has got nowhere. None of the authorities seems willing to take the group's disarmament initiatives seriously. The group's members decide that a planned campaign of some kind of violent disruption is necessary to get the authorities to listen. They want to be as certain as they can that no one will be physically injured or killed in the process. They want their violence to be mainly directed towards the property of arms manufacturers, but they will not be deterred by the possibility of injuring or even killing people in the process. A Canadian plant which manufactures parts for the cruise missile is selected as the first target. A bomb will be set off near the front entrance of the plant and the organization will take credit for it in the hope that its pleas for nuclear disarmament will be heard. The members know that innocent people working in the plant might be injured or killed. To minimize the risk they choose a time in the early hours of the morning when only a skeleton staff will be working in the plant, and they plan to phone in a warning in time to evacuate the plant before the bomb explodes. The agreement is struck and the plans laid. John's friend, Bill, is one of the team chosen to hide the bomb and set it to go off at the agreed time. Bill needs to have someone to make the warning phone call for him, and asks John to do it as a favour for a friend. John sympathizes with the group's frustration with civil disobedience, but seriously questions whether any act of terrorism is a way to bring about peace. He also fears that despite precautions some innocents might be hurt or killed. He tries to persuade Bill to abandon the plan. He argues that once terrorism is adopted as a means to achieving the ends of the peace movement, the distinction between property and people will become meaningless and the integrity of the movement will be compromised. But Bill remains determined to go ahead. What is the morally right thing for John to do?[1]

Some dilemma raises several important ethical questions. First, is it morally right to help a friend commit an act of terrorism? Or, more generally, is it ever morally right to use violence or terrorism in the pursuit of peace? Or, more generally still is it ever morally right to use violence or terrorism to promote a just cause? The answers we give to these questions will, as we know, depend on the ethical systems we use to give us our answers. If we rely on utilitarianism, which makes social utility the first principle of ethics, then we would think it morally right to help a friend commit the act of terrorism. If we rely on Kantianism, which makes respect for persons the first principle of ethics, then we would think it morally wrong to help a friend commit the act of terrorism. The theories tend to arrive at different conclusions in part because the utilitarians are consequentialists who hold that the rightness or wrongness of actions is determined by the actual consequences, while the Kantians hold that the rightness or wrongness of actions is determined by the motive or the intended consequences of the agent. The utilitarians are thus led to support the principle of expediency – the end always justifies the means – while the Kantians adopt the Pauline principle that evil may not be done that good may come of it. The two traditions have radically different attitudes towards the principle of sanctity of human life.

First, let's see how a utilitarian might arrive at the conclusion that it is morally right to help a friend commit an act of terrorism. The first stage in a utilitarian justification of aiding terrorism would be to provide a utilitarian defence of the peace movement. Is war ever justified on utilitarian grounds? There is always a prima facie utilitarian case against war because of the great suffering it causes. War would be acceptable for the utilitarian only if the alternatives caused more suffering than the war. For the utilitarians, the choice with respect to war is always between the lesser of two evils. So each situation would have to be given a cost/benefit analysis, to decide whether the war would be morally acceptable or not. For the utilitarians, the Second World War against Germany was justified, because of the great evil the Nazis' regime presented to the democracies and the world. However, the devastation a nuclear war would produce makes it morally wrong for the utilitarians. It's true that utilitarian arguments were used by President Truman to justify the atomic bombings of Hiroshima and Nagasaki at the end of the Second World War. The use of nuclear weapons minimized human suffering because it brought the war to a speedy end and saved countless lives. This was valid then, but not now because at present we possess more lethal nuclear arsenals. The situation is radically different, and current circumstances make nuclear war unthinkable.

Some utilitarians believe that the idea of a limited nuclear war which could be restricted to the use of tactical weapons and confined to the battle field is not a realistic option. There is no way of preventing a limited war from developing into a full scale nuclear war. The idea of retaining nuclear weapons as a deterrent is also unrealistic. For a threat to be real, it must be effective. So a nuclear threat must involve the real intention to use nuclear weapons. On utilitarian grounds this is an unacceptable risk. Unilateral nuclear disarmament appears to be the only reasonable course. The utilitarian would also argue that countries such as Canada and the UK should have nothing to do with nuclear weapons. They should become nuclear-free zones. There should be no cruise missile testing in their air space and they should probably withdraw from NATO. The avoidance of nuclear war is so important for the utilitarian that it would justify the use of terrorism provided terrorism really did bring about peace.

Second, since terrorism is a criminal act, a sound utilitarian argument for breaking the law is required. The utilitarians believe we have a duty to obey the law, because a system of law is a socially useful practice. A lawful society is more likely to maximize happiness and minimize suffering than a lawless society. To legalize terrorism would be absurd because it would undermine the rule of law. A legitimate government has a legal right to enforce its policies and the laws which express them. Naturally, the duty to obey the law is contingent on whether the law is just or unjust, that is, whether it is conducive to the general happiness. Although utilitarians support the rule of law, they also believe we have a duty to change the law or government policy if they are morally wrong. If legal means fail, they believe we ought to resort to civil disobedience first, and sometimes even to terrorism. So the utilitarian would support terrorism as a means for political action, if the goal to be achieved was of very great value and terrorism actually did bring about political change. The ends which both John and Bill want to achieve are to avoid nuclear war and to bring about world peace, which would produce great happiness. The pursuit of peace would justify the use of terrorism because peace would cause less suffering than war, especially nuclear war.

Violence poses a special problem for the utilitarians, because they are committed to the principle of non-maleficence: don't harm others. This principle generates secondary rules like don't inflict injury and pain on others. Because someone always suffers when we resort to violence, the utilitarians would normally be reluctant to use it to achieve their goals. Nevertheless, the utilitarian can never be an extreme pacifist, someone who holds that the use of violence in any circumstances is always wrong. In practice the principle of non-maleficence, when properly expressed, means 'minimize human suffering', not 'never cause human suffering'. As Jan Narveson has effectively argued, pacifism is logically incoherent for the utilitarian.[2] It implies that violence can never be used to prevent more or greater violence, that we must reject our legal and moral right to protect ourselves against the violence of others. There is always a prima facie utilitarian case against the use of violence, because of the pain and suffering it causes. But there are situations where non-violence can cause more pain and suffering than violence.

Consider the following hypothetical case. A deranged sniper has barricaded himself on top of a central building overlooking the campus and pedestrian mall of a large university. He opens fire on the crowds below, killing and wounding several people, including women and children. Others, again including women and children, are pinned down on the campus by the continuous and indiscriminate rifle fire. A SWAT (Special Weapons and Tactics) team from the local police force arrives. They find that the sniper is so well positioned and protected that they cannot even get to the wounded and dying in the open campus, far less put him out of action. One of the police sharpshooters is able to get himself into a position were he can get a clear shot at the sniper, but only at his head. Having tried to talk him down from his perch to no avail, the officer in charge orders the sharpshooter to take the sniper out. He does, killing the sniper instantly.[3] In this situation it seems clear that killing the sniper will cause less suffering and death than passively allowing him to continue his murderous rampage. So even the highest level of violence can be justified in certain circumstances on utilitarian grounds. It would be inconsistent for the utilitarian to argue that violence ought never to be used to prevent violence. Terrorism doesn't always cause suffering; when it does, it can still bring about the greatest happiness for the greatest number. So the use of terrorism in the cause of peace can be justified on utilitarian grounds provided it actually does bring about peace.

The utilitarian must also consider the negative consequences of using violence in the cause of peace. If violence is used and innocent people are harmed or killed, the peace movement could be easily criticized as hypocritical, believing in peace yet resorting to violence. Terrorism can be counter-productive and the goal of peace could be harder to achieve. What have the terrorist campaigns of the IRA in Ireland, the PLO in the Middle East, or the FLQ in Canada achieved? None of these organizations has achieved its goals. What they have done is to alienate much of world opinion. Even people who are sympathetic to their causes are turned away by the indiscriminate car bombings, hijackings and hostage takings. Violence in the cause of peace is clearly self-defeating. Surely non-violent campaigns, like civil disobedience, would be a more effective strategy for the peace movement. However, if peaceful methods fail to be effective, as Bill believed they were in Canada at the time, the utilitarian could try a course of selected terrorism, for example targeting property rather than people. Peaceful methods may work in some contexts but not in others. The utilitarians would point out that civil disobedience was an effective tool for Gandhi against the British in India, but it has not been an effective tool for the black majority living in South Africa. Narveson has argued that non-violence is generally an ineffectual method of bringing about political change. This is especially true in the face of aggressors who are often moved to further violence when met by non-violence.[4]

A utilitarian faced with an unjust law or an immoral government policy cannot justify violence as a political strategy unless the following conditions are met:

1 The end will bring about a great good or eradicate a great evil.
2 All legal democratic means have been tried and exhausted.
3 All forms of non-violent protest, such as civil disobedience, have been tried and exhausted.
4 Violence must be used in a way which keeps it from being self-defeating; for example, violence should be directed at property rather than people where possible, and harm should always be minimalized.
5 Terrorism, which involves the deliberate harming or killing of the innocent, can only be a very last resort.

Unless John can show that using terrorism wouldn't work in this context, he must agree with Bill that terrorism is the lesser evil. He ought then to agree to make the warning phone call, and allow his friend Bill to carry out his terrorist mission.

Even if a utilitarian held that terrorism was morally wrong, he could still think it was right to help a friend commit an act of terrorism. Let's see how this would come about.

Whether a utilitarian will help a friend commit an act he thinks immoral will depend on whether doing so would cause greater happiness than not doing so. In this case helping Bill would appear most likely to cause the greatest happiness and the least suffering. Utilitarian friendships are based on mutual advantage. It's a case of you scratch my back and I'll scratch yours. As long as they can use each other beneficially, their friendship will last. So if John refuses to help Bill, their friendship might well be lost and John could no longer expect Bill to help him in the future. This consequence is certain given Bill's fanaticism and desire for absolute loyalty. On the other hand, if John helps Bill he could possibly endanger the peace movement and he could be caught for aiding a crime. However, endangering the peace movement is not that certain. Many things could alter the course of events. For example, the bomb could turn out to be a dud and no act of terrorism would occur and there would be no public exposure. In any case the warning call would minimize the possibility of harm. Even if Bill were apprehended by the police, he would not be likely to involve John. Since the long range consequences are unclear, the utilitarian cost/benefit analysis would favour the short range. It appears to come down in favour of John helping Bill with his act of terrorism.

That was a utilitarian response to the dilemma. Now let us look at a Kantian response. The Kantian would think it's morally wrong to help a friend commit an act of terrorism because to do so is inconsistent with the principles of sanctity of human life and respect for human rights, and the Kantian concept of friendship.

The Kantians, like the utilitarians, believe that nuclear war is morally wrong, but they do so for different reasons. For the Kantian, nuclear war is immoral because it is inconsistent with the principle of sanctity of human life: all human life is sacred, no matter what its quality. For the Kantian, human life is intrinsically valuable, hence it is morally wrong to assault or kill human beings. Kantians are either extreme or moderate pacifists, but both types agree that nuclear war is immoral.[5] Extreme pacifists believe that there is no exception to the rule against killing or violence. The extreme pacifist believes that it is even wrong for an individual to take a life to save a life. The prohibition is absolute. On this strict view suicide, capital punishment, euthanasia, abortion, killing in self-defence or to protect the innocent, and all wars would be considered immoral.

The moderate pacifists hold that it is consistent with sanctity of life to take a life in order to save a life. They believe that killing and violence are wrong except in self-defence, or to protect the innocent. Consider the following example. A young woman returns home to her apartment late one night. As she enters the apartment she is violently assaulted by a man who has been lying in wait for her. She is dragged to the bedroom and flung on the bed, where her assailant tries to rape her. During the struggle she manages to get hold of a revolver which she keeps in her bed-side table. She shoots and kills her attacker. The police charge her with manslaughter, but an able defence attorney successfully pleads self-defence, and the women is exonerated.[6] This is a clear case of self-defence which justifies the killing from a moderate pacifist perspective. The moderate pacifist would also agree with the utilitarians that the sharpshooter in the earlier example did the right thing in killing the sniper. What the sharpshooter did was to save innocent people, not commit homicide. Here is a clear case of protecting the innocent.

The moderate pacifist accepts the doctrine of the 'just war'.[7] War can be justified if it is either in self-defence, to repel an aggressor, or to protect the innocent, to repel aggression against a peaceful, less powerful state. As G.E.M. Anscombe has ably argued, even just wars must be fought by moral means.[8] There must be no deliberate killing of the innocent. James Rachels uses the following example to illustrate Anscombe's argument:

> Suppose a military commander ordered that a city be bombed. Then the death of innocent people would be the direct and intended result of the bombing, and that bombing would not be permissible. On the other hand suppose that the commander ordered that a munitions factory be bombed but, since the bomb sights are not perfect, he knows that some bombs will inevitably fall on nearby civilian homes. In this case the deaths of the innocent people will be a foreseeable but unintended by product of the bombing raid against the factory, and so this bombing may be justified.[9]

So if a military commander bombs a munitions factory knowing innocent people will be killed this is not immoral. What is immoral is to kill the innocent intentionally. To terror-bomb cities and indiscriminately kill innocents and combatants alike is morally wrong. Certainly the use of atomic weapons is wrong because they kill the innocent. Tactical nuclear weapons might pass the test because they are intended to kill combatants and not civilians. However, a nuclear war would always involve the use of the complete nuclear arsenal, so nuclear war can never pass the test of the just war and must always be condemned. Nuclear deterrence policy doesn't fare much better. To be effective, as utilitarians have pointed out, the policy must involve the will to use nuclear weapons, and it is just as wrong to threaten to use immoral means to conduct a just war as it is actually to use them.

The argument does presuppose that there are innocents in modern war. The innocents in war are those not directly involved in the use or the production of arms. These include women, children, the sick, the elderly, farmers and medical personnel. In modern total war, which involves the whole population in the war effort, the distinction between combatants and non-combatants is more difficult to draw. Nevertheless, even in so called total war the children, the aged, the sick, the farmers and medical personnel would remain innocents. They are not intentionally doing anything which endangers the combatants. The problem becomes even more complicated when children, the aged and hostages are used as 'shields' to protect combatants. Even here the innocents are clearly identifiable, even if they have been put at higher risk by some of the combatants in the war.

The scholastic doctrine of double effect which Anscombe relies on to establish her position holds that the unintended but foreseeable killing of the innocent in war is morally permissible but not the intentional killing of the innocent. The Kantians are concerned with intentions, the utilitarians with results. It is the one who intentionally kills who does the wrong; the victim is always guiltless. So the Kantian concludes that nuclear war is morally wrong and it is also wrong to use terrorism, which could involve the killing of the innocent, to avoid nuclear war.

At the centre of the dilemma for the Kantian is the principle of sanctity of human life: all human life is sacred or possesses intrinsic value, no matter what its quality. This principle is, as Keyserlingk has pointed out, central to our systems of both morality and law, and is not easy to interpret.[10] On one interpretation this principle is thought to entail an absolute rule against taking human life. This would prohibit suicide, capital punishment, euthanasia, abortion and killing in self-defence or to protect the innocent. This is the position of the extreme pacifist. This position, when it is derived from the principle of sanctity of life, does not appear to be inconsistent, as Narveson has argued.[11] In fact it appears perfectly consistent. Surely one cannot logically assent to sanctity of life and condone killing in some circumstances. Extreme pacifism may be inconsistent on utilitarian grounds, but not necessarily on Kantian grounds. Utilitarians assent to the principle of sanctity of human life because life is a necessary condition for the possibility of happiness. Quality of life is important for the utilitarian, and not just biological life.

There is another side to the principle of sanctity of human life. The principle requires us not to kill but it also requires us to save, preserve and promote human life. Its prescriptions are positive as well as negative. Unless our moral universe is irrational, these two aspects of sanctity of life cannot conflict as they do in the present dilemma. Can extreme pacifism cope with the positive aspects of sanctity of life? Kantians could reformulate the principle as follows: we have an obligation to save and foster life, but we cannot use violence or killing to do so. In the sniper case this would imply that we ought not to kill the sniper or even use any violence to prevent him from wounding and killing the innocent. We can try to get the innocent out of harm's way, and we can risk our lives to do so, but we cannot use direct violence against the sniper. If there is no other way out of the dilemma, as in the sniper example, we must simply accept our deaths or the deaths of the innocent. It is the sniper who commits the crime, not us. This could be seen as an application of the Pauline principle: you cannot do evil in order to do good. According to the extreme pacifist, you have a right to self-defence but not to kill. The woman in the attempted rape case was right in trying to defend herself, but wrong to kill. Again, the good end does not justify immoral means. This interpretation of the principle of sanctity of life appears too radical. It denies our rights to self-defence and to protect the innocent. It renders us powerless in the face of evil. It arbitrarily ranks not killing above preserving innocent life.

Given our ordinary moral experience, moderate pacifism, i.e. no killing or violence except in self-defence and to protect the innocent, is a more plausible interpretation of the principle of sanctity of human life. What the principle proscribes is no killing of, or violence against, the innocent. In practice this would allow us to combat evil, but would require us to use only appropriate force and avoid unnecessary violence. We would have a right to use as much force as necessary in self-defence or to protect the innocent, but not normally to kill. You can sit on the aggressor or disable him, but taking his life would be a last resort. Consider the following example. A man returning home from work early interrupts a burglar ransacking his house. He goes to

his study, picks up his gun and accosts the burglar. The teenage
burglar turns his back and flees. The home owner tells him to stop or he
will fire. The burglar continues to try to escape. The home owner fires
and kills him. The police charge the home owner with murder.[12]

The moderate pacifist would argue that a citizen has a right to
protect his property as well as his person but cannot use unnecessary
force to do so. In this case, once the burglar had fled the premises the
home owner's property was safe and there was no reason to use deadly
force. On the other hand, in the attempted rape and sniper cases it
seemed that this last resort was necessary. The moderate interpretation, although clearly more adequate than the radical interpretation
of the principle of sanctity of human life, would still not condone
nuclear war or terrorism, because these involve the intentional killing
of the innocent.

The moderate interpretation of the principle of sanctity of life is
consistent with the Pauline principle of never doing evil in order to do
good. The Kantian would argue that in these cases the intention of the
sharpshooter was to protect innocent lives, and of the victim of assault
to protect her own life. The deaths of the sniper and the rapist were
foreseeable but unintended consequences of these morally permissible
activities. The killing of the sniper was not a case of murder because it
was not intentional in the strict sense. What the sharpshooter was
doing should be properly described as saving lives. The killing of the
rapist was not a case of manslaughter because it was not intentional in
the strict sense. What the woman was doing was protecting herself. It is
possible then to use the principle of double effect as a principle of
consistency for a Kantian system of ethics. After all it is the intended,
and not simply the actual, consequences which are relevant for the
Kantian, and it is the intended, not the unintended, consequences
which provide the correct description of what an agent is doing.

The Kantian would also reject the distinction which some urban
terrorists draw between violence directed against property and
violence directed against people. If acts of terrorism are directed
against property, this cannot be a breach of the principle of sanctity of
life, even if innocent people are accidentally harmed or killed. This
could be a foreseeable but unintended consequence of the act of
terrorism, making it consistent with the principle of double effect.
Nevertheless, it is still a breach of the principle of respect for persons.
To violate someone's property is to violate his or her person, even if his
or her life is not directly threatened. The act is still inconsistent with the
Pauline principle that you cannot do evil to bring about good. For the

Kantian, unlike the utilitarian, the end does not necessarily justify the means. So the Kantian would say that John should not help Bill commit the act of terrorism. He should not make the warning phone call even if the peace group's act does not put innocents at risk.

The Kantians, like the utilitarians, believe we have a duty to obey the law only when it enforces morally right conduct. So the duty to obey the law is contingent on the law being just. However, the idea of legalizing terrorism makes no more sense for the Kantian than it does for the utilitarian. To legalize terrorism is absurd because it could undermine the rule of law. A legitimate government has the right to enforce the laws which express its policies. Like the utilitarians, the Kantians support the rule of law, and they also believe we have a duty to change government policy if those policies are morally wrong. We have no absolute duty to obey an unjust law, one which is inconsistent with the principle of respect for persons or sanctity of life. If legal means fail, the Kantian would say that it is morally right to use civil disobedience to achieve change. This is morally acceptable because it is passive and does not involve the use of violence. Civil disobedience may provoke violence on the part of the authorities, but it is not violent in itself. The Kantians believe that political terrorism is immoral because it is inconsistent with the principle of sanctity of life and the principle of respect for human rights. Terrorism is an illegitimate means of violence because it involves attacking the innocent intentionally.

This stand is consistent with both moderate and extreme pacifism. Both views reject terrorism. It is not inconsistent for a Kantian to argue that it's wrong for a individual to fight violence with violence, but morally permissible for the state to fight violence with violence. Violence involves assault on another person's body. To use force on another person's body without his or her consent is morally wrong because it fails to respect that person's moral autonomy. This is why rape is wrong for the Kantian. The state has a duty to see that the moral rights of its citizens are protected and to use sufficient force to protect them from violence when necessary. For John to help Bill violate other people's rights is wrong for the Kantian, and the fact that John and Bill are friends would make no moral difference.

A Kantian friendship, unlike a utilitarian one, is based on mutual respect, not mutual advantage. The basic obligation in a Kantian friendship is concern for the other person's moral well-being. It is not just to help the other person when he or she wants help. Hence it would be wrong for Kantians to help a friend do something they believe to be immoral. Friends also have a duty to develop and respect each other's moral autonomy. On the one hand, John would have a duty to express his disapproval of Bill's proposed act of terrorism. On the other hand, it would be wrong of Bill to insist that John help him, because he would be disrespecting John's moral autonomy. A Kantian friendship would not allow John to help Bill perform an act of terrorism. John should not agree to make the warning phone call.

That was a Kantian analysis of the dilemma. Now, let's sum up both viewpoints. In this dilemma, we had a conflict between the utilitarian consequentialist principles of non-malevolence and expediency, and the Kantian non-consequentialist principles of sanctity of life and respect for human rights. The utilitarians are not pacifists but they believe that the suffering of a nuclear war would outweigh the suffering caused by an act of terrorism. Utilitarians might support unilateral disarmament in the belief that it could prevent nuclear war and so produce the least suffering for everyone on the whole. The utilitarians also believe that friends are there to help each other when they are called on. Friendship is based on the mutual advantage it provides the partners, so John ought to help Bill even if this indirectly involves aiding a criminal act.

The Kantian, however, thinks it is morally wrong for John to help his friend commit the act of terrorism. For the Kantian terrorism is an illegitimate means of violence because it involves harming the innocent and/or violating the sanctity of persons and their property. The Kantians, like the utilitarians, hold that nuclear war is immoral – but they do so for different reasons. Nuclear war is immoral for the Kantians because it's inconsistent with the principle of sanctity of life. Whether one develops the principle in terms of extreme or moderate pacifism the results are the same: nuclear war is immoral because it involves the deliberate killing of the innocent. For the same reasons, Kantians reject terrorism as a morally acceptable way to achieve peace. One can resort to civil disobedience to try to change an immoral law or social policy, but not terrorism. Once more we arrive at a familiar result. Both theories produce different but inadequate answers to the dilemma. The utilitarians abandon the principle of sanctity of human life when they embrace terrorism in the cause of peace. The Kantians leave us powerless in the face of evil, like nuclear war. Once again both solutions are deficient in important values and reach states of affairs which are less rich and coherent than we would desire. Some progress in extricating ourselves from the dilemma might be made if we consider the role which consequentialist and non-consequentialist principles play in determining the way the dilemma is dealt with.

The Kantians are non-consequentialists, who hold that the rightness or wrongness of actions depends on the motives or intentions of the agent, hence for the Kantian we can only be held responsible for the intended and not the unintended consequences of our actions. The utilitarians, on the other hand, are consequentialists, who hold that the rightness or wrongness of actions depends on the actual consequences. Hence for the utilitarian we can be held responsible for all the consequences of our actions, whether intended or unintended. Both views appear to be untenable.

One of the basic differences between the utilitarians and the Kantians is the roles they assign to the intended and the actual consequences in moral reasoning. For the utilitarians, the rightness or wrongness of actions is determined by the actual consequences rather than the intended consequences, as is the case for the Kantians. The theory of actual consequences leads the utilitarian to assert what appear to be unacceptable paradoxes. Consider the following examples. First, someone, A, has wanted to get rid of his arch rival C for some time. At a boating party he gets an opportunity to do this. C falls off the boat and because he cannot swim is drowning, when A happens by. There is a life-saver hanging on the ship's rail. A tosses the life-saver at C, ostensibly trying to save him but in reality trying to hit C on the head in order to drown him and make it appear like an accident. Fortunately for C there is a sudden change in the wind and the life-saver lands nearby. C grabs it and is saved. Second, at the same party a second person D falls off the boat, as another guest B happens by. Again there is a life-saver handy. B throws the life-saver at D to save him from drowning. B has every reason to believe that in these circumstances this is the best way to try and save D's life. Unfortunately for D there is a sudden change in the wind and the life-saver hits him on the head, causing him to drown. The utilitarians would have to conclude, paradoxically, that A did the right thing – saved C's life, even though he intended to kill him – while B did the wrong thing – killed D, even though he intended to save him. The Kantian on the other hand would have to conclude the opposite, that A did the wrong thing – tried to kill C, even if he actually saved C's life – and that B did the right thing – tried to save D's life, even though he actually killed him.

Both these analyses are counter-intuitive. Although no theory is logically committed to making itself consistent with ordinary moral judgements, it surely must square in general with our moral experience. The utilitarians need to supply an explanation of the paradox if the theory of actual consequences as the test of right and wrong is to be maintained. Similarly, the Kantians must produce an explanation of their paradoxes. G.E. Moore, following suggestions first developed by J.S. Mill, has argued that the theory of actual consequences as the test of right and wrong can be saved if we recognize that we make different sorts of moral judgements and use different criteria to establish them.[13]

We make moral judgements about people's characters as well as their conduct. We also make judgements about moral responsibility, and we assign moral praise and blame. Moore argued with considerable ingenuity that the intended consequences were relevant for judgements about persons, and for moral responsibility, but the actual consequences remained the test of right and wrong. The proper way to interpret the two previous examples would be as follows. We should say in the first case that A did the right thing, saved C from drowning, but he should not be given credit or praised for what he did. In the second case we should say that B did the wrong thing, drowned D, but he should not be held responsible or blamed for what happened. By distinguishing different types of moral judgement from each other, we dissolve the paradoxes and bring the theory into harmony with ordinary moral experience. We do not, however, dissolve all the paradoxes the theory entails. If we look at utilitarianism as a decision-making theory rather than a theory for post mortem moral judgements, more problems arise. The theory implies that we ought to choose that course of action which will maximize happiness and minimize suffering. If the actual consequences turn out badly through no fault of our own, then we cannot be held responsible for the unintended consequences of our actions.

The same follows from Kantian theory, because it is concerned initially with virtue, not conduct. The Kantian theory puts the emphasis on the motives and intentions of the agent rather than the consequences of actions. It is because they start with judgements about the goodness and badness of persons that the Kantian's claim – that intentions, not actual consequences, are the fundamental criteria for moral judgements – gains its initial plausibility. Surely everyone, including the utilitarians, would agree that the motives and intentions are relevant for moral judgements about character and for ascriptions of moral responsibility. Both Mill and Moore would concede this. Where they would still differ with the Kantians is on judgements about the rightness and wrongness of actions. These they believe do depend on the actual rather than the intended consequences. But the Kantian would argue that our moral world is co-extensive with our conduct and our conduct is determined by our intentions. What we do not intend is not part of our conduct, so it is absurd to include the unintended consequences as a criterion for determining the moral worth of our actions. The proper way to interpret the two cases is as follows. First, A did the wrong thing in trying to kill C. What A did was to try to kill C, and in doing so accidentally saved him. To say that he saved C from drowning is to fail to describe his action properly. Saving C was an unintended consequence of his action, for which he cannot be held accountable. Second, B did the right thing in trying to save D. What B did was to try to save D's life and, in doing so, accidentally drowned him. To say that B killed D is to fail to describe his action properly. Killing D was an unintended consequence of his action, for which he cannot be held accountable. As with the doctrine of double effect, the Kantian doctrine implies that moral agents can only be held responsible for the intended consequences of their actions.

Donagan has argued effectively against interpreting the Pauline principle, that evil is not to be done that good may come of it, in terms of the doctrine of double effect.[14] He argues correctly that this does not achieve its original goal of facilitating ethical decision-making and, more importantly, it implies that we cannot be held responsible for the unintended consequences of our actions: 'Finally the doctrine underlying all forms of the theory of double effect is that what lies outside the scope of man's intentions in acting does not belong to his action, and so is not subject to moral judgement.'[15]

Moore's solution to the problem of the role of the intended and the unintended consequences in moral reasoning is attractive in many ways. It draws attention to the fact that we do make different kinds of moral judgements and that we do emphasize different criteria in justifying them. But it, like the doctrine of double effect, implies that we cannot be held responsible for the unintended consequences of our actions and this is clearly false. Consider the following case. An anaesthetist accidentally overdoses a patient during surgery and the patient dies. The anaesthetist was apparently reading a book and not paying attention to his machinery. He certainly did not deliberately try to kill the patient. The patient's death was an unintended consequence of his actions. Is the anaesthetist morally responsible for the death of the patient? He was certainly thought to be legally responsible, because a medical malpractice suit was brought against him by members of the patient's family who thought he had acted negligently. Even if the family lost its case the anaesthetist could be held morally responsible, because reading a book during surgery certainly looks like moral negligence.

Consider a second case. A driver is speeding along a suburban street when a child darts out in front of her car from behind a parked car. The driver swerves to avoid the child, mounts the kerb and hits a pedestrian who later dies in hospital of injuries sustained in the accident. Again, the driver did not intentionally kill the pedestrian. The pedestrian's death was an unintended consequence of her actions. Should the driver be held morally responsible for the death of the pedestrian? She was certainly held legally responsible, because after an investigation the police charged the driver with careless driving. Even if the driver were not convicted in court she could still be held morally responsible, because she was speeding in an area where children were likely to be playing.

Cases of medical malpractice and careless driving clearly show that we do hold people both legally and morally responsible for the unintended as well as the intended consequences of their actions. We can be held responsible for our carelessness and our professional negligence. Conduct and personality cannot be as sharply divided from each other as utilitarianism and Kantianism imply. Both theories hold that what lies outside the scope of an agent's intentions lies outside the scope of his or her moral responsibility. But this is inconsistent with our moral experience.

If we look at the paradox from an idealist perspective, the dichotomy between the intended and the actual consequences dissolves, because both are relevant to all moral judgements. The idealist sees morality essentially as the development of personality. So it should not surprise us that when we talk of holding people responsible for the unintended consequence, we start talking about personality traits, like carelessness, and negligence. Our actions are always functions of our personalities, and it is conduct viewed in this way for which we are held responsible. In this sense the Kantians are correct to place the theory of virtue, rather than the theory of conduct, at the centre of moral theory.

The utilitarians, like the Kantians, have a theory of virtue. Utilitarians define virtue as a trait of character which benefits the self (personal virtue) or others (social or moral virtue). They define a vice as a trait of character which harms the self (personal vice) or others (social or moral vice). Prudence would be an example of a utilitarian personal virtue; imprudence an example of a utilitarian personal vice. Prudence tends to produce happiness and imprudence to produce unhappiness. Benevolence would be an example of a utilitarian social or moral virtue; malevolence would be an example of a utilitarian social or moral vice. Benevolence tends to promote the general happiness and malevolence to promote general unhappiness. For the utilitarian, virtue is a means to happiness. It has no intrinsic value. It possesses only instrumental value. A virtue in one context might be a vice in another context. Courage might be a virtue in generally peaceful societies, because it would be conducive to the agent's happiness yet involve minimal risk. But in warlike societies it might be a vice: because of the high level of violence which these societies display, it would be conducive to the agent's misery.

A Kantian defines virtue as a trait of character which facilitates rational moral conduct towards the self (personal or moral virtue) and towards others (social virtue). Courage would be an example of a Kantian personal or moral virtue; cowardice would be an example of a Kantian personal or moral vice. We need courage to act morally in the face of strong fears. Honesty would be an example of a Kantian social virtue; dishonesty would be an example of a Kantian social vice. We need to be truthful and open with others if we are to treat them as rational moral agents who possess intrinsic value. This might put us at greater risk, but we must learn to control our selfish desires in order to treat others with the impartiality rational moral agents require. For the Kantian, virtue is an end in itself. It is universal and non-contextual. What is a virtue for one person is a virtue for any other moral agent. The conscientious person does his or her duty because it is the right thing to do, and not to gain rewards or to avoid punishment. The conscientious need to have their desires under control if they are to act in accordance with rational moral principles. If virtue is to be achieved, reason must repress desire.

The idealist would reject both the utilitarian and Kantian concepts of virtue and vice. For the idealist, a virtue is a personality structure which facilitates the moral development of the agent (personal moral virtue) and the growth of social relationships (social moral virtue). A vice is a personality structure which inhibits or retards the moral development of the agent (personal moral vice) and the growth of social relationships (social moral vice). For the idealist, moral virtue is simultaneously personal and social. Courage, for example, would remain a personal virtue because we require it in order to face risks and dangers in realizing any personal goals we may set for ourselves. But it would also be a social virtue because communities, which are composed of individual moral agents, need to be brave in order to realize any social goals they may set for themselves. Benevolence, for example, would also remain a social virtue. We need to care for others if society is to organize its institutions in ways which will encourage, rather than inhibit, the moral development of its members and itself. But it is also a personal virtue. Self-love is as necessary for moral growth as is the love of others. People who do not love themselves are not likely to be able to love others. People who do not love others are not likely to be able to love themselves. Love of self and love of others are mutually dependent. The notion that personal and social virtue are onto-logically distinct, as utilitarianism and Kantianism presuppose, is untenable.

The idealist concept of virtue differs radically from the utilitarian concept because it does not draw a sharp distinction between personal and social or moral virtue. They can be distinguished from each other but they are organically related, as persons are to the communities they create. The idealist concept of virtue also differs radically from the utilitarian and Kantian concepts because it tries to harmonize reason, will and desire rather than having desire master reason and will or reason and will repress desire. The virtuous person has a healthy, growing personality, one which is becoming richer and more har-monious. For the idealist, virtue is intrinsic both to human well-being and the well-being of the communities that humans create.[16]

The Kantian principle of double effect achieves consistency by redescribing actions in such a way that their undesirable consequences are excluded, but this is an artificial way of escaping our moral responsibilities. Using the mechanism of redescription to interpret the Pauline principle is clearly inadequate. It makes it too easy for moral agents to wash their hands of the unsavoury consequences of their conduct. We require the intended consequences to give a correct description of what any agent is actually doing. A tried to kill C, not to save him. B tried to save D's life, not to kill him. It is intentionality which both describes and explains our conduct, even if it does not always justify it. The principle of redescription, if used as a method for justifying conduct morally, would make us search for answers in the wrong direction. We would look for excuses, rather than for creative solutions to our moral problems. In situations like those of the demented sniper and the violent rapist, there appears to be little choice but to do the lesser evil. Here the Pauline principle must give way to the principle of the lesser evil. Here we come face to face with our limitations, with understandable moral failure. The Pauline principle has not been abandoned. We simply are unable to apply it. We have done our best to avoid evil and this is all that can be expected of a finite moral agent. We tried, but the urban terrorists did not try hard enough. Terrorism is not moral heroism, but a failure of the moral imagination.

Chapter 6

Gentle exits

Three friends of assorted ages serve as volunteers in a nursing home and a chronic care facility in a hospital. They are very concerned about the suffering of aged, bed-ridden patients who no longer are able to function in any normal fashion or relate to anyone in a meaningful way. Each of them has also lived through trying months and years watching her own aged parents suffer a great deal of pain and frustration as they gradually lose their hearing, their eyesight, the use of their limbs and mental powers. The three friends talk a great deal about the dangers of living too long and each decides that at an appropriate time she will commit suicide so as not to get caught in a nursing home or terminal care facility. They agree to help each other if help is needed. When the oldest of the three reaches the age of 82 she decides the time has come and asks for the assistance of one of her friends. She plans to run her car engine in her garage with the door closed. The only problem is that the door can only be closed from the outside. She has informed her grown family about her plan to commit suicide when the time comes, but has explained that she would not involve them in the details or let them know the precise time she would act. The family were reluctant to accept her idea, but knew her determination and came to respect her decision. She tells her family, who check daily on her, that she is going away for a week to visit a friend, which she often does, and arranges with her friend to come along at an agreed time to close the garage door. The friend keeps her promise to help and does as requested. Did she do the morally right thing?

   In this dilemma there are three considerations which are important. First, the three friends have promised that they would aid each other's suicide if one of them wanted help. Second is the consideration of the legal status of aiding suicide. Third, there's the question of whether we should ever make promises to commit an illegal or immoral act.

We can begin the analysis of the dilemma with the example of Canada providing the legal context. In Canada, aiding suicide is an illegal act which involves considerable personal risk. It is no longer a criminal offence in Canada to attempt to commit suicide, but it is a criminal offence to counsel, aid or abet suicide. As the Law Reform Commission of Canada notes: 'Section 224 of the Criminal Code states that anyone who aids, abets or counsels suicide is liable to imprisonment for fourteen years. The criminal offence of attempted suicide was abolished in 1972.'[1] This is the reality for Canadians and it is likely to remain so in the foreseeable future, as aiding suicide is not likely to be decriminalized. The Law Reform Commission of Canada, in its definitive report on the issue, has recommended that aiding suicide should remain a criminal offence: 'The Commission recommends that aiding suicide not be decriminalized, and that section 224 of the Criminal Code be retained in its present form.'[2] So anyone in Canada who promises to aid a suicide is promising to commit an illegal act. This raises the last consideration, whether we should ever enter knowingly into contracts or make promises to perform illegal or immoral acts?

Whether we keep a promise to help a friend commit suicide will depend on whether we think it right to promise to commit illegal or immoral acts, and whether the risk is worth it. The answers to all these questions are, as we know, theory-dependent. If we rely on the utilitarian tradition we would be likely to keep our promise to our friend and aid his or her suicide. If we relied on the Kantian tradition it is likely that we would not help our friend commit suicide. Let us look at the Kantian perspective first, then the utilitarian. Kantians would tend to hold that it was wrong to make the promise in the first place and so it ought not to be kept. Let's see how they might arrive at this conclusion.

We can begin with the question of promising to perform an illegal act. Kantians believe, as we saw earlier, that we have a duty to obey the law because it enforces fundamental moral values.[3] For the Kantian, the duty to obey the law is contingent on the law being just, that is, whether it enforces morally acceptable conduct. So first we need to ask whether the current law against aiding suicide is just or not from a Kantian perspective. The Canadian law against aiding suicide would be just for the Kantian if suicide were immoral. If suicide were immoral then aiding suicide would be immoral, because helping someone carry out a wrongful act is immoral. It is inconsistent with our duty to further the moral development of others. If it were not immoral then the current law would be unjust and it would be morally permissible to break it. We thus need to settle the morality of suicide first before we can determine whether we should promise to do an illegal act.

The Kantians believe suicide is immoral because it is inconsistent with the principles of sanctity of human life and respect for persons. Kantians would argue that to commit suicide is inconsistent with our duty to ourselves because it is contrary to our natural instinct for self-preservation. Kantians believe we all have a strong innate desire to live. This one argument is similar to the traditional Judaeo–Christian one against suicide. In Judaeo–Christian cultures, suicide presents a difficult problem because our religious values have inculcated in us such a strong revulsion towards it. Judaeo–Christians argue that we have a duty to God not to take our own lives. Life is a gift from God and it is not up to us to decide when to abandon it. God created the natural universe and to interfere with nature is always immoral. For Judaeo–Christians, suicide is an unnatural act and so immoral. This Judaeo–Christian teaching colours in profound ways much of our contemporary discussion of suicide.

In the Kantian tradition, the rightness or wrongness of an action is determined by its accord with morally acceptable rules. A rule is shown to be morally acceptable if it can be consistently universalized, that is made into a rule valid for all rational agents. Because all human beings are rational agents, all human life is valuable no matter what its quality. The principle of the sanctity of human life in turn implies, as we have seen, a strict rule against taking the life of an innocent human being. There are no exceptions to it, neither in war, nor in civilian life. Since suicide is a breach of the sanctity of human life, it will always be morally wrong.[4] In order to understand the Kantian's uncompromising attitude towards the value of human life, let's look at a related example.

A baby is born with Down's Syndrome. Doctors tell the parents that the child is likely to be severely damaged and have a poor quality of life. The baby also has a hole in its heart and an intestinal blockage which, if not removed, would lead to the baby's death within a very short time. The parents request the doctor not to operate so the baby may be allowed to die. Is the parents' request ethical?[5]

There are two questions raised by this dilemma. First, is it ever morally right to withhold medical treatment from a newborn child, even when the life to be saved will be of poor quality? Again the fundamental question is: is life always sacred no matter what its quality? If not, how do we determine quality of life? What criteria should we use? Is a life of chronic and acute suffering worth living? Second, when someone is unable to speak for his or herself, as the newborn child is unable to, then who decides? The parents? The doctors? The state? Does anyone have the right to judge the worth of another human being's life? From a Kantian perspective it would be morally wrong to withhold life-saving medical treatment from the handicapped baby, because this would violate the principles of respect for persons and of sanctity of human life. It would deny the child's right to life, and should be considered criminal negligence on the part of the doctors.

Let us see how the Kantian might arrive at this conclusion. Kantians think it would be wrong to withhold life-saving treatment from the baby because to do so would be inconsistent with the principle of respect for persons. Respect for persons implies assent to the principle of sanctity of human life. To allow someone to die when we could save her or him is to disrespect them as persons. Even if people are mentally or physically handicapped, their lives are not worthless. Because human life is intrinsically valuable, human life is valuable no matter what its quality. However, since all human beings are mortal, natural death is not an evil for the Kantian. It is an intrinsic part of human life. Death is life's alter ego. On the other hand, premature death is always an evil for Kantians, hence they hold that we have an obligation to try to extend life as long as possible. Again, heroic measures are not required as that would show disrespect for natural death. The Kantian would frown on practices like that of deep freezing corpses in the hope that future scientific technologies would restore them to life. Endless temporality is not eternal life.

For the Kantian, we give a moral principle substance when we live in accordance with it. Moral principles are universal prescriptions, and not merely descriptive generalizations. If we hold that human life is sacred, it follows that we ought to save human life wherever possible. To say human life is sacred and to refuse to save a life when the means are available indicates a lack of sincere commitment to the principle. Sincerity is fundamental to Kantian morality. For the Kantian, when we adopt a principle we must try to live in accordance with the rules it generates. In this case the relevant rule is that we should save human life wherever possible. Everything possible should be done to save the child. To do otherwise is simply moral hypocrisy.

The Kantian would point out that the principle of sanctity of human life is basic, not only for our medical ethics and medical law but for our general morality and criminal law.[6] It informs the moral life of our society. The principle of sanctity of human life is the reason we require doctors to save life and the reason for our recognition in law that all human beings have a right to life, no matter what its quality. It makes no difference if a person is physically handicapped or not. Allowing the handicapped baby to die is a violation of its right to life and so is morally wrong.

The Kantian would also argue that the case presents a problem with respect to informed consent. Should we withhold or stop life-saving treatment when a patient is unable to give informed consent? Such action might be considered murder. As the Law Reform Commission of Canada notes: 'At the present time however, physicians and lawyers are generally unable to predict with any certainty how the provisions of the present Criminal Code would in fact be applied in a case involving cession of treatment.'[7]

The famous Karen Ann Quinlan case in the United States is typical of this dilemma.[8] Karen was severely injured in an accident. She was rushed to hospital and attached to a respirator. She never regained consciousness. After a reasonable period, her parents asked the attending physician to stop the treatment and allow Karen to die a natural death. The doctor refused because Karen was comatose and could not give informed consent. The parents took the matter to court. Their legal counsel argued successfully that the parents were just carrying out Karen's own wishes and that this was equivalent to informed consent. The court agreed and ordered the treatment to be discontinued.

The Kantians would agree with the court's decision because they think people have a right to be allowed to die. Kantians hold that patients have a moral right to refuse any medical treatment, including life-saving treatment. Although killing someone is inconsistent with sanctity of life, allowing someone to die if they refuse treatment is not. The distinction between killing and letting die, between active and passive euthanasia, is important for the Kantian. It's the intention of the action and not the actual consequences that matter morally for the Kantian. Another example will illustrate the Kantian position.

Suppose a patient is dying of cancer and the disease is in a very late stage. The chemotherapy she is taking slows the progress of the disease but does not cure it. The side-effects are both painful and distressing. Would it be consistent with the principle of sanctity of life for her to stop her treatment, leave hospital and return home to die? Kantians would agree it would be, provided she did not do anything directly to shorten her life, like taking poison. That would be suicide, something the Kantians think is immoral. If you commit suicide you intentionally kill yourself, but if you stop useless medical treatment you are simply allowing nature to take its course. No one is required to use heroic methods to prolong dying. So the Kantians believe it's morally right to allow someone to die, providing it's his or her decision to do so. When there is refusal based on informed consent there is no problem for the Kantians. Hence the Kantian would be generally sympathetic with the recommendations of the Law Reform Commission of Canada, that cessation of treatment should be distinguished from aiding suicide and euthanasia proper and that only the latter two be retained as criminal offences.[9]

In the 1992 case of Nancy B, the young Quebec woman won the legal right to be disconnected from the respirator which was keeping her alive. This would still be a borderline case for the Kantian, because it was not clear that she was terminally ill or that her treatment represented extraordinary measures to keep her alive.[10]

But what happens in cases where there is no informed consent? Is it morally right to let people die then? Another case will make the Kantian position clearer. Let's take someone who has suffered irreversible brain damage in an accident and who is being kept alive by lung and heart machines and intravenous feedings. Let's say he's been comatose for several days. He can't breathe on his own. There are no spontaneous movements, no response to stimuli and his electro-cardiograph is flat. There's no possibility of him giving consent for treatment and there's no one available who can give proxy consent. It's up to the doctor to decide. In one sense the patient is alive, at least biological life is present. But is there human life? If a physician were to shut the patient's life support system down, would he be committing murder? The legal answer to this is not clear. In Canada, for instance, the Law Reform Commission of Canada proposed legislation in 1981 which would resolve this legal problem, by giving a more precise set of criteria for the determination of death.[11] But would it be morally wrong?

Suppose Canadian criminal law were reformed in a way which would make it clear that no crime was being committed if a doctor shut down the life support systems in a case like this. If there were no legal impediments, would it still be morally wrong for the doctor to do so? If we give sanctity of human life our highest value the answer would be yes, it would be wrong. When there is no possibility of getting consent, Kantians would say we must do everything possible to respect a person's physical integrity. So we must keep the patient biologically alive. Even brain death is insufficient to justify cessation of treatment. Euthanasia is always morally unacceptable. When we deal with handicapped newborns, we are faced with a similar situation. If we allow the Down's Syndrome baby to die, we are doing so without its consent. The Kantian would say that allowing the baby to die could never be morally justified. The baby has a right to life, like any other human being. Everything possible must be done to keep it alive, and only when this has been done can we let nature take its course.

Kantians do have problems with their first principle here, because strictly speaking newborn children, the mentally incompetent and comatose adults are not 'persons', i.e. fully functioning moral agents. If human rights are based on the principle of respect for persons then only persons – that is, rational moral agents – would be protected under the principle of sanctity of human life. If interpreted strictly, the principle of respect for persons would exclude the mentally handicapped, children and foetuses from the moral community. They would not have moral or legal standing, and no moral or legal right to life. One solution, for the Kantian, is to consider these people as potential persons who have the capacity to be persons, but who are at present not functioning fully. They would then be the bearer of rights, including the right to life, but not to all other rights, e.g. informed consent. The alternative would be to make the principle of sanctity of human life the supreme principle, taking precedence over respect for persons. This would mean that the term person or human being would refer simply to any creature who was a member of the human species. Donagan has suggested that we treat the handicapped, children and foetuses as rational animals who are impaired, or not fully developed, rather than potential persons. This would establish their basic human rights, like the right to life, and allow us a way of determining what other rights they might have. 'What could be made of somebody who professed to rate the state of rational agency as of supreme value, but who regarded as expendable any rational creature whose powers were yet undeveloped.'[12] Either of these solutions would appear to solve the problem for the Kantian, and they might in fact be mutually compatible. Talking about rational animals is after all just another way of talking about rational moral agents or persons. Talking about potential persons is just another way of talking about developing rational animals.

Kantians would also argue that allowing handicapped babies to die will further our prejudice against them. The handicapped already have a difficult time getting a fair break from the non-handicapped.[13] If given a chance they can make a valuable contribution to the lives of others. The mentally handicapped are well known to be warm, loving people who bring emotional richness into the world. The Kantians would say that no one has the right or the capacity to judge the value of another person's life. If we can't judge the value of the life of a Down's Syndrome baby, neither can we make that judgement for any newborn afflicted with a disease which might bring early childhood death. These babies also have a right to life and so everything possible must be done to keep them alive. Once everything has been done and if the baby no longer responds to treatment, then and only then the baby can be allowed to die.

That was a Kantian response to the first question, now let's look at the Kantian response to the second question: who should make the decision to withhold treatment – the parents, the doctor or the state? In most societies the health and well-being of any child is primarily the responsibility of the parents and not the doctors.[14] A doctor must get permission from the parents in order to treat a child. The Kantians generally approve of this arrangement, because they believe parents ought to be primarily responsible for their children's care. The parents then would appear to be the natural people to make the decision. Not to allow them to do so could be an infringement of their rights as parents. The Kantians would point out, however, that parental rights over children are not absolute. Children are part of the Kantian moral universe and have rights as their parents do. Parents are not allowed to neglect, abuse, fail to educate their children or to kill them. The Kantian would argue that in the case of the Down's Syndrome child society ought to restrict the parents' rights because we are dealing here with a child's right to life. The Kantian would point to the way our legal system has dealt with conflicts between freedom of religion and the right to refuse life-saving medical treatment as a way of supporting their viewpoint. An example will illustrate their point.

The Jehovah's Witnesses believe blood transfusions are immoral. They believe they are a form of cannibalism which is prohibited by the Bible. To accept a blood transfusion is to endanger the soul, although this teaching has been questioned by some members of the sect.[15] Witnesses often refuse to sign consent forms for blood transfusions for themselves or their children, even in situations where life is at stake. Through a series of legal actions, in Canadian courts, for instance, the

Jehovah's Witnesses won the right to refuse life-saving treatment for themselves. But they failed to establish the right of parents to refuse life-saving treatment for their children. If children are involved, the attending physician can get a court order to proceed with the blood transfusion without the consent of the parents. The Kantian would agree with the court's decisions concerning children, because it is immoral to deny a child its right to life. The Kantian would say that it's morally wrong for a parent to refuse life-saving treatment for his or her child. Life-saving treatment ought to be given.

Because it would condone suicide, the Kantian would be less sympathetic with the decision to allow adults to take their own lives on religious grounds. If we are to take sanctity of life seriously, we might have to place limits on religious freedom in order to protect human life in all circumstances. If we start by allowing people to take their own lives for whatever reason, it will not be long before we start taking the lives of the innocent and defenceless because we judge their lives to be of poor quality. The slippery slope from suicide and aiding suicide to euthanasia, like a bobsleigh run, is steep, fast and dangerous. The principle of sanctity of human life needs to be carefully protected. Although allowing someone to die a natural death is morally acceptable, suicide and euthanasia are always morally unacceptable. Kant recognized that suicide is often contrary to our duties to others:

> To be sure, suicide can also be held to be a transgression of one's duty to other men, as, for instance, the transgression of the duty of one of a married couple to the other, of parents to children, of a subject to his government or his fellow citizens, and, finally, of man to God by forsaking the station entrusted to him in this world without being recalled from it.[16]

In the main dilemma in this chapter, the woman appeared to have fulfilled all her obligations to others, even if her family was reluctant to accept the idea of her suicide. She had put her public affairs in order and had made her peace with God. So taking her own life would not appear to be a breach of her duties to others.

Kant also recognized that there was a problem with so called heroic suicides:

> Bitten by a mad dog, a man already felt hydrophobia coming upon him. He declared that since he had never known anybody cured of it, he would destroy himself in order that, as he said in his testament, he might not in his madness (which he already felt gripping him)

bring misfortune to other men too. The question is whether or not he did wrong.[17]

Kant sometimes treated these cases as suicide. More frequently he wondered whether they should be called cases of self-murder proper, because the basic goal of the agent was not self-destruction but the good of others. He was reluctant to accept these as cases of justified suicide, as Donagan does, because of their heroic altruism. Donagan argues that suicide is morally permissible in circumstances in which suicide relieves others of a duty which they cannot carry out and survive. He cites the famous Captain Oates' case: 'The suicide of Captain Oates, in Scott's antarctic expedition, in order not to retard his companions as they struggled back to their depot, is rightly considered an act of charity as well as of courage.'[18] Since they were not truly cases of suicide, such instances did not represent genuine exceptions to the prohibition against suicide for Kant.

Kantians also hold that suicide is always contrary to our duty to ourselves. The principle of respect for persons requires not only that we treat others as ends in themselves, but ourselves as well. It is relatively easy to see what would be involved in treating others as ends in themselves, as rational moral agents. We could not, for example, treat others merely as a means to our ends or to the ends of others – such as helping a friend to commit suicide in order to gain an inheritance, rather than to secure a dignified death for him or her. But what would it mean for me to use myself as a means to further my own ends? This appears to be impossible. To understand Kant here we need to consider the concept of self-respect. We certainly can lack respect for ourselves. There are certain forms of behaviour which are beneath the dignity of a rational moral agent. We cannot demean ourselves in order to gain success. We cannot sell ourselves into slavery and still retain our respect for our autonomy. Anyone who is contemplating suicide must surely have a poor self-image, must believe his or her life is worthless, otherwise why consider ending it? It is essentially an irrational act. The elderly lady in this dilemma must surely be depressed and frightened at the prospect of spending her old age in what she sees as a dreadful state. She sees her life as worthless. She is emotionally unstable, and so it is impossible for her to assess her future happiness rationally. But no human life is ever completely worthless. All human beings are moral agents who possess intrinsic value and hence dignity. Suicide is morally wrong because it necessarily displays disrespect for ourselves as moral agents. It is only when grief or other strong emotions cloud our reason that we think otherwise. Suicide is always morally wrong because it expresses a disrespect for all moral values. It is the personal negation of everything which makes human life valuable.

Even in the case of the terminally ill, Kant would reject suicide and active euthanasia. It would be morally wrong to deliberately kill oneself or to have a friend or a physician take direct action to terminate one's life. Euthanasia, even with someone's informed consent, is always morally wrong. The Kantian would accept passive euthanasia. The terminally ill should be allowed to die a natural death without heroic medical intervention and as painlessly as possible. Easing the suffering of the dying is both morally and legally acceptable. The Kantians would support the hospice movement and the concept of death with dignity. They would also generally support the recommendation of the Law Reform Commission of Canada which allows for passive euthanasia for the terminally ill only, but retains aiding suicide and active euthanasia as criminal offences.

The Kantian argues that since suicide is immoral it would be wrong to promise to aid a friend's suicide and there is no reason for changing the current Canadian law against aiding suicide. For the Kantian, the law is just and to break it would be immoral. Aiding suicide is really a form of mercy killing in disguise. So in this situation the morally right thing to do is to break the promise to aid the friend's suicide. That ends the discussion of a Kantian response to the dilemma. Now let us look at a utilitarian response.

Utilitarians would tend to agree that the promises made in the dilemma were morally acceptable and should be kept. Let's see how they might arrive at this conclusion. The utilitarians hold that suicide is morally permissible because it is consistent with the principles of social utility, individual liberty and quality of life, hence aiding suicide would also be morally permissible. Presumably the woman who planned her suicide thought death was preferable to life in a nursing home, so aiding her suicide would maximize her happiness and minimize her suffering. Her suicide would harm no one. She had the consent of her relatives and close friends, and had properly arranged for all her public and private obligations. She was going to die in the near future anyway, and the sole remaining question concerned the quality of her remaining life and death. Aiding her suicide would involve committing a criminal act and a utilitarian would have to consider this as well. From a utilitarian perspective is it ever right to make promises to commit illegal or immoral acts? Let's start with the question of promising to carry out illegal acts. We saw in the last chapter that the utilitarians believe that we have a duty to obey the law because it is a socially useful practice.[19] They view the law as a means of producing the greatest happiness of the greatest number. The utilitarians take a more liberal view of the relation between law and morality than the Kantians do. They are legal positivists who hold that the state should not enforce morality. It should preserve the social order because we all need peace and security if we are to fulfil any of our wants. Law for the utilitarian is based on power, not morality. The two are quite distinct and should be kept separate. But they also hold that the duty to obey the law is contingent on whether the law is just or not, whether it is conducive to the general happiness. So we need to ask whether the current Canadian law against aiding suicide is just or unjust from a utilitarian perspective.

For the utilitarian, the present Canadian law against aiding suicide is unjust because it produces unnecessary suffering, especially in the case of the terminally ill. Utilitarianism has intellectually fuelled the liberal reform movement which has been the hallmark of our modern social history. Its adherents have championed the development of more humane and civilized attitudes towards the poor, the weak, the disadvantaged and disenfranchised. They have been in the forefront of the fight against slavery, racism, sexism, and for more humane treatment of prisoners. It should not surprise anyone then to find them leaders in the 'right to die' movement, which is concerned with the plight of the terminally ill. They would strongly disagree with the Canadian Law Reform Commission's recommendation that aiding suicide be kept in the criminal code.[20] They would agree with groups like the Hemlock Society, who want aiding suicide decriminalized.[21]

The principle of individual liberty, do as we please so long as we don't harm others, supports the right to die as well as the right to life. It is our life and each of us must have the final say concerning its quality. This gives us the right to commit suicide, if we desire to do so. This in turn gives us the right to help when we need it. It makes no difference to the utilitarian if the help is active, directly killing on request by a rational agent, or passive, allowing the person to die. The state should provide for that right by decriminalizing aiding suicide. Both active and passive consensual euthanasia should be legalized, and exit houses, as well as hospice centres, should be made part of comprehensive medical treatment. Even the Law Reform Commission of Canada recognizes the absurdity of decriminalizing attempted suicide and not decriminalizing aiding suicide:

After all, it is argued, a person who seeks to end his life is legally free to do so, since the law today no longer punishes attempted suicide. If the person is unable to perform the act himself, is it not illogical to treat the one who assists him as a criminal?[22]

We must, of course, be aware that a law which decriminalized aiding suicide could be abused. The elderly and the very ill are vulnerable and can be easily abused. There is a need for vigilance certainly, but this is not a sufficient reason for denying the right to a dignified and beneficent death, as the Canadian Law Reform Commission's recommendations do.

Since the current law is unjust the utilitarian would, as we have seen, seek to change the law by morally acceptable means, but if the law could not be changed, as appears to be the case in this dilemma, then it would be morally acceptable to defy the law and keep the promise to aid the friend's suicide. In this situation it would reduce human suffering, it would be an act of mercy. For the utilitarian then, it would be morally permissible to promise to help a friend commit suicide, even if this would involve committing an unlawful act.

For the utilitarian it would always be wrong to promise to perform an act we think immoral, one which did not maximize human happiness and minimize human suffering. It would also be immoral to ask a friend to do something she believes to be morally wrong. So whether it's right or wrong to promise to help a friend's suicide will depend upon how we view the morality of suicide. The utilitarian attitude to suicide is complex, but most utilitarian writers hold that suicide is morally permissible under certain circumstances. It is not an intrinsic evil. It is not intrinsically wrong but it is not always right. David Hume, in his famous essay 'On Suicide', provided perhaps the best utilitarian justification of suicide.[23] Hume argued that if there was a complete moral prohibition against suicide, then it must be because we owe a duty to God not to take our lives, or we have a duty to others not to take our lives, or finally we have a duty to ourselves not to take our lives. But none of these duties always obtains, so an absolute prohibition against suicide cannot be defended.

In his essay, Hume did not give us a definition of suicide, but in order to assess his arguments properly we need to have one. We can define suicide, following Richard Brandt, as the deliberate doing of something which results in the agent's death.[24] This definition would include so called heroic and altruistic suicides, in which the basic intention is to protect others from harm rather than to destroy one's own life, as in suicides proper. The definition is clearly not morally neutral, because it is described in such a way that it is the actual consequences of the action, rather than the intentions of the agent, which decide the morality of an act. The definition has a clearly utilitarian bias.

Is suicide, in this sense, a breach of our duty to God? Hume argues that it is not. Life, according to this argument, is a gift from God and it is not up to us to decide when to abandon it. God created the universe and to interfere with nature is always immoral. The heart of the argument is the claim that suicide is unnatural. Hume argued that suicide is not unnatural or immoral, because it is natural for humans to alter nature for their own benefit.[25] We dam rivers for power. We farm. We build cities. We inoculate people against disease. If tampering with nature was always wrong, then all technology, including the practice of medicine, would have to be abandoned. If it is wrong to shorten our lives through suicide, it is wrong to lengthen them through medicine. People are essentially technological creatures, natural tool makers who alter nature for human benefit. The real problem is not whether suicide is natural or unnatural but whether it is in our interest or not. Suicide is not always wrong even on religious grounds.

Hume also argued that suicide is not necessarily a breach of our duties to others.[26] First he pointed out that suicide does no direct harm to others. If it harms anyone directly it is the agent. It's true that the agent may no longer be able to help others, but it is also true that she would no longer be a burden for others. Hume recognized that suicide can indirectly harm others. However, we may be in a situation where we have no relatives or friends, as the very old or the terminally ill often are, and hence would not harm others if we committed suicide. In situations where we have no duties to others, suicide would be permissible because it concerns only ourselves. Normally this is not the case. More frequently people have friends and relatives whom they have obligations towards, as in this dilemma. In this situation we would be required to arrange our affairs in ways which would fulfil our obligations to others. If we arrange our affairs so that our friends and relatives are not harmed, as was the case in this dilemma, then suicide is permissible. For the utilitarians, suicide is morally permissible if we have fulfilled our duties to others, but is never required.

The utilitarians would point out that suicide, although never morally required, could be morally desirable. There are heroic suicides. Take the famous case of Captain Oates, cited by Donagan. Captain Oates, a member of the famous Scott expedition to the South Pole, was injured during the desperate attempt to return to base camp after reaching the Pole. He was slowing the expedition down because he had to be pulled on a sledge. He decided that no one would make it back if they continued to help him, so at night, while the others slept, he stole out of the tent into a blizzard and disappeared. As it turned out, his heroic suicide was futile because everyone in the expedition perished anyway. Or take another example. A pilot crashes his plane in a field to avoid smashing into a populated area: another heroic suicide which is perhaps morally commendable, even desirable, but not required. Suicide then is not only morally permissible but under the right circumstances can be morally commendable. It is not always a moral evil, as most of us are taught to believe. Nor has it always been viewed as an evil in other cultures. Ritual suicide was considered morally acceptable in classical Rome and in prewar Japan.

Hume also argued that suicide is not necessarily contrary to our duties to ourselves.[27] Suicide would be immoral for the utilitarian if it involved a breach of duty to others. If there are no duties to others, then it would be morally permissible to commit suicide if one wanted to. For the utilitarian, once the question of moral obligation to others is settled there are no other moral questions to ask. There are only questions about individual happiness. For the utilitarian, there are no duties to the self.

In the first place, a duty to the self is self-contradictory. We can only have duties to others. To say, 'I have a duty to do X' implies that I can be compelled to do it. If I have broken a contract with others I can be forced to comply with it. The idea of coercion is implicit in the meaning of the phrase 'moral obligation'.[28] It makes sense to say, 'I have a duty to others to do X,' but not 'I have a duty to myself to do X.' We cannot make contracts with ourselves, as we can with others or the state. Can I, for example, take out a loan from myself which I promise to repay? If I fail to make good my promise, who will force me to comply? Myself? Only the promisee can release the promiser from the promise. But if I am both promiser and promisee, I can always release myself from the promise, which nullifies the contract.[29] For the utilitarians, to be obliged means that we can be coerced by others to perform or to refrain from performing certain acts. Since coercion implies force from outside, it makes no sense to talk about self-coercion, or duties to the self.

Second, suicide is a private, not a public act. The utilitarians draw a sharp distinction between a public moral world and a private non-moral world. They believe in the principle of individual liberty: everyone has a right to do as they please so long as they don't harm others. Our lives, and our deaths, are ours to do with as we please. Morality for the utilitarians is essentially social rather than personal. Hence for them all moral problems can be reduced to questions concerning the legitimacy of social control. The utilitarian would argue that social control over suicide is not appropriate because it's a private matter, which concerns the individual first and society only secondly. Suicide is a private act which belongs to the world of individual freedom rather than the world of social control. Once questions concerning public morality or duties to others are settled, there are no further moral questions to answer. There remain only questions about individual happiness, but these strictly speaking are not moral questions. Prudence and morality are separate spheres. Suicide is not really a moral question at all. It is a matter of individual preference and society should not only respect but support people's private decisions, especially those of the terminally ill.

In the case of the Down's Syndrome baby, the utilitarians would agree with the decision of the parents not to allow surgery. Life is worth living only when it possesses an acceptable balance of happiness over unhappiness. In this case the balance is unacceptable and life expectancy very short. For the utilitarian, death is always an evil.[30] What makes death an evil for the utilitarian? It cannot be a positive evil because a non-existent person cannot suffer. Our not being born cannot be an evil because it cannot be experienced. So why should death be an evil? Perhaps it is the process of dying which is evil, because it normally involves suffering? However, as long as death is painless it is not evil. It must then be a negative evil. Death is an evil because it deprives us of all present and future happiness. Someone who is seriously crippled in an accident suffers a misfortune not only because of his or her present pain but because he or she is limited with respect to future goods. Death is the ultimate limiter. Life is intrinsically valuable because we value the experience of certain states of consciousness. It is the quality of experiential life which decides its value. Premature death is an evil for the utilitarian. A short happy life might in some cases be preferable to a long life of chronic suffering, but normally the longer we live the better. The utilitarian would condone the practice of deep freezing corpses in the hope that future resurrections would continue happy lives, provided the technology is not the wishful scientific fiction it appears to be.

The utilitarians argue that the principle of sanctity of life only makes sense if it is interpreted in terms of quality of life. Unlike the Kantians, the utilitarians believe that we are not morally obligated to keep a brain dead person alive. The utilitarians argue that the value of human life can't be measured purely in biological terms. Its value can only be measured in terms of the quality of life experience, an experience which includes consciousness and the capacity to feel and suffer. It follows that since a brain dead person no longer feels or suffers, we are not morally obliged to sustain mere biological life.

The Kantian distinction between 'killing' and 'letting die', between active and passive euthanasia, is not morally relevant to the utilitarian. It would make no difference for the utilitarian if a terminally ill cancer patient did something directly to shorten her dying. The utilitarian is primarily interested in the actual rather than the intended consequences of actions. Killing or letting die are merely different means to the same end. The utilitarians would agree that the courts in the United States were right to allow the family and physicians to disconnect Karen Quinlan from her life support system. They would agree with the Kantians that she should be allowed to die. But they would go further than the courts and the Kantians, and disconnect the intravenous feeding apparatus which continued to keep Karen biologically alive after the main life support systems had been removed.[31] For the utilitarian, it doesn't matter what you do as long as you reduce human suffering. For the utilitarian, the terminally ill patient who refuses further treatment and returns home to die does the right thing because she avoids unnecessary suffering.

The utilitarian would also argue that the Kantian places too much importance on informed consent. The fact that a dying patient is incapable of giving informed consent is not a reason to allow her to suffer. Why should we be so cruel? The utilitarians suggest that in cases like this we must do for the dying patient what any reasonable person would want to have done to her. The utilitarians believe no reasonable person would want to be kept alive to experience prolonged suffering near the point of death. The rational person would expect us to be compassionate and end the suffering. They kill horses with broken legs, don't they? Why deny humans the same concern?

For the utilitarian, the parents would be justified in allowing the Down's Syndrome baby to die, as long as the consequences produced more happiness than suffering. Utilitarians would consider not only the implications for the child, but also for the parents, the siblings, the health professionals and society as a whole. What for example would be the social, psychological and economic costs of looking after a severely damaged child? The utilitarian would argue that there's nothing morally wrong with aiding the natural death of a terminally ill child, either actively or passively. Euthanasia or mercy killing is not always wrong. The utilitarians would generally be antagonistic to the cautious approach of the Canadian Law Reform Commission towards legal reform in this area.[32] All the nice legal distinctions they wish to draw between cessation of treatment and euthanasia do little to ameliorate the suffering of the terminally ill, whether adult or child, whether they can give consent or not. Pandering to the moral sensibilities of the crowd may be politically prudent but it is morally unacceptable.

The problem with a disease like Down's Syndrome is that it's not easy to predict how severe the handicap will be, or how poor the quality of life. So in the case of the Down's Syndrome baby, the main problem for the utilitarian would be predicting the extent of the handicap. If the disease is one which tends to produce more serious problems, like a rapid deterioration of the nervous system, or some other gross malformation which leads to early death, then the problem is easier. As Rachels points out, this was the situation in the 1983 case of Baby Jane Doe in the USA: 'But Baby Jane Doe's case is different: her "handicap" is so severe that she will not be able to have a normal life – in fact she will not be able to have a human life at all.'[33] For the utilitarians, these cases are similar to those of other terminally ill patients and they would say there's nothing morally wrong with allowing or aiding the death of the child. However, such a decision can only be made on the basis of an accurate diagnosis of the child's disease.

So much for the utilitarian answer to the first question – ought medical treatment be withheld from the Down's Syndrome child? They would say yes, on the basis of an expected poor quality of life. Now let us examine their response to the second question, who should make the decision to withhold treatment – the parent, the doctor or the state?

The utilitarians would hold that the parents should decide, because they are more likely to act in the interest of the child than either the health professional or the state and that it should be legally permissible for the attending doctor to withhold life-saving treatment from a handicapped newborn at the parent's request.

The principle of the sanctity of human life is certainly a fundamental moral principle which must be taken seriously. However, if we are to treat the sick and the dying with humanity, the principle needs to be interpreted in terms of the quality of life. Once it is agreed that there is no hope for a happy life, as was the case in the main dilemma, it would be morally permissible to promise to aid suicide and the promise should be kept.

Since there is normally a prima facie case against suicide, the utilitarian holds that we should try to prevent suicide if possible. If we are in a position to prevent someone's suicide we should try to do so. We are justified in doing so until we can determine if the person's decision is a rational choice. If the person believes she has no hope for a happy life, then it is morally permissible for her to commit suicide. If we think that her judgement is mistaken we should not aid her suicide, but we should not interfere with it either. In this dilemma the utilitarian would say that the morally right thing to do would be to keep the promise to aid the suicide, because everyone agrees that there is no hope for a happy life in this case. It is not as if the friend was dealing with a total stranger.

The only remaining question for the utilitarian is whether promises to friends should take precedence over self-interest. For the utilitarian, prudence is a value but not a moral value. There are no duties to the self, only duties to others. Our duties to others are established by applying the principle of social utility: maximize happiness/minimize suffering. The general justification for keeping our promises is that the practice is conducive to the general happiness. Of course what is good for the majority may not always be good for the individual. If keeping a promise is not in someone's self-interest, then we have a reason to break it, but only if doing so will not undermine this useful practice.

In the situation described in this dilemma it's not likely that breaking the promise would have any effect on the general practice. Hence it would be permissible to break the promise provided the risk to the promiser was not too great. The only risk in keeping the promise is the possibility of being caught committing a crime, that of aiding suicide: a crime which the utilitarians believe shouldn't exist anyway.

The risk in not keeping the promise is that the promiser might want the help to be reciprocated some time in the future, or that the third friend would deem the promises of the second unreliable in the future. The prudential calculus would appear to be in favour of keeping the promise and aiding the suicide. So in this dilemma the utilitarian analysis would conclude that the right thing for the woman to do is to keep the promise to aid her friend's suicide. That ends the discussion of the utilitarian response to the dilemma. Now let's sum up both the Kantian and utilitarian responses to the dilemma.

This dilemma involved a conflict between the Kantian principles of respect for persons and sanctity of life, and the utilitarian principles of social utility, individual freedom and quality of life. The Kantian believes that suicide is immoral, hence a promise to aid suicide is also immoral and should not be kept. The Kantian also sees no reason for changing the current law against aiding suicide in countries such as Canada and the UK. For the Kantian, the law is just and to break it would be immoral.

The Kantians would also hold that euthanasia, the active taking of another person's life on compassionate grounds, is always morally wrong. They would see no reason for changing the existing laws against euthanasia. For the Kantian, the law is just and should not be broken. The Kantians, however, think there is nothing wrong in allowing someone who is terminally ill to die a natural death without heroic medical intervention. Passive euthanasia is morally acceptable to the Kantian but active euthanasia is not.

On the other hand, the utilitarian believes that suicide is morally permissible because it is a private act. Morality has nothing to do with it. So long as we have fulfilled our duties to others we are free to take our own lives if we want to. Hence a promise to aid suicide should be kept if we think the person we have promised has no hope for a happy life. This is especially so if the promise was part of a reciprocal contract between friends. The utilitarians want aiding suicide to be decriminalized, as suicide is in Canada. They also hold that euthanasia is morally acceptable under certain conditions. They want the current law against euthanasia changed, so our society will be able to deal more humanely with the terminally ill and with patients suffering unbearable pain. Active, as well as passive, euthanasia is morally acceptable to the utilitarian.

In order to make some headway with this dilemma we need to concentrate on the incoherences which emerge in the patterns of moral reasoning on both sides. The Kantian arguments may appear to be more vulnerable than those of the utilitarians, because their moral opinions are more obdurate. But the utilitarians have their problems as well.

We need to note first that the Kantians reach their position by accepting a rigid interpretation of the principle of sanctity of human life, and giving it absolute precedence over the principle of respect for persons. They treat their principles as if they are completely incommensurable. We must choose between them. It is a case of either/or and we cannot have both. But these principles are not necessarily inconsistent with each other. First, respect for persons commits us to a form of the principle of individual liberty. If we respect persons as moral agents, we must recognize that they have a right to decide for themselves whether it is right or wrong to take their own lives. So long as they do not limit or interfere with the autonomy of others they must be free to decide for themselves. Moral freedom is a necessary condition for moral self-realization. This much we can grant to the utilitarians. But we would not be giving the utilitarians everything. Instead of dividing our lives into a private non-moral world and a public moral world, as the utilitarians do, we would be dividing our lives into two different but interrelated moral worlds. We would recognize a personal moral world, as well as a public moral world.

This new division would express in a different way the utilitarians' proper concern with our freedom to control our own destinies. In this view the greater the freedom, the greater the moral responsibility. Thus suicide would be a matter of personal morality and not simply a matter of doing as we please. We would have duties to the self as well as duties to others. To say, 'I have a duty to myself' is not inherently self-contradictory. As Kant argued, obligations and promises are self-contradictory only if obligation is defined by external coercion, if it directly involves the idea of social control. If I borrow money and promise to repay it, I am morally obligated to keep the promise, even if the promise can't be enforced. I still owe the money. I borrowed it, and the moral obligation to repay still stands. It is reason, not fear of punishment or hope of reward, which binds moral agents. Morality is not simply a matter of social control, but of acting in accordance with right reason. It is our reason that binds us, not the threats of others, hence we can meaningfully talk about duties to the self as well as duties to others.[34]

Morality and law are intrinsically related but they are not equivalent. Part of morality needs to be enforced by law. If an act is immoral, this is a necessary but not a sufficient reason for legal prohibition. Part of morality needs to be enforced within other social institutions. Professional ethics witnesses to this. Institutions like universities, for example, have a moral life of their own. On occasion they need to enforce the values, like academic honesty, which are intrinsic to them. But there remains a part of morality which belongs to our private life, which should be beyond the reach of social control. Moral agents need freedom in order to grow. This is recognized by the utilitarian principle of individual liberty: do as you please as long as you don't harm others. It is also recognized in the Kantian principle of autonomy: do as you please as long as you don't interfere with or limit the freedom of others. Both theories recognize the need to maximize freedom and minimize social control. An idealist theory would reformulate the principle of freedom as: do as you please as long as you don't harm others or unnecessarily limit their freedom. The real problem, as Mill recognized, is not whether we should be absolutely free or absolutely controlled but how to determine the limits of social control.[35]

To define moral obligation solely in terms of coercion instead of reason reduces morality merely to matters of social control. It reduces morality to law and to other quasi-legal methods of social control. Morality is more than social control, because there are immoral laws and morally inadequate social practices. We need freedom to criticize our laws and social practices rationally. Morality is not simply a matter of power relations between people. Might and right are not the same thing. Politics and ethics, although intimately related, are distinct.

To admit there are duties to the self would require a radical revision of utilitarian theory. Utilitarians would have to hold that matters of personal happiness were also a part of morality, and suicide could still be consistent with our duty to the self. If a person has no hope for a happy life, as is the case for many terminally ill patients, then it would be morally permissible, even right, for her to take her own life. She should be free to take her own life if she wants to. For the utilitarian, the principle of sanctity of human life must be interpreted in terms of the principle of quality of life. Life is only worth living if it provides a satisfactory balance of happiness over suffering. In most cases optimism is more justified than pessimism. So there is normally a prima facie case against suicide on utilitarian grounds. The most important question for the utilitarian is always whether we can be sure that the quality of life judgement, that someone has no hope for a happy life, is sound. It is this which justifies suicide and aiding suicide on utilitarian grounds.

On this the Kantians and utilitarians are not really that far apart. The principle of self-respect may not be inconsistent with this sort of death with dignity.[36]

For the Kantian, like the utilitarian, there is normally a prima facie case against suicide. Because suicide is the negation of all human value, the Kantians always have a strong moral reason against it. The Kantians appear to me to be right on this point. But they seem to be wrong in thinking there can be no rational suicides, that suicide can never be consistent with the principle of respect for persons. Certainly the contract between the three friends in this dilemma was a rational contract. So in this sense it was consistent with respect for the self as a rational agent.

On the other hand, modern technology has made it possible for many more people to live longer. The discovery of miracle drugs, the invention of heart pumps and pacemakers, dialysis machines, techniques for organ transplant and, more recently, the artificial heart have reduced the evil of premature death to narrow limits. But the quality of many of those extended lives has been extremely poor. People are kept alive longer, but they often suffer not only great pain but a loss of self-control or diminished mental capacity. In all such cases this means a loss of human dignity. In this case, directly taking one's life is surely consistent with maintaining self-respect. To avoid or to help someone avoid an undignified death is surely consistent with the principle of respect for persons.

There are residual doubts here. Are we ever in a position to say that happiness and moral agency are over? Possibly. Is such deep pessimism ever justified? Possibly. But surely hope is a virtue and despair a vice? Still, the way we die is a personal moral matter and the freedom to make this decision, unencumbered by social control, is essential for our full self-realization. We have a right to a gentle exit, but before we exercise that right we should perhaps take seriously the advice of the great Welsh poet Dylan Thomas, who wrote:

Do not go gentle into that good night
Rage, rage against the dying of the light.[37]

Chapter 7

Moral quandary

A passenger-cargo ship foundered and sank off the coast of New-foundland in a storm. Two large life boats managed to get clear before the ship sank. One of the life boats was overloaded and soon began to take on water. The first mate in charge of it thought it would sink unless its load was lightened. He decided that the only way to do this was to throw a number of its passengers overboard. He reasoned that the three members of the crew were needed to man the large life boat, that women and children should be saved and that married couples should not be split up. The rest were expendable. The mate and the crew threw 13 passengers overboard. The boat stopped taking on water, and a few hours later its occupants were rescued. The mate was later tried and convicted for multiple homicide and sentenced to life imprisonment. Did the mate do the morally right thing?[1]

The basic question raised by this dilemma is whether it's morally right in an emergency to sacrifice lives in order to save other lives. A related and equally difficult question is also raised: in emergencies who should decide, if anyone, who should live and who should die? The life boat dilemma dramatizes the most difficult type of dilemma human beings have to face. We are finite creatures with limited knowledge and power, hence we sometimes find ourselves in a moral quandary, a situation in which our choices are very restricted. No matter what we do we appear to be doing something wrong. We cannot rationally resolve the dilemma we face, yet we must act.

The way the life boat dilemma is resolved will, once again, depend on the ethical traditions we rely on to give us our answers. If we rely on the utilitarian tradition, which makes the principle of social utility the first principle of ethics, we would hold that it was morally right to throw some people overboard in order to save the rest. The utilitarians would also argue that the first mate was right to take the responsibility for deciding who should live and who should die. In these unhappy circumstances we must choose the lesser evil. These are hard choices to make. They leave us with unresolved feelings of remorse, sadness and rage. Still, hard choices must be made. The defence in the actual trial used this utilitarian approach to make its case. If we relied on the Kantian tradition, which makes the principle of respect for persons the first principle of ethics, we would hold that the mate did the morally wrong thing in sacrificing some to save the rest. Even in terrible situations we cannot do evil in order to do good. Nor should the first mate have taken it upon himself to decide who should live and who should die. No one has the right to decide that. The prosecution in the trial used this essentially Kantian approach to establish its case.

First let's look at a utilitarian approach. How does it arrive at the conclusion that the mate did the morally right thing? For the utilitarian, saving lives is morally right as long as the consequences of doing so are better than the consequences of letting people die. Generally a utilitarian will want to maximize life because this will produce the greatest happiness for the greatest number in the long run. The utilitarians would support the rule maximize human life/ minimize human death, because life is a necessary condition for the possibility of human happiness. If there is no one alive to feel pleasure or pain, then we cannot try to maximize the former and minimize the latter. Of course it is unrealistic to think, given the human condition, that we can eliminate suffering. Our aim should rather be to maximize happiness/minimize suffering.

Normally for the utilitarians, all human lives have equal value. In maximizing human happiness we must give equal value to the interest of everyone affected by our actions. James Rachels, for example, argues that a minimum conception of morality requires that we try to guide our conduct by reason while giving equal weight to the interests of each individual: 'first, that moral judgements must be backed by good reason; and second, that morality requires the impartial consideration of each individual's interests.'[2] But in life boat situations all human lives cannot be treated with equality. In deciding whom to save utilitarians would rank individuals according to their social utility. That is, they would decide which individuals, if saved, would produce the greatest happiness for the greatest number, with a minimum of suffering. In a crisis, the utilitarian would be committed to weighing the social value of individual lives. In this case the criteria used were that married couples, children and women should be given preference, presumably because the first mate believed the family is basic for human happiness.

To assess people according to their social utility appears grossly immoral because in our Judaeo–Christian culture we believe that everyone is equal in the eyes of God. We therefore have no right to play God with the lives of others. The utilitarians would defend their position by pointing out that we often do assume that right, and we believe that it would in some circumstances be immoral to do anything else. Wouldn't it be wrong to save no one when many lives could be saved by sacrificing a few? In a crisis we must choose the lesser evil. A couple of other examples will make the utilitarian position clear.

The life boat situation is analogous to other life and death situations, like deciding who should receive medical care on the battle field, or who should be given scarce life-saving medical treatment, or whether we should help poor countries struck by famine and other disasters. Let's look at the battle field first.

In the First World War, casualties were so great that the front line medical teams could not treat them all. They had to decide who should receive medical treatment and who should not. The French medical corps rejected both random choice and the rule of first come, first served. These were thought to be inefficient ways of handling manpower in time of war. Instead they invented a system called Triage, which classified wounded soldiers into three categories.[3] First were those who had a good chance of surviving and being able to return to the battle field if treated immediately. Second came those who had a good chance of surviving without immediate treatment. Third were those who had a poor chance of surviving and would never be able to return to the battle field. Soldiers in the first category, that is those who had a good chance of surviving, were treated first. Those in category two, who would survive without immediate treatment, were put off till later. Members of category three were simply left to die. Civilian casualties and wounded enemy soldiers would automatically be classified as class three. Triage proved to be a useful system because it saved the most soldiers for the front line. A nice utilitarian solution to the problem of battle field casualties.

A similar situation to that on the battle field arose with the invention of artificial kidney machines. These machines are used to rid a patient's blood of waste products when the kidneys malfunction because of disease. As is often the case with new medical technologies, there is never enough to satisfy demand and this produces typical cases of scarce resources.

In the 1960s the artificial kidney centre at a major American hospital initiated a large scale treatment programme for people with fatal kidney disease.[4] At the beginning of the programme there were more patients than there were machines. Since medically there was no way to choose between the patients, the hospital set up citizens' panels to select candidates for treatment. The panels were informed that data concerning each applicant – like age, sex, number of dependants, occupation, wealth, education – were readily available. The panels were then asked to decide which data they thought were relevant and, on the basis of the data, which patients were worth saving and which were not, a truly utilitarian procedure.

Since not all the patients could be saved, the hospital authorities thought this was the fairest and most democratic way to proceed in making such non-medical decisions. At least some lives would be saved, and this would be consistent with the principle of maximizing life and minimizing death. For the utilitarian, it would simply be immoral to deny treatment to everyone when some could be saved. Using the criterion of social utility may appear harsh – after all we are dealing with life and death here. Yet if we don't use some criterion then we have to let everyone die, which is surely just as unacceptable. If not social utility then what other criteria should we use? We have to decide. In some situations we have to make hard choices.

The utilitarian position can be made clearer if we look at another example of moral decision-making in difficult situations, one in which the approach is not counter-intuitive – as it frequently is. Suppose a poor African country is struck by a famine. Its population is already ravaged by civil war and is ill equipped to handle another disaster. The International Red Cross sets up a famine relief organization and asks other countries to contribute. Without help from rich western nations, thousands will perish from starvation. Ought we to contribute to the relief effort, and how much should we give? The utilitarian would argue, as Peter Singer has, that we have a natural duty to help others in need and that maximally we ought to contribute as much as we can to the victims of famine. We ought to give until we reach the level of marginal utility. We should give until we are as poor as they are. Minimally we ought to give to the victims of famine as long as it costs us little or nothing morally, i.e. as long as in helping others nothing equally bad happens to us and no wrong is done.[5] Let's see how a utilitarian, like Singer, would arrive at this position.

First the utilitarian would argue that starving to death is intrinsically evil. Suffering and death from lack of food, shelter and proper medical care is surely an evil. On this we can all agree. Further, the principle of utility – maximize happiness/minimize suffering – places us not only under an obligation to promote the good of others, it also places us under obligations not to inflict harm on others and to prevent harm or evil from happening to others. Consider the following example cited by Peter Singer.[6] A man is out for his Sunday walk in his newly dry-cleaned suit. He comes across a baby who has fallen face down in a paddling pool. The baby is unable to right itself and its mother is preoccupied with her other child and is unaware of her baby's distress. If the man does not help, the baby will drown. Instead of helping the man walks away, because he does not want to get his clean suit muddied by the water. The baby dies and the public is outraged by his callous act. Surely we have a duty to help others in distress when helping involves little or no great cost to ourselves. A dirty suit is surely a small price to pay for saving a baby's life. The utilitarian would be equally outraged. If we can prevent a great harm to others, with little or no cost to ourselves, then we ought to do so. This is a minimal requirement of the principle of utility. Hence if we can prevent the death of others from starvation by contributing to famine relief, we ought to do so, especially if this can be done with little or no cost to us.

Second, the utilitarian would argue that allowing the victims of famine to starve to death, when they could be saved, is tantamount to killing them. Consider the following example cited by James Rachels.[7] Smith is the sole heir to a fortune held in trust for his 6 year old nephew. He plans to murder his nephew while he gives him a bath on a day when he is looking after him. Smith drowns the child in a bathtub and makes it appear like an accident. Compare Smith to Jones, who is in a similar situation with his nephew. He, like Smith, will inherit a good deal of wealth if his nephew dies. He also plans to drown his nephew in the bath and make it appear accidental. However, when he enters the bathroom to murder him, his nephew slips in the tub, knocks himself out and slips unconscious beneath the water. He could be easily saved by his uncle, but Jones stands by idly while the child drowns. Smith killed his nephew, Jones allowed his nephew to die. Are Smith and Jones equally culpable? Legally they might not be, but the utilitarian would argue that morally they are. The actual consequences were the same. Their charges died.

Morally there is no difference between killing someone and allowing them to die. If you don't help the victims of famine, you might as well kill them. If we can prevent great harm from occurring to another, especially when there is little cost to us, then we ought to do so. There is much that we in rich countries can do to help the poor and starving in underdeveloped countries, especially in times of famine, at little cost to ourselves. Luxuries abound in countries in the west, and surely we can give some of these up to help others without much cost to ourselves. A luxury is by definition something we can give up without any great hardship to ourselves. Do we really need that second colour TV set, or that second car? Possibly we might if we are going to compete in our fast paced modern world. There is probably nothing which could not be identified as a luxury for someone. It may not be possible to define a luxury independently of a context. What is a luxury for one person could well be a necessity for another. Yet surely most of us have luxuries, things we personally could do without and suffer no great loss. To sacrifice some of our luxuries to help others is a minimal requirement for the utilitarian. If we are to take seriously the injunction to give equal consideration to the interests of everyone affected by our actions or inactions, then we would be required to give a great deal more. If we are not to be selfish and if we are fully to maximize human happiness and minimize human suffering, we must give until there is nothing left to give.

For the utilitarian, the allocation of scarce medical resources in war or peace or famine must be based on the full implementation of the principle of social utility. The hospital administration and the French medical corps did the right thing. The first mate also did the right thing when he saved most of the passengers in the life boat at the cost of sacrificing a few.

That finishes the analysis of the utilitarian response to the question of whether the mate did the right thing by sacrificing some lives to save others. Now let us look at the utilitarian response to the second question: who should decide in emergencies who is to live and who is to die? The utilitarian answer to this question will depend on the circumstances. The utilitarians believe that democratic decision-making procedures, like the citizens' panels, tend to maximize happiness and minimize suffering. They hold this because in a democracy, theoretically at least, the interests of the governed are the same as those who govern. In a democracy the people elect the government. The government is responsible to the people, and hence is likely to reflect their interests. There is no guarantee of this in a monarchy or a dictatorship.

The utilitarians would approve of the citizens' panels deciding who should get the kidney machines. This is a democratic procedure which should maximize human happiness. They would also approve of the

French medical corps' decision to use the Triage system for treating wounded soldiers. Although democratic procedures are generally to be preferred, in this case a dictatorship would be more likely to maximize human happiness, assuming that maximizing the number of soldiers fit to fight and so winning the war would achieve this. What works in theory does not always work in practice.

In a war there is never time to make democratic decisions; that is why armies work on an authoritarian basis. A democratic army would be very inefficient. Finally the utilitarians would have supported the mate's decision to take charge of the situation and try and save as many lives as possible. The life boat case is more like the situation on the battle field than the situation faced by a citizens' panel in a hospital. There would be no time on a life boat to deal with the situation in a democratic way. By the time a decision was made, the life boat would have sunk and everyone would have been lost. Frequently in situations of crisis someone needs to take charge and hard decisions have to be made quickly. On utilitarian grounds the actions of the mate are defensible.

That completes the analysis of the utilitarian response to the dilemma. Now let us take a look at the Kantian response. The Kantians would hold that the first mate did the wrong thing in sacrificing some lives to save others, because what he did was inconsistent with the principles of sanctity of life, equality and respect for persons.

The Kantians believe that each human life possesses intrinsic value no matter what its social utility. Being old or a bachelor or poor does not make a person's life less valuable than others, who may be young, married or wealthy. The Kantian would point out that everyone in the life boat was innocent. None of them was responsible for the sinking of the ship. The innocent should never be sacrificed to save the lives of others. It is always morally wrong to do evil for the sake of good. The end, no matter how good, never justifies the use of immoral means.

The Kantians would also argue that what the mate did was unfair. The Kantians believe that everyone has a right to life and that everyone ought to have an equal chance to survive. In throwing some people overboard, the mate violated their right to an equal chance to survive. The Kantian would argue that if the only way to save some was to kill others, then perhaps everyone should have died together. It should have been all or none. Or at least some form of random choice should have been used.

The action of the mate also violated the principle of respect for persons. The lives of those tossed overboard were taken without their consent. Had they agreed to sacrifice their lives for the sake of those who remained in the life boat this would perhaps have been different. Or if everyone had agreed to draw lots, then those who lost would have at least participated in the decision to die.

Kantians would also hold that the captain and other members of the crew have a professional responsibility to try to save their passengers before they save themselves. But this duty would not include killing some passengers so that others could survive. If the first mate and his crew could save the passengers by jumping overboard themselves, the Kantians might approve. They believe that the sacrifice of one's own life for another's is morally permissible. If this action would save the passengers, then the first mate and his crew have a professional duty to go down with the ship. These are not suicides but acts of heroism or conscientiousness.

The system of Triage adopted by the French medical corps for treating wounded soldiers would also be rejected by the Kantians. They believe that all the wounded have an equal right to treatment and the medical teams must treat everyone until medical resources run out. The same treatment should also be given to civilian casualties and wounded enemy soldiers. Adhering to this principle of treating everyone equally would require that casualties of war should be dealt with on a first come, first served basis.

The Kantians would also morally disapprove of allocating scarce medical resources on the basis of a patient's social usefulness. Kantians hold that every citizen has a right to a fair share of a country's resources, so every citizen has an equal right to life-saving medical treatment. Medical professionals have no right to deny treatment to people because they are old, poor or uneducated. Social utility is irrelevant in life and death situations. The treatment should again be allocated on a first come, first served basis or by some form of random choice.[8] Given that all the patients had an equal chance of survival if they were selected, a lottery would probably be the best way to select patients for life-saving treatment.

Kantians would also argue that the question of what obligations we have to the victims of famine is not as straightforward as the utilitarians suggest. Helping others is more often a question of charity than moral requirement. We can require people not to harm us, but can we require people to benefit us? I may give money to a beggar and that is perhaps morally desirable, but the beggar has no moral claim on my money. He has no moral right to my good offices. Can we demand that others love us? There is something odd about trying to coerce someone to love us. Rejected lovers are perhaps to be pitied, but they have no right to another's love.

The Kantians believe that we have a complex set of moral relations to others. We have duties of justice to others as well as duties of non-maleficence and beneficence. Then of course there is charity. They would accept the general principle that it is morally permissible, and desirable, to help others in need when this costs us little or nothing, or when nothing equally bad happens to us or our dependants and no wrong is done. To fail to come to the aid of the drowning baby just to keep a suit clean would be morally repugnant to the Kantian. But in other cases our duty to others is less clear. Consider the following example.[9]

Bob needs a kidney transplant to survive. George, the man's brother, is located, and he agrees to tests to determine if he would be a suitable donor for a kidney transplant. The tests turn out positive, and arrangements are begun for the operation. George, in the meantime, has second thoughts about the transplant and refuses to go ahead with the surgery. He has a deep rooted fear of operations to begin with, and his family has convinced him that the risks are too great. Bob and his family plead with George and his family for George's kidney. They argue that the risk is not that great. The doctors have performed so many transplants that the operation is now considered routine. Besides it is his brother's life which is at stake. Surely George has a moral obligation to help someone in need, especially a close relative. If he does not go through with the operation he will be killing his brother. This accusation leads to a huge family fight. The two sibling families have never got along very well, and now George's family is accusing Bob's family of harassment. Bob becomes so angry with his brother that he takes him to court and sues him, claiming he has a legal right to his brother's kidney. After a bitter trial, that embarrasses and hurts George, the court rules against Bob. The presiding judge however chastises George for his uncharitable behaviour. Shortly after the trial Bob dies of kidney failure. George suffers great remorse over the death of his brother, but always maintains that he has done nothing wrong.

As far as the Kantian is concerned, George has done nothing wrong. He has no obligation of justice towards his brother that would require him to donate his kidney. Bob has no moral right to George's kidney. There is also doubt as to whether he has a duty of beneficence towards Bob. The cost to George of the loss of a kidney and the risk of the surgery would have been very great. There was no real guarantee that the kidney would not have been rejected even if the operation had been a success. According to the Kantians, we have a duty to ourselves to preserve the biological integrity of our bodies. It would, for example, certainly be wrong for us to sell any of our organs for money. It would only be in very special circumstances that it would be morally permissible to donate an organ to save someone else's life. At best, for George to have given his kidney to his brother would have been a heroic act of charity. Certainly it could not be an act which was morally required, and the judge should not have reprimanded George in public for failing to donate his kidney, no matter how morally desirable the donation might have been.

Similarly, in the case of the victims of famine the Kantian would argue that we are not morally required to help. If we contributed anything to famine relief, it would be an act of charity not of duty. Aiding the victims of famine would not be an act of justice. Certainly persons must be treated fairly, but everyone does not have a right to an equal share of the food or other goods which the rich countries produce. Merit and individual effort are as important as simple equality in determining distributive justice. We have a right to what we have earned or created with our own effort. It is our food, not theirs! They have no more rightful claim on it than the beggar has on our money. One could perhaps argue that because of the historic economic exploitation of the poor countries by the rich during the colonial period, poor countries of the third world now have some legitimate claim on our aid. Reciprocity is certainly a rule of justice, and for the Kantian would apply in general to foreign aid. With respect to famine the case may be more complex. If a country mismanages its economy, it is not the fault of others if disaster occurs. If a business corporation mismanages its affairs, we allow it to go bankrupt. It's not our responsibility to save people from bad economic planning. We may help out of charity, but again no one has a right to our aid. The victims of famine have then no right to our help.

Helping the victims of famine is also not a duty of non-maleficence, of not harming others. For the Kantian, allowing someone to die and killing them are not morally equivalent. If we do not help the victims of famine, some will surely die – but this is not murder. Because there is no intentional killing, it is absurd to say that failing to help is the moral equivalent of murder, as the utilitarians do. The Kantian would agree that in the cases of Smith and Jones there was moral culpability in both cases. In both cases the men acted from a morally bad motive; namely, greed. However, Jones' conduct is relevantly different from the person who fails to help the victims of famine, for the latter had no intention of killing the victims. Jones could more properly be said to have set out to kill his nephew, rather than allowing his nephew to die, but events made this unnecessary. One was clearly a breach of our duty of non-maleficence, the other is not. Helping others in need is then not a duty of non-maleficence.

Nor is helping others in need necessarily a duty of benevolence. In the first place everyone does not have an equal claim on our benevolence. Surely our obligations to our family, friends and fellow citizens take precedence over our obligations to foreigners and strangers. If we had to choose between feeding our own children and allowing a starving Ethiopian child to die, then surely we are required to attend to the needs of our own first. It would be immoral to neglect our children in order to attend to the needs of other people's children. This is certainly a difficult choice to make but everyone, according to the Kantian, including Ethiopian parents, has a moral obligation to care for their offspring. It is the Ethiopian parents who are responsible for their own child's death, not us. Although we have a general obligation to bear children, we ought only to bring into being children we are capable of providing for. Some sensible policy of voluntary birth control should be instituted by all countries so that famine could be avoided. If countries know that they can rely on others to help them out when famine strikes them they may become overly dependent on aid from the richer countries, who already control their own populations.

Famine relief also encourages the richer countries to take an overly paternalistic attitude towards poorer countries. Paternalism undermines economic and cultural self-reliance. Paternalism assumes that we need others to look out for our well-being. It leads to a lack of individual and national self-confidence. We start blaming others for our failures. We passively accept our plight. If this happens, poor countries then fail to take responsibility for their own well-being and continue to be dependent on the paternalistic alms of the rich countries. False benevolence creates low self-esteem in its recipients and inhibits their growth. It may seem cruel, but the poor might be better off if they were left to fend for themselves. You do no one any favour if you destroy their self-reliance. Famine relief then is not necessarily even a duty of beneficence. It might not even be a matter of charity.

For the Kantian, acts of charity are morally permissible if they can be carried out without great cost to ourselves and those we have strong contractual relationships with: our family, friends and fellow nationals. If famine relief required us to neglect those duties, then it would be morally wrong to be charitable in these circumstances. Garrett Harding, a population biologist, has argued that this is in fact the case.[10] He suggests that our planet Earth is like a life boat in the ocean. It has a limited carrying capacity. If it becomes overloaded, if population outstrips the food supply, then everyone in the boat is endangered. Is this a case once again of everyone or none for the Kantian? The answer is no, because in this situation we have to choose between our strict obligations to ourselves and our kin and being charitable to others. Here our charity must begin at home.

For the Kantians, famine relief is not a duty of justice or non-maleficence or beneficence or, if Harding is right, even a matter of charity. So the Kantians would argue that the French medical corps, the hospital administrators, the Red Cross and the first mate all did the wrong things. That finishes the Kantian response to the question of whether the mate did the right thing by sacrificing some lives to save others. Now let us look at their response to the second question: who should decide in emergencies who is to live and who is to die?

Like the utilitarians, Kantians are also strong defenders of democratic systems of government, because totalitarian and paternalistic systems of government are inconsistent with the principle of respect for persons. Unlike the utilitarians, they are uncompromising in their adherence to democracy. There are no situations where autocracy is morally justified.

The first mate did the wrong thing in ignoring democratic procedures even in this emergency situation. The Kantians would support the idea of a voluntary army run essentially on democratic lines. The system of Triage for treating wounded soldiers would only be acceptable if it had the consent of the army and the people. Although the idea of citizens' panels would appeal to the Kantian, they could not be used to decide who should live and who should die. The purpose of a democracy is not to produce the greatest happiness of the greatest number, but to protect individual and minority rights. For the Kantian, no one has the right to decide who is to live and who is to die, even in emergencies. The hospital administrators had no right to usurp the basic right of the patients to decide their own fates. It is either everyone or none, or first come, first served.

For the Kantian, our first obligation in an emergency is always to save as many lives as possible, but not at the expense of the lives of others, because that would be inconsistent with the principle of the sanctity of life. The Kantians also hold that no one has a right to decide for others who should live and who should die since that fails to respect others as persons. They would conclude that the mate did the wrong thing in taking charge of the situation and deciding who should be thrown overboard.

That finishes the analysis of the utilitarian and Kantian responses to the dilemma. Now, let's sum up. In this dilemma, we have a conflict between the utilitarian principles of utility and expedience and the Kantian principles of sanctity of life, equality and respect for persons. For the utilitarian, the end – maximizing human happiness and minimizing suffering – justifies the means – throwing passengers overboard. In a crisis we are morally required to do the lesser evil. Sometimes we find ourselves in situations where no matter what we do, we will do evil. There is no way to do good without at the same time doing bad. Still, we must act. We must make hard choices. We may not like it, we have to choose. In a utilitarian moral universe there exist incommensurable moral dilemmas.

In crisis situations we must choose to do the lesser evil. If utilitarians are to be consistent then they must say that, paradoxically, doing evil is sometimes the right thing to do. This was the situation that the first mate found himself in, as did the French medical corps in the First World War and the hospital administrators with their kidney machines. The principle of the lesser evil is not an ad hoc principle which the utilitarians simply tack on to make their theory coherent. It is implicit in the principle of expedience. A utilitarian moral universe is ultimately irrational.

The utilitarian would also hold that the mate was morally right to take control of the situation and make the decision about who should be thrown overboard. In emergencies, authoritarian or paternalistic decision-making procedures are more likely to maximize happiness and minimize suffering. In most situations the utilitarian would support democratic procedures because they tend to maximize happiness and minimize suffering. Hence the utilitarian would support the idea of citizens' panels selecting patients for scarce medical treatment on the basis of their social utility.

The Kantians, on the other hand, would argue that the first mate did the wrong thing when he opted to throw some of his passengers overboard in order to save the remainder, because his actions were inconsistent with the principles of sanctity of life, equality and respect for persons. For the Kantian, every human life has intrinsic value and so all lives are equally valuable. You cannot take a life to save a life. You cannot do evil in order to do good. The end, however good, does not justify the use of immoral means. Even in situations of crisis you are not allowed to do evil. The person who allows someone to die in order not to do evil does nothing wrong. In fact he or she is doing the right thing. If Kantians are going to be consistent then they must hold that allowing evil to occur is sometimes the right thing to do. The Pauline principle, never do evil in order to do good, is not simply an ad hoc principle that the Kantians add to make their theory coherent. It is implicit in the principle of respect for persons.

In a Kantian moral universe there exist incommensurable moral dilemmas. Evil can flourish like the green bay tree and the morally good person can only look on in dismay, wringing his or her clean hands. A moral universe which required moral agents to do evil intentionally would be absurd. A rational moral agent can always refuse to do evil. The mate should have tried to save all his passengers rather than sacrificing the few for the many. One does not have to choose the lesser evil, because one can always choose to do no evil. So no one should have been thrown overboard. Similarly, scarce medical treatment should be distributed either on a first come, first served basis or by a lottery, certainly not on the basis of an individual's value to society or to the progress of a war. It would even be wrong to act charitably towards others if this required us to fail in our duties to ourselves. Because evil is allowed to flourish, the Kantian moral universe also appears to be irrational.

The Kantian would also hold that the mate did the wrong thing when he took it upon himself to decide who should be thrown overboard. For the Kantian, totalitarian or paternalistic decision-making procedures are always wrong, no matter how efficient. Everyone has a right to life and no one has a right to decide when other people should live or die. Democracies are designed to see that such basic human rights are never violated.

The Kantians and the utilitarians approach crisis dilemmas in radically different ways. For the utilitarian, the central principle which guides hard moral choices is the principle of the lesser evil. For the Kantian, it is the Pauline principle of never doing evil in order to do good negatively interpreted: let evil flourish, as long as the agent does no evil. Both theories recognize that there are incommensurable moral dilemmas. Both lead to the view that the moral universe is ultimately irrational: a paradoxical conclusion for theories which presuppose that there must be a rational solution to every dilemma which must be available to any normal rational enquirer.

In contrast, an idealist moral universe would ultimately be rational. The principle of self-realization, and the twin criteria of richness and integration it generates, implies that there can be no incommensurable moral dilemmas. This idealist vision of the moral universe may appear to be counter-factual. Surely some of our moral dilemmas, like that of the life boat, are incommensurable. The idealist, however, makes a distinction between theoretical and practical incommensurability. For the idealist, theoretically there can be no incommensurable dilemmas. Idealism presupposes that the moral universe is rational. But like the utilitarians and Kantians, idealists recognize that in practice there can be incommensurable dilemmas. This is how they would interpret the life boat situation. They would agree with the utilitarians that we can be faced with tragic choices. Given our finitude, we have limited powers both of thought and action; hence some of our choices will involve doing evil. But they agree with the Kantian that when we do evil we must accept that we have done wrong, even though we did our best not to do evil. We assume that the moral universe is rational even if we fail to understand how it all fits together. In a crisis we must go beyond the merely negative form of the Pauline principle. We must try to seek out alternative possibilities and not sit idle in the face of evil. We must always be as inventive as possible. In all of the examples we have discussed, this failure of creativity is evident. The first mate should have paid more attention to the principle of respect for persons and tried more democratic means to arrive at a course of action. The hospital authorities should have made some attempt to involve the patients and their families in the process of deciding who should have access to scarce medical treatments. Surely there are more imaginative ways for us to deal with the problem of famine in poor countries, such as the World Food Bank and the Green Revolution.[11] Can we not help in ways which will develop self-reliance and self-esteem in the recipients, rather than destroying these qualities? Are there no more imaginative ways we can deal with the Malthusian problems of population growth and the world food supply? Still, in some cases even when we have done our best to be morally creative we may have to do evil. For this we will surely feel remorse, but if we have tried our best we cannot be fully blamed. This is the human tragedy we all have to learn to live with.

Chapter 8

Women's voices

Anne-Marie, a 28-year-old black woman, and Helen, a 32-year-old white woman, both apply for a job as a waitress with a particular outlet of a large restaurant chain. Both woman have approximately five years' experience as waitresses and both are willing to work weekends. Helen, who had a high school education, does much better on the aptitude tests which the chain uses as part of its hiring policies than Anne-Marie, who had only a public school education. Anne-Marie is also enrolled in a government programme to upgrade her working skills. Anne-Marie is married but has no children, while Helen, recently widowed, is the mother of two young boys. The chain management, in response to recent government pressure, has instituted an affirmative action policy. At present, at the outlet where Anne-Marie and Helen have applied there are about 10 per cent minority employees. The goal of the affirmative action programme is to have 20 per cent minority employees. Individual franchises are allowed considerable flexibility in implementing the programme. The branch manager decides, in this instance, to comply with management's general affirmative action policy and hires Anne-Marie. Helen, who is unable to find employment, is forced to apply for public assistance in order to support herself and her two small children. Did the branch manager do the morally right thing?

The question raised in this dilemma is whether it is ever morally right to use skin colour or race as a criterion in hiring employees. To understand the dilemma we need to fill in some historical background. When he hires a black person, the restaurant manager is taking affirmative action to try and redress the wrongs of previous discrimination. Canadian society, for example, has been a racist and sexist society, although not as extreme as typical racist societies like

Nazi Germany, modern South Africa or the southern United States. As the Ontario Human Rights Code Review Task Force noted:

> Until the mid 20th century, discrimination was open, blatant, and legal in Canada. As late as 1940, the Supreme Court of Canada ruled that property rights gave owners the power to refuse service to persons because of their colour. [Christie vs. York Corporation][1]

Once racism and sexism were recognized as immoral, and as pervasive in our culture, we had to decide what to do about it. Do we simply make discrimination on racial or sexual grounds illegal, and enforce this through the courts and human rights commission, as we do now in Canada, or do we need to take more positive action to create a non-racist/non-sexist society?[2] Affirmative action programmes, like the one instituted by the restaurant chain, are designed to correct the disadvantages minorities have suffered as a result of historic and systemic discrimination. The way we answer the manager's dilemma will, as we know, depend upon the general ethical tradition we rely on. If we depend on the utilitarian tradition, we would agree that the restaurant manager did the right thing when he hired the black applicant over the white. If we depend on the Kantian tradition, we would hold that the restaurant manager did the wrong thing when he hired the black applicant.

First let's look at a utilitarian response to the dilemma, then at a Kantian response. Utilitarians believe that racism and sexism, discrimination on the grounds of colour, race or sex, are real, historic, systemic and morally unjustified. They believe that racism is immoral because they think that a non-racist society will maximize happiness and minimize suffering and that a racist society will minimize happiness and maximize unhappiness. Hiring practices based on racial discrimination are also inconsistent with the utilitarian principles of distributive justice: basic needs, just reward and impartiality. The utilitarian believes that goods ought to be distributed in proportion to individual merit, once basic human needs are met. In a non-racist society everyone, no matter what their colour or race, ought to have an equal opportunity to acquire goods and wealth. All human beings have the same basic need for physical security, health, food, shelter and sexual companionship, hence their interests must be treated equally in calculating consequences or formulating social policy.[3] For the utilitarian, the principle of equal opportunity is essential to achieve economic justice.

Utilitarians would say a society based on these principles of distributive justice would tend to produce a stronger economic system than one based on racial discrimination. Businesses which hire the best qualified people will produce better products, provide better services to customers and increase productivity. Economic prosperity will produce more happiness for a greater number. So utilitarians have strong reasons for supporting a society based on individual merit, once basic needs have been met. Such a society could not be racist.

The utilitarians would support the idea of affirmative action as a way of bringing about this non-racist society. Since minorities have been discriminated against in the past, utilitarians believe that preferential treatment is now needed to create a non-racist society. If minorities are to be integrated into the economic mainstream of society they need to have equality of opportunity, and affirmative action programmes will help them achieve this. It would not be enough for the utilitarian simply to make racial discrimination illegal and leave this to the courts to enforce. Even programmes of moral education, designed to teach racial equality, which are in place in our publicly funded schools, although welcome, would not be sufficient.[4] Affirmative action programmes would need to be introduced to integrate racial minorities into the mainstream of society. Positive goals would need to be created, in which quotas, based on proportionality, set out clearly defined objectives. For example, if 20 per cent of the population is black and 10 per cent oriental, then 20 per cent of the positions in the work place would have to be reserved for blacks and 10 per cent for orientals.

Universities and other institutions of higher education will also have to set aside a specific percentage of places for minorities, especially in professional schools such as medicine and law, as was done, for example, at the University of California and at York University in Canada. This will ensure that a proper number of racial minorities become college graduates, doctors and lawyers.[5] According to the utilitarians, these places would have to be reserved for minority groups even though many of their members may be less qualified than some members of the dominant group. People who have been subjected to racism for long periods of time are faced with disadvantages which have become part of their way of life. They are often undernourished, poorly housed and undereducated, and frequently suffer from low self-esteem which robs them of the motivation necessary to succeed. Minorities will not be able to find their proper place in society unless these problems are solved. The utilitarian would support affirmative action programmes even if these always involved reverse discrimination, i.e. discrimination against the dominant social groups in a society which results from the preferential treatment given to minority groups in affirmative action programmes. The utilitarians would argue that these radical steps ought to be taken to redress historic wrongs against racial minorities. They would also have to take into account the negative consequences of affirmative action programmes.

If affirmative action programmes led to hiring less qualified people, the quality of workmanship and service could be impaired, and this would have a negative effect on the economy and the targeted institutions. Requiring businesses or other social institutions to hire a specific percentage of racial minorities could also aggravate the racial problems they are designed to correct. The dominant group might come to resent the policy, especially if jobs or places for equally or better qualified people are lost, and creating a non-racist society would be made that much more difficult. Though affirmative action programmes may produce more jobs or increase the number of professionals among minorities, they could have a negative effect on the self-image of minorities. Many might feel that they hadn't merited their jobs and suffer a further loss in self-esteem. The utilitarian would certainly have to agree that in the short run there might be some undesirable consequences, but that in the long run the balance of happiness over unhappiness would still favour affirmative action. Affirmative action programmes are after all only temporary, and when successful they would no longer be required. By then our society would have become non-racist.

The utilitarian would also argue that there are times when a useful purpose can only be served by discrimination. An example will illustrate the utilitarian point. Suppose we wanted to find out how a multicultural society works? A social scientist tells us the best way to do this is to use small groups which reflect the cultural mix of the society being studied. Suppose the society is 70 per cent white, 20 per cent black and 10 per cent oriental. Then 70 per cent of our subjects would have to be white, 20 per cent black and 10 per cent oriental. We would have to discriminate on racial grounds against some of the applicants who applied to participate in the studies, as soon as our quotas had been filled. Here we would be rejecting people simply because of their colour or race. If we didn't maintain these quotas there could be no study because racial inequality is part of the study's scientific protocol. Similarly, the utilitarians would say, the only way to create a non-racist society would be to discriminate temporarily against the dominant group, which is what happens in an affirmative action programme. So they would conclude that the restaurant manager did the right thing in hiring the black rather than the white woman.

The utilitarian would add that it was the analogy between racism and sexism which led to the creation of the modern women's liberation movement. Discrimination against women in many western societies, like discrimination against racial minorities, was until recently also open, blatant and legal. Women were discriminated against in the work place. They had to take menial jobs where they received much lower wages than men, even for work of equal value. Only grudgingly were they admitted into institutions of higher learning and the professions of medicine, law, politics, the church. It was not until 1917 that Canadian women received the right to vote. Since the black person in our particular dilemma is also a woman, this means she will be in double jeopardy living in a sexist as well as racist society. She will be discriminated against both on the basis of her colour and also because of her gender.

The utilitarians would tend to support the radical wing of the women's liberation movement. The radicals hold that women have been sexually repressed in society because all laws relating to the control of reproduction were created and imposed on women by men. Even the basic institutions of our society, like marriage and the family, are essentially sexist in their eyes. Women are allowed to realize themselves only as lovers, wives and mothers; everything but these male-dependent roles is largely taboo. They believe that all women in our society are essentially prostitutes, selling themselves to men for economic security.[6] In order to achieve true equality for women in our society, the radicals believe that massive affirmative action programmes are necessary.

Our sexist society is also supported by a sexist educational system which programmes women for their dependent and inferior roles in which they can only realize themselves as lovers, wives and mothers of men. In a sexist society the relationship between men and women is controlled by sexual stereotyping. The female is seen as a helpless, passive, emotional, dependent, family-oriented person. The male is seen as powerful, aggressive, rational and sexually promiscuous. Since both images are stereotypes, they lead to alienated and destructive forms of sexual relationships. The main goal of the male becomes the conquest and repression of the female. This is graphically expressed in the sexual violence which dominates modern pornography. Love becomes the war of the sexes.

The bias against women even reaches into our scientific research and theories. Carol Gilligan, for example, has argued convincingly that modern theories of moral education and morality are gender-biased.[7] Gilligan has demonstrated, for example, that Kohlberg's work on moral development presupposed a male bias. Kohlberg maintained that morality develops through a series of fixed stages which are both individually and culturally invariant.[8] Each stage is characterized by a distinct mode of thinking about and responding morally to the world. Each stage represents a more adequate way of relating both intellectually and morally to the world. There are three main stages of development.[9] Stage one is the pre-conventional stage and is mainly hedonistic and egotistic. In it the child is essentially concerned with the pleasurable and painful consequences that actions have for itself. The child learns, mostly by trial and error, what is in its selfish interest and what is not. Stage two is the conventional stage and is mainly one of social conformity. In it the child acts in accordance with the morality of the social groups to which it belongs: the family, peer groups, churches, schools and the state. Morality is now essentially social, and includes the interests of others as well as the self. Moral thinking becomes mainly non-consequentialist. Rightness and wrongness are now determined by conformity and non-conformity to conventional moral rules, rather than by their consequences. Moral rules are seen to apply equally to everyone in the society. The rules of fair play become important. The morality of law and order replaces that of selfish hedonism. Stage three is the post-conventional stage and is mainly one of personal universal morality. This is the stage of mature moral adults who think for themselves in terms of universal moral principles which apply to all rational moral agents, first in terms of the utilitarian principle of social utility and finally in terms of Kantian principles of justice, like equality, fairness and universal human rights. Morality at this stage is no longer relative to a particular culture but applies universally to all humankind.

Gilligan does not dispute the stage theory itself. She agrees that men generally developed the way Kohlberg's theory describes. What she criticizes is the way the theory has been applied to the moral development of women. She argues that women do not develop morally in the same way as men do, hence it is unfair to criticize them from the perspective of male models of moral development. Women's morality differs both in form and substance from masculine morality. Women's morality is one of care and benevolence rather than justice. Women are programmed for love; men for justice. In discussing the difference in responses of female and male subjects to moral dilemmas, Gilligan notes: 'Instead, Amy's judgements contain the insights central to an ethic of care, just as Jake's judgements express the logic of the justice approach.'[10] Women also approach moral dilemmas with a different methodology. Again referring to the differences in responses by female and male subjects to dilemmas, Gilligan writes:

> Thus in Heinz's dilemma these two children see two very different moral problems – Jake a conflict between life and property that can be solved by logical deduction, Amy a fracture of human relationship that must be mended with its own thread. Asking different questions which arise from different conceptions of the moral domain, the children arrive at answers which fundamentally diverge, and the arrangement of these answers as successive stages on a scale of increasing moral maturity calibrated by the logic of the boy's response misses the different truth revealed in the judgment of the girl.[11]

Women tend to think concretely and contextually while men tend to think in terms of abstract moral rules. Men are logical, social and legalistic in their moral orientation; women are emotive, intuitive and interpersonal. Women's morality differs from masculine morality in form as well as content. According to Gilligan these differences begin to appear at least in stage two. In this stage morality for women is equated with caring for others and in sacrificing the self for the well-being of others. It is not primarily concerned with justice, law and order, as is the case with men. Even here women's thinking has already begun to diverge from men's. Women's moral thinking is primarily intuitive and emotive rather than abstract, logical and rule-bound as male thinking is. In stage three there is a maturing of both feminine and masculine morality. Women, like men, move towards a universal morality that is not culturally dependent. This morality, however, is different from masculine morality. It is still a morality of care rather than justice, but it includes the developing female agent. It remains contextual rather than abstract. Since it does not give priority to the abstract principles of justice that mark masculine morality, its full flowering appears to be fundamentally more utilitarian than Kantian.[12] Kohlberg's selection of a form of Kantianism over a form of utilitarianism as the highest stage of moral development appears to be a product of the gender bias in his theory.

The affinity of utilitarianism with feminist perspectives can be illustrated by focusing on the abortion debate. This is a good example to use because Gilligan thinks that mature feminine moral thinking expresses itself most clearly when women are faced with the decision to have, or not to have, an abortion.[13] To examine this we need to outline the debate from radically opposing positions, which I shall call 'radical pro-choice' and 'radical pro-life'.[14] These positions contain three sets of claims, plus a general thesis about the relation of law and morality. First there are legal positions about the legality or illegality of abortion. Second, there are propositions about the legal, moral or ontological status of the foetus. Is the foetus a person or not? Third, there are propositions about the morality of abortions. Is abortion morally right or wrong? The ontological and moral claims are normally thought to provide rational support for the legal claims. These claims should be viewed as historically rather than logically linked. They do not mutually entail each other. There are certainly natural affinities between the claims. Adopting one tends to support the other. Radical pro-choice makes the following three claims:

1 Abortion on demand up to viability ought to be legal.
2 A person is legally and morally present at viability.
3 Abortion is morally permissible.

Let's look at the legal position first. Abortion on demand up to viability ought to be legal. When women began to free themselves from their bondage to men and to strive for a non-sexist society, they came to see that unless they had complete control over their bodies they could never be free from male domination. It was their reproductive systems which had enslaved them. A non-sexist society would involve, among other things, the right for women to have free access to contraceptive techniques and abortion. The first step towards the creation of a non-sexist society would be to reform the legal systems, which were gender-biased. In Canada, prior to 1969, non-therapeutic abortions were illegal. To participate in one was to commit a criminal act. Abortion needed to be decriminalized if women were to gain control of their bodies. Canadian women took much longer than their American cousins to achieve this goal. With the Roe vs. Wade decision in 1973, American women won the right to abortion on demand. The American Supreme Court ruled that anti-abortion laws were un-constitutional because they violated a woman's right to privacy and because a foetus was not legally a person which had rights comparable with an adult woman.[15] Canadian women did not gain this right fully until 1988. Between 1969 and 1988, largely as a result of pressure from women's groups, the law was changed to allow abortions if the pregnancy endangered the life or physical or mental health of the mother, provided it was performed by a qualified doctor, after approval by a hospital abortion committee. Abortion was decriminalized in Canada in 1988, and there is now de facto abortion on demand in Canada.[16]

Pro-choice supporters marshalled a significant body of legal argument in defence of their position. First they pointed out that in Canada, as in many other countries, a foetus is not legally a person until viability, or birth. Section 206 of the Canadian Criminal Code states: 'A child becomes a human being within the meaning of this Act when it has completely proceeded, in a living state, from the body of its mother'.[17] Second, they argued that any law which denies or limits women's access to abortion violates the existing rights of Canadian women. They pointed out that women have a right to medical autonomy. Abortion is a medical procedure and women, like men, have a right to refuse or to initiate any treatment they and their doctors deem necessary for their well-being. If we do not take the right of patients to refuse treatment seriously, then not only is the freedom of women threatened but the whole of democracy is. Once the state gets control over its citizens' bodies through the medical profession and the hospitals, the demise of democracy is imminent.[18] The pro-choice movement also pointed out that anti-abortion laws violate a woman's right to privacy.

Moreover, women have a right to enter freely into agreements with their spouses or partners and doctors to raise a family as they see fit, to determine the size and quality of their families. Finally, the pro-choice movement appealed to the legal right of self-defence. This is important because the appeal to women's existing rights are much stronger if taken in conjunction with the lack of foetal rights. If the foetus were to be granted rights, then the legal debate becomes one of conflicting rights and not simply taking existing rights seriously. With the introduction of the self-defence argument, feminists were able to argue that the mother's rights would take precedence over the rights of the foetus when it endangered her or her family's life or well-being.[19] We are legally allowed to use as much force as is necessary, including killing an aggressor, in order to defend our lives.[20] Of course the analogy between an aggressor and a foetus may not hold, because the latter is innocent. The foetus does not intend to harm anyone. The intent to do harm is, however, not essential to the plea of self-defence, because we are also allowed to defend ourselves from psychopaths who are about to kill us, even if this is an unintended consequence of their insanity.[21]

In any case, the assumption here is that a case can be made for giving the foetus rights, especially a right to life. Just because a foetus does not have legal standing at the moment does not mean that it should never be given legal standing. However, according to the radical pro-choice position there is no reason for granting the foetus legal standing. This is substantiated by their second claim that a person comes into being only at viability. A person is a rational moral agent and a foetus is certainly not a fully developed rational moral agent, hence it cannot have any moral rights. Technically a foetus is part of a woman's body, much like a kidney or a piece of tissue. Kidneys and body tissue do not have rights. One cannot even argue that a foetus is a potential person, because this implies that an unfertilized ovum would also have rights.[22] If a foetus cannot have moral rights, then it cannot have legal rights.

There is, however, a major internal problem with this pro-choice position because it appears to be inconsistent with the principle of social utility: maximize happiness and minimize suffering. The principle of social utility implies that the criterion for moral standing is the capacity to suffer or to be happy, to feel pain or pleasure. At viability the foetus clearly possesses this capacity, hence it would have moral and presumably legal standing. The newborn baby has a right to life and this justifies our view that infanticide is immoral and should remain a criminal offence. However, if we strictly apply the criterion of personhood then infanticide, as Michael Tooley has so ably argued, would be morally and possibly legally acceptable.[23] Consistency requires that sentience be taken as the criterion for moral standing for the utilitarian. If this is the case then the utilitarian would have to grant the foetus moral standing when it acquires the capacity to feel pain, somewhere around or between five or six months into its development. This would mean that utilitarians would have to distinguish morally between early and late abortions. Early abortions would automatically be morally permissible, but late abortions would not.[24] Although not biologically the same as a human organ or tissue, the foetus in its early stages of development is morally the same. How this moral position translates into a legal position is complex, but even if some two-tiered legal position was accepted it could still be a form of abortion on demand. The rights of the mother would clearly take precedence over the rights of the foetus in late pregnancy, because the foetus would still not be a creature with self-conscious wants until at least viability.

There are moral arguments which the pro-choice movement can rely on to establish the moral permissibility of late abortions. The pro-choice movement argues on basically utilitarian grounds that abortion is morally permissible but not morally required. It is a matter of freedom of choice. To deny women the right to an abortion is a serious breach of the principle of individual liberty: maximize freedom and minimize social control. Women, like men, should be allowed to do as they please so long as they don't harm others or interfere with their liberty. A woman's freedom depends upon having full and free control over her procreativity. She needs the right to enter freely into agreements with her partner or spouse to raise a family and to determine its size and quality. The principle of individual liberty establishes a woman's right to medical autonomy and the pursuit of personal happiness. It also establishes her right to privacy.

Getting married, becoming pregnant and having children is a private, not a public, matter which concerns the woman first, her spouse or partner second, her doctor third, other members of her family fourth, and society in general last, if at all. The state should have no direct concern in these matters. The question of whether to carry a pregnancy to term is essentially a private matter and probably not a moral matter at all. It is certainly not a public matter. The principle of individual liberty defines the relations between the public and private spheres of our lives. It defines the limits of the state's interference in the affairs of consenting adults. Abortion falls within the domain of a woman's private life, and to deny her access to abortion is an unwarranted breach of her right to privacy.

In a democracy, people have a right to raise a family and are responsible for both its size and quality. To have children is morally permissible but is certainly not required. There is not, nor ought there to be, compulsory motherhood. If people decide to raise a family, their first responsibility is to have children only when they can take care of them properly. It would be morally wrong to bring in to the world children we are not prepared to look after. All children should be wanted children who will be cared for. Our basic responsibility is the quality of life of our family.

Since quality of life is always central to utilitarianism, the principle establishes a prima facie case against abortion. As long as there is a prospect for a happy life for all concerned, then abortion would be unjustified. This holds whether we treat the decision as a private moral one or a non-moral choice concerning personal happiness. As R.M. Hare has so aptly shown, there should be no abortion of a potentially happy person.[25] Hare demonstrates this by appealing to the 'golden rule': do unto others as we would want them to do unto us. He points out, correctly, that this general rule implies the less general rule: do unto others what we are glad was done to us. If we are glad that our parents did not abort us, presumably because we've had happy lives, then we should not abort a potentially happy person. Life for the utilitarian is only valuable when it possesses a certain quality, a proper balance of happiness over unhappiness. It is experiential life and not merely biological life which is important for the utilitarian. The question of abortion will only arise then in cases where the quality of life of those immediately affected by carrying a pregnancy to term is threatened; for example, when the life or health of the mother is endangered, or in teenage pregnancies, or when the pregnancy is a result of rape or incest, or if the mother is mentally handicapped, or if the foetus is terminally ill or severely damaged. Abortion must be determined in terms of quality of life. Quality of life judgements, in turn, are extremely complex and situation-dependent, hence they are best left to the pregnant woman in consultation with her partner and doctor. They are more likely than the state to understand what is in the best interests of their families.

To return to our original dilemma of whether or not affirmative action programmes are morally right, it comes as no surprise to find that in a discriminatory society black women are victims of discrimination more often than their white sisters. In order for women to prosper, the radicals believe we need to restructure our basic social institutions completely through affirmative action programmes at all levels. If a society is to be fully affluent, access to jobs must depend on individual merit, once basic needs have been satisfied. Free access to abortion is a necessary condition for satisfying the basic needs of women. A non-racist/non-sexist society requires both equal opportunity and abortion on demand. For the utilitarian, racism and sexism are morally wrong. Affirmative action programmes are morally justified. Reverse discrimination is also morally justified. Temporary discrimination against the dominant group is necessary to create a non-racist, non-sexist society. The restaurant manager did the right thing in hiring Anne-Marie, the black woman, and discriminating against Helen, the white woman.

That was a utilitarian response to the dilemma, now let's look at a Kantian response. The Kantian would hold that the restaurant manager did the wrong thing when he hired the black woman rather than the white. The action was unjust because it is inconsistent with the principles of respect for persons, human rights and equality. The Kantians believe, like the utilitarians, that racism is immoral. But they do so for different reasons. Their rejection of racism is simpler, more

direct and more compelling than the utilitarian rejection because it is
not mediated by the principle of social utility.

For the Kantian, racism is essentially the denial of human rights.[26]
Human rights are fundamental and universal. They apply equally to
all human beings simply because they are persons. They are not earned
rights like those we get by completing a degree in law or medicine.
They are what classical philosophers called 'natural rights'. Racism
violates the natural right of every human being not to be discriminated
against on the basis of race or colour, a right which is guaranteed by the
Canadian constitution.[27]

Racism is also inconsistent with the principle of equality. To be
treated equally means to be treated as an equal but not necessarily to
be treated the same. In situations of scarce resources everyone ought to
be treated the same, but in other situations this interpretation of
equality would not be fitting. For example, we do not consider it unfair
to give disabled people preferential parking arrangements. If they
aren't given preference they will have severely restricted access to
facilities that others take for granted. Equality, however, does imply
the principle of equal opportunity, and on this the Kantians and
utilitarians agree. Everyone should be treated the same unless there is a
morally relevant difference between them. Racism is inconsistent with
equality because there is no morally relevant difference which justifies
a different treatment of the non-white minorities. The differences cited
by the racist, like lack of intelligence, discipline, sensitivity or industry,
are false.[28] If non-white races are generally less educated or poor it is
because they have not had an equal opportunity to get an education to
enable them to compete in our economic system. It is surely wrong to
punish or handicap people for things over which they have no control.
Any violation of the principle of equal opportunity is a violation of
democratic egalitarianism.

Although racism is immoral for the Kantians, they would not
support the idea of affirmative action. The fair opportunity rule
appears to be a negative right, i.e. it guarantees non-interference with
human freedom or liberty.[29] It would appear to require only limited
interference by the state with its citizens to enforce it. Discrimination
on the grounds of race or colour certainly ought to made illegal and
equal rights should be enshrined in the constitution, as they presently
are in Canada and the USA.[30] They should also be vigorously enforced
by the courts and human rights commissions. However, the Kantians
would not support affirmative action programmes, because that would
be treating equality rights as if they were positive rights, rights which

are guaranteed by massive intervention by the state in the lives of its citizens.

Affirmative action programmes are immoral because they involve reverse discrimination. For the restaurant manager to reject a white person simply because of her colour is reverse discrimination. Reverse discrimination occurs when a member of a dominant group is discriminated against because of his or her race or colour, to make up for previous discrimination against a racial minority. For the Kantian, turnabout is not fair play. The Kantians would point to cases like the Bakke case in the United States to confirm their view.[31] This case concerned the Davis Medical School of the University of California, which in the late 1970s introduced an admissions programme to increase the number of doctors from minority groups: Asians, blacks, Mexican Americans and American Indians. The school set aside a number of places for these minority applicants which assured them places in the medical school but at the expense of more qualified white students. Allan Bakke was one of the rejected white applicants. He took his case to the Californian courts and finally to the Supreme Court of the United States. The American Supreme Court ruled in favour of Bakke, stating that the Davis Medical School had denied Bakke's right not to be discriminated against because of his colour, which in this case was white. The Davis special admissions programme was ruled unconstitutional and the school was required to allow Bakke into its medical programme. Bakke eventually graduated from Davis and is currently practising medicine in New York State.[32] The Kantians would agree with the American Supreme Court's ruling because they believe that discrimination in any form is immoral and ought to be illegal.

Kantians would also agree with utilitarians that sexism, like racism, is morally unacceptable. But again they do so for different reasons. Women are persons and they have the same natural rights as men, and they must be treated with equality. The Kantians would strongly support ideas like equal pay for work of equal value because these ideas express their ideal of equality. They would also support programmes designed to give women higher profiles in the professions and to protect them from male violence. But the Kantians would agree with feminists like Ann Dummet who argue that the analogy the radical feminists draw between racism and sexism is not valid.[33]

In the first place Dummet pointed out that women in our society were never treated as badly as blacks. They were never legally deprived of all their human rights. They were never slaves who lost their right to life. Dummet also argued that treating women differently from men is not necessarily a breach of the principle of equality. There is a functional difference between men and women which may be relevant. Women may have as much intelligence, courage and emotional stability as men, but only women can bear and nurse children. Dummet argues that this difference does not justify depriving women of their rights, but it does mean that women's equality must not be achieved at the expense of marriage and the family. The struggle for equality must not radically alter the basic structures of our society. The institutions of marriage and the family should be based on democratic rather than totalitarian and paternalistic models, in which men are the rulers and women expected to be obedient servants. The principle of equality can function as the basic moral principle in these institutions as it should do in the state. Marriage and the family may need to be reformed to express the principle of equality properly, but they do not have to be abandoned. There is no need to adopt a so called feminist ethics, as Gilligan and others have argued for. It is certainly true that women may in fact be taught different social roles and to a certain degree a different morality. Women are taught to be good wives and mothers, while men are taught to be good husbands and good fathers. The former roles tend to develop a contextual ethics of care, the latter a universalistic ethics of justice. This does not mean that we need to abandon universal ethics for the irrationalism of particularism, or that women need to remain mired in an emotional tribalism which defeats the higher stages of moral development. Women are perfectly capable of reaching Kohlberg's higher stages of moral development if given the opportunity to do so.[34]

The Kantians would reject the idea of a feminist ethics. We do not require one ethic for women and another ethic for men. Ethics, because it is based on universal moral principles which are valid for all moral agents, including women, is necessarily unisexual. The rejection of feminist ethics by the Kantians would come as no surprise to radical feminists, because Kantianism, with its emphasis on rules, justice and rights, is seen as the paradigm of masculine ethics.[35] The affinity which feminists see between masculine and Kantian perspectives can be illustrated by focusing on the abortion debate once again. The 'radical pro-life' position appears to have a male bias.

The 'radical pro-life' position, like the 'radical pro-choice' position, contains three sets of claims, plus a general thesis about the relation of law and morality. First there is a legal position on the legality or illegality of abortion. Second there are propositions about the legal, moral, or ontological status of the foetus. There are claims about the morality of abortion. Again the moral and ontological claims are thought to provide rational support for the legal position. Radical pro-life makes the following three claims:

1 Abortion ought to be legally prohibited.
2 A human being (person) is present from conception.
3 Abortion is always morally wrong.

Radical pro-life represents the status quo which existed in Canada prior to 1969, and in the United States prior to 1973. It also represents the conservative backlash which developed in Canada and the United States once women had won the right to have abortion on demand. Let's look at the legal position first.

Radical pro-life holds that abortion ought to be legally prohibited. Its supporters argue that the foetus is legally a human being or person from conception, hence it has full legal status and rights from conception. It has the same rights as any other child, including the right to life. Abortion is murder and should be treated as the criminal act which it is. Further, radical pro-life supporters argue that in cases of conflict foetal rights take precedence over women's rights. They do not deny that women have the legal rights which radical pro-choice argues for, but they suggest that these rights need to be weighed against the rights of the foetus. The rights of the unborn should take precedence over the rights of the born because they are innocent and defenceless. The rights of pregnant women, although real, are limited, like the rights of any parents. Parents are not allowed to abuse or kill their children. In some countries they are not allowed to refuse life-saving medical treatment even on religious grounds.[36] Even an adult's right to refuse medical treatment isn't absolute. The public interest sometimes requires that individual rights be overridden. In many countries we can be treated for highly contagious diseases like bubonic plague without our consent.[37] No one has absolute control over his or her own body; to demand this is surely unreasonable. There is no right to infanticide.

Pro-life legal arguments have so far not proved to be very strong in Canada and the United States, where the courts have ruled that anti-abortion laws violate women's rights to medical autonomy and privacy, and that the foetus is not legally a person until viability or birth.[38] Because a foetus is legally not considered a person, it does not follow that ontologically or morally it is not a person who ought to be given legal standing. After all it was only recently that the law recognized that women were legally persons who had the same rights as men. As the supporters of pro-choice know, women only gained the right to vote in Canada in 1917.

Radical pro-life argues that the foetus is a human being onto-logically from conception, hence it ought to have both moral and legal standing. The idea that a human being is present from conception has obvious links to the Judaeo–Christian view that a soul is present from conception. This needs, however, to be translated into a secular position before it would be relevant in a multireligious democratic culture like Canada. The most common secular interpretation of this theological view is that biologically a unique genotype is present from conception.[39] The pro-life ontological argument is clearly stronger than the legal arguments. The foetus is not like a piece of human tissue or a kidney or an animal. It is a human being who is physically dependent on its mother's body for its existence but it is ontologically distinct. Hence there can be no automatic ownership, as there is for the mother's tissues and bodily organs like kidneys. Because the foetus has a unique genotype it is a human being, a member of the species *homo sapiens*; this secures its humanity and surely gives it some sort of moral standing. It clearly falls under the umbrella of the principle of sanctity of human life, so it does have moral standing and ought to have legal standing. Pro-life arguments have led the courts in both Canada and the United States to consider giving the foetus some sort of legal standing.

There appears to be a conflict here between the principle of sanctity of life and respect for persons. A foetus is clearly a human being in the biological sense, but it is not a rational moral agent. Since it is not a person in that sense it cannot have moral or legal standing[40] but, according to this argument, neither would a child or a comatose adult or someone who was mentally handicapped. However, children, the mentally handicapped and comatose adults are recognized as pos-sessing rights. In Canada and the United States they do have both moral and legal standing. This suggests that the principle of sanctity of life is more fundamental than the principle of respect for persons.

An alternative solution for the Kantian would be to argue that although a person is not present from conception a potential person is. What exists from conception is a creature who has the capacity to develop into a person. A potential person, like a child, someone who is mentally disabled or a comatose adult, must be respected as a person. All in these categories would have moral and hence legal standing. They would all possess rights, but these would apply in different ways from other adult persons because they could not give informed consent. The concept of a potential person itself does have problems. Thompson, for example, has argued that since an unfertilized ovum is also a potential person contraception, like abortion, must be considered morally wrong.[41] Thompson and others who argue this way are clearly mistaken, because we trace the beginning of each individual human life to conception. The fertilized ovum creates a new human life, a rational animal who has the capacity to develop into an adult moral agent. Hence contraception and abortion are not necessarily linked through the conception of a potential person.[42]

Radical pro-life also appeals, like radical pro-choice, to moral arguments to support its claims for the moral and legal impermissibility of abortion. The basic principle which it appeals to is that of sanctity of human life. Each human life is sacred and an end in itself. All human life has value no matter what its quality. The principle of sanctity of life is fundamental to both our morality and law. It is from this principle that we derive our rules against killing people and the basic human right to life. Abortion always involves the taking of an innocent and defenceless human life. It is always a serious breach of sanctity of life, and hence is always morally wrong. The appeal to sanctity of life clearly establishes a prima facie case against abortion. Both radical pro-choice and radical pro-life agree that there is always a prima facie moral case against abortion. Radical pro-life must also establish that there are no exceptions, that this prima facie case can never be overridden, to establish a complete ban on abortion.

Radical pro-life argues that the sanctity of life always takes precedence over individual liberty. Individual liberty is often overridden in both law and morality. We are not allowed to murder or assault or rape people. Individual liberty is not absolute as radical pro-choice appears to claim. A simple appeal to liberty cannot justify abortion. We cannot split the world as the utilitarians want to do into a public moral world and a private non-moral world. We cannot escape our moral responsibility to others so easily. Morality has a private as well as a public sphere, and our law ought to reflect this, especially with respect to private activities between consenting adults, like doctors and their patients.

Abortion then is always wrong. There are no exceptions. Because a child may endanger the health of the mother is no reason for killing it. The self-defence argument does not work in the case of abortion because the foetus is not intentionally trying to harm the mother. Because a child is mentally or physically handicapped, is the result of rape or incest, or is unwanted, are not valid reasons for killing it. The mother, after all, must take responsibility for the consequences of her sexual activity. But what is involved in sexual responsibility? Does sexual responsibility mean celibacy, at least outside of marriage? Sexual responsibility could also mean using proper birth control. If the object is to prevent unwanted pregnancy, then logically sexual education and birth control technology must be made freely available. If radical pro-life is to take sexual equality seriously it will have to adopt the latter interpretation of sexual responsibility. But in any case accidents will occur and the abortion question will reappear.

One might think it is cruel to bring an unwanted child into the world, but unwanted children can always be adopted by loving couples. In all these cases the foetus is innocent and so should not be harmed. The only possible exception arises in cases where the foetus is a threat to the mother's life. Even here, where we have to choose between two human beings, the weight of the argument falls on the side of the innocent child. In these cases if we save the mother we must kill the child, but if we save the child we would allow the mother to die. The death of the mother would be an unintended but foreseeable consequence of saving the baby. By saving the child rather than the mother no evil is done.

Moving from the Kantian position on abortion back to our original dilemma, the Kantians would not support affirmative action programmes for women which involve reverse discrimination based on gender, colour or race. For the Kantians, reverse discrimination is quite as immoral as discrimination. So they would hold that the restaurant manager did the wrong thing in rejecting the white person simply because of her colour.

That was a Kantian response to the dilemma. Now, let us sum up. This dilemma involved a conflict between the utilitarian principles of social utility and just reward, and the Kantian principle of respect for human rights and the principle of equality. The Kantians believe, like the utilitarians, that racism and sexism are immoral but they do so for different reasons. For the Kantian, racism and sexism are immoral because they are inconsistent with respect for human rights and equality. There is no need to develop a feminist ethics. The utilitarians believe that racism and sexism are immoral because racist and sexist societies produce more unhappiness than happiness. There is a need to develop a feminist ethics to replace traditional ethical theories which are male-biased. The utilitarians support the idea of affirmative action programmes even when these involve reverse discrimination. To achieve a non-racist, non-sexist society the utilitarians believe radical action is needed. This is why they support abortion on demand. The Kantians would argue that no matter how desirable a non-racist, non-sexist society may be, it would be wrong to try to achieve this goal through immoral means. They would not support achieving these goals through affirmative action programmes which involve reverse discrimination, nor through abortion. So the utilitarians would say the restaurant manager did the right thing to hire the black woman and the Kantians would say he did the wrong thing.

Once again we arrive at a situation in which incommensurable ethical theories produce inadequate responses to crucial moral problems. The liberal utilitarians are willing to undermine the principles of fairness and respect for life in order to create a non-racist, non-sexist society. The conservative Kantians make the achievement of a non-racist, non-sexist society virtually impossible with their negative uncompromising moral attitudes. It is not surprising then that the current debates concerning affirmative action and abortion have turned ugly. In order to make any headway with these dilemmas we need once again to put on an idealist thinking cap and concentrate on the incoherences which emerge in the moral reasoning of both sides in the debate.

Let's look at some Kantian problems. In the abortion debate the radical pro-life position depends on accepting the view that a human person is present from conception and that sanctity of human life is a moral absolute. The problem here is that this argument is valid only if sanctity of life is thought to take precedence over respect for persons, and this is disputable. The principle of respect for persons is capable not only of establishing the immorality of murder but of assault and rape as well. Take rape, for example. Rape is not considered wrong because it is a breach of respect for life, but because it is inconsistent with respect for persons. It is wrong to have sexual relations with anyone without consent. Rape violates this fundamental rule of sexual morality. Before we accept the radical pro-life position we need to determine which value is more fundamental, respect for life or respect for persons. A strong case can be made in favour of respect for persons. We need to ask what is it about human life which makes it intrinsically valuable? The religious answer, that it is a sacred gift from God, is not sufficient, because we still do not know why God values human life. One of the reasons we value human life is because we value sentience. Human life is valuable because humans have the capacity to experience a wide range of feeling and thought and to express these in action. Love. Rationality. Creativity. These are the characteristics which define our humanness and give human life its intrinsic value. These characteristics are implicit in the principle of respect for persons. Sentience, passion, rationality and creativity are all aspects of personhood, of what it means to be a moral agent. Respect for persons, then, appears to be more basic than sanctity of life, especially if the latter is construed purely biologically. This also suggests that the two great principles, respect for persons and utility, which dominate so much of our contemporary moral debate, have much more in common with each other than we imagine.

The concept of quality of life is an intrinsic part not only of the principle of utility but of respect for persons. We cannot deal with abortion dilemmas unless we recognize the importance of quality of life. This much we must grant to the utilitarians and feminists. But the utilitarians and feminists have their problems too. The radical pro-choice position depends on the view that a person is not present until birth, hence the foetus has no moral standing. This view appears to be indefensible. This much we can grant to the Kantians. We do not need, however, to agree with the Kantians that a person is present at conception, a view which is equally untenable. It is more likely that what we have at conception is a potential person. Although a person is not present at conception, a potential person clearly is. Once fertilization has taken place, a natural process is set in motion which, barring accidents or abortion, will result in the birth of a human child. So the principle of sanctity of human life is involved in some degree with respect to the conceptus. A potential person must be granted moral standing of some sort.

To have an abortion is a difficult moral choice and there must be strong moral reasons for doing so. Both utilitarians and Kantians agree that there is always a prima facie case against abortion, so the central moral problem becomes: under what circumstances is abortion morally permissible? These circumstances always involve questions of quality of life. The mother's health is in danger. The pregnancy is the result of rape or incest. The foetus is seriously damaged or deformed. The family cannot ensure the quality of life any parent is obligated to give to every child. Abortions based on ugliness or the wrong sex would be difficult to justify morally, because quality of life has no intrinsic relevance in these cases.

The decision to abort, as feminists like Gilligan rightly point out, is complex and not easily decided by abstract ethical methodologies. An idealist methodology, which tries to give harmonious expression to conflicting values, is clearly more appropriate. An idealist moral epistemology is necessarily androgynous. This complexity also suggests that the mother, in consultation with her partner and physician, is the best person to make this difficult moral decision. The principle of individual liberty is implicit in both the principles of utility and respect for persons. Where possible, we ought to maximize human freedom and minimize social control. Idealism allows us coherently to hold a morally restrictive position and a legally permissive position with respect to abortion.

With respect to social change we can generally agree with the Kantians that we ought not to bring about change by immoral means. A non-racist, non-sexist society is morally better than a racist, sexist society. But to achieve this by social programmes which involve reverse discrimination is morally unacceptable. We need to be more creative in the way that we adopt means to ends. Perhaps affirmative action programmes which involve reverse discrimination are not the only way to create a non-racist or non-sexist society. There is no reason why we can't reach the same goal with affirmative action programs which don't involve reverse discrimination. For example, universities who want to ensure that minorities have equal access to professional schools could set up programmes so the minorities could compete on an even basis with other applicants. In this way, society as a whole would carry the burden of redressing past wrongs, rather than placing it on individuals who may never have discriminated against anyone in their lives. Creativity is intrinsic to the Pauline principle of never doing evil to bring about good.

Chapter 9

Global ethics

Multinational corporations often appeal to ethical relativism as an excuse for using business practices which enhance profits but would be morally questionable in their home country, and which are frequently exploitative in the host country in which they are operating. Factory workers in third world countries are often paid wages which are considerably less than those paid to factory workers doing the same work in the multinational's home country and they often work with lower safety standards than those accepted in the home country. These practices are thought to be justified not only because cheap labour and lower safety standards produce higher corporate profits, but because these are the going rates and the accepted safety standards in the host country. But can a difference in cultural norms justify what appear to be unjust and exploitative business practices? To address this question it's necessary to examine in some detail moral dilemmas which arise from a conflict of moral norms between countries doing business with each other. First let's consider the following example which I have entitled 'The Candu Affair'.[1]

During the late 1960s and early 1970s Canada was having difficulty in selling its Candu nuclear reactor. It had been previously sold to India, but Australia, Mexico and Japan had bought from the competitors, the Americans or British. The failure to succeed in international markets was traced by management to poor marketing practices, rather than the quality of the Candu atomic reactor or to Canada's more stringent non-proliferation safeguards. It became obvious to the Atomic Energy Commission (AEC) that a more aggressive marketing campaign would be needed to improve its position in this highly competitive international market. The most effective way to do this was to use commercial agents who knew the foreign countries in which sales could be made. The survival of the industry was at stake, as were many jobs. In addition, there was concern about the already large financial investment Canada had made in the nuclear power industry. The new marketing procedures were introduced. The senior manager responsible for this new marketing campaign soon learned that the commercial agents who had been engaged to help make sales in Argentina and South Korea needed to use AEC money to bribe government officials in these countries if sales were to be made. Bribery was widespread in these countries at the time and Canada's NATO competitors appeared willing to use bribery to gain sales. The question facing the AEC management was: is it morally right to bribe foreign government officials to get an international business contract? The more general question raised in this dilemma is whether it is ever morally right for business people to secure international contracts by bribery.[2]

The way the AEC management answers the question will, as we know, depend on whether it relies on utilitarianism or Kantianism to give it its answer. The utilitarians we know are consequentialists, for whom the rightness or wrongness of actions depends on the actual consequences and who subscribe to the principle of utility: maximize happiness/minimize suffering. Kantians, on the other hand, are non-consequentialists, for whom the rightness or wrongness of actions depends on the motives of the agent and who subscribe to the principle of respect for persons: always treat persons as ends in themselves and never merely as a means.

Kantians are also strict objectivists who hold that moral judgements are independent of the person making the assertion, while the utilitarians tend to be subjectivists who hold that moral judgements are relative to the perspective of the individual moral agent. This observation holds true in spite of the fact that utilitarians have developed philosophically interesting objective forms of the theory. The fact that there are no subjective forms of Kantianism, as there are of utilitarianism, indicates that the theoretical debate between subjectivism and objectivism is internal to utilitarianism but not to Kantianism.[3] The utilitarians have to make a case for objectivism, while the Kantians cannot logically be anything else. Because of this utilitarians have always been more tolerant of diverse moral opinions than the Kantians have. Kantians tend to be more dogmatic in morals than the utilitarians are. The utilitarians have also generally been more sympathetic towards the doctrine of moral relativism, which holds that moral judgements are culturally dependent. Ethical relativism is attractive to the utilitarian because it appears to have a strong basis in fact and lends support to the idea of moral tolerance.[4]

Moral diversity appears to be a fact. Ritual suicide is morally acceptable in some societies but not in others. Bribery is morally tolerated in some countries but not in all. In some countries it is morally permissible to file false income tax returns, while this is morally unacceptable in others.

Our moralities also appear to be culturally determined. If someone grows up in a western society it is very likely that his or her morality will have a broadly Judaeo–Christian character. Even utilitarianism, which made a determined effort to abandon that religious tradition and to develop a rational scientific morality, has often been described as a secular form of Christianity. John Stuart Mill recognized the affinities and argued that when properly understood utilitarianism was completely compatible with Christian morality.[5] One modern American theologian, Joseph Fletcher, holds that a form of utilitarianism contains the essence of Christian morality.[6] These considerations give strong support to the idea that the rightness and wrongness of actions depend, in some important way, on the societies in which we grow up. For the utilitarian, morality is essentially social. It is something which is imposed on the individual by society and which restricts individual freedom. So it is not surprising that to the utilitarian morality is culturally determined.

Ethical relativism is also attractive to the utilitarian because it supports the idea of moral tolerance. Surely all cultures, like individuals within a society, have a right to moral self-determination. President Gorbachev was justifiably angry when President Reagan began to tell him what was morally wrong with Soviet society when they first met a few years ago. What right did Reagan have to lecture Gorbachev on human rights? Surely no more than Gorbachev would have to lecture Reagan or anyone else on human rights. This position is right not because Gorbachev or Reagan is insincere, or has a poor record with respect to human rights, which may be true in both cases. It's not a matter of the pot calling the kettle black, but of recognizing that the moral values of all cultures should be treated as equally valid. Why should we assume that Canadian or American or Swedish society is morally superior to Soviet society? Why should we assume that the Judaeo–Christian values of western cultures are morally better than the values of say Canada's native peoples, or the Australian aborigines? To claim this is nothing more than cultural conceit. We are not dealing here with scientific disputes which can be resolved by appeal to objective facts. In moral disputes there are no objective facts to appeal to. We have only the opinions of moral agents. Utilitarianism's affinities with subjectivism give it the flexibility to deal with the facts of the moral world.

Kantians, on the other hand, are more sympathetic to ethical universalism, which holds that moral judgements are dependent on universal natural norms which are valid for all humankind.[7] Universalists claim that moral diversity is superficial and that natural norms do exist. They point out that all known human societies recognize parental obligations towards children. The notion of the 'good mother' is present in all cultures.[8] Everywhere it is understood that parents have a moral responsibility to care for their offspring. There is of course some diversity as to what constitutes good child care. For example, is the child's spiritual well-being to be considered more important than its material well-being? But these disputes do not involve rejection of the general obligation for child care. At any rate all cultures appear to reject wanton cruelty towards children, even if they do not always agree as to what constitutes child abuse. Is physical punishment always a form of child abuse, as Swedish society maintains, or is mild physical punishment morally acceptable? The incest taboo also appears to be universal, although there is some disagreement as to who is to be considered close kin. Are first cousins to be included in the ban against sexual relationships with close kin? There also appear to be exceptions to the rule, but these are related to fertility rites, or are restricted to some royal families, and are not seen by the communities where they occur as breaches of the taboo. All known societies try to control group aggression, even if the level of violence which is morally acceptable varies considerably among cultures.[9] The universalists argue that the existence of natural norms can be explained by the nature of human beings.

The fact that universal moral norms exist should not surprise us, because we all share a common human nature. All humans desire security, food, shelter, sex and progeny. We all experience pleasure, pain, fear, love, hate, jealousy, pity and remorse. Most importantly, for the Kantian, we all think and make moral judgements. Conscience is universal and innate. Morality, like breathing, is natural to humankind. Rational moral agents are likely over time to discover the same moral universals.

The affinity of utilitarianism with ethical subjectivism and relativism, and of Kantianism with ethical universalism, will tend to make them accept conflicting answers to the Candu dilemma. In this case I want to suggest that if the AEC officials rely on the utilitarian tradition, which makes social utility the first principle of ethics, they would think it is morally right to secure the international contracts by bribery. If, however, they rely on the Kantian tradition, which makes respect for persons the first principle of ethics, they would think it is morally wrong to do so.

Let's look at a utilitarian analysis first. The line of reasoning outlined here was the one actually followed by the management of the AEC and those who defended the AEC's activities when the debate over its international conduct became public. The defence was always conducted along utilitarian lines. So again we are basing the hypothetical utilitarian position on arguments used in the real case.

The utilitarians would say that it's morally right to bribe in these circumstances because doing so would produce the greatest happiness for the greatest number. It is consistent with the principle of utility. The AEC is a crown corporation in which a lot of Canadian tax payers' money has been invested. The Candu atomic reactor is Canadian-designed and produced, and is one of our best high-tech products. The continued success of the AEC depends on capturing a section of the overseas market, as the domestic market is already saturated. The survival of the AEC is economically important for Canada. It will produce a good return on our investment, create jobs for both skilled and unskilled workers, keep research in physics fully funded and help establish our reputation in international markets.

The countries in which Canada builds power stations will also benefit. Many of these countries are poor and are just developing their industrial potential. They need the electric power to get their manufacturing started and to modernize their agricultural pro-duction. The new power stations will also create jobs in countries where jobs are badly needed. The utilitarian would argue that the benefits of selling the Candu reactor to foreign countries are so great that it would be cowardly not to bribe in order to get the contract. For the utilitarian, the end justifies the means. Sometimes we must make hard choices and do the lesser evil.

The utilitarians would also have to consider the long range difficulties of resorting to bribery in international trade. The practice might produce a political and economic backlash against Canada, especially if these business policies tended to support the repressive political regimes which were in power in these countries. If the regimes were overthrown by more democratic ones, these new governments might well turn to other countries for economic support, and these long range economic consequences could make the risks of using bribery too high. Of course, these long range consequences are more difficult to predict with the same accuracy that we can predict short term consequences, hence they have less immediate relevance. Cost/benefit economic analysis tends to favour short term gain and the possibility of long range pain. Utilitarian business people are rarely futurologists. In the real case the short term benefits actually materialized. The new marketing policies were a resounding success. The AEC sold nuclear reactors to both Argentina and South Korea, and everyone involved benefited. The long term pain, however, did not materialize. Argentina and South Korea moved in different degrees towards democratic government and this has had no dire consequences for Canadian international trade.[10]

The utilitarians would also argue that bribery is not intrinsically wrong. Canadians may believe bribery is immoral, but it is not thought of as immoral in all countries. In some countries, bribery is just another way of doing business. The Canadian economy is a free-market economy. The idea of fair competition is important because the buyer is looking for the best product at the best price. If sales people in such an economy start using bribes to get contracts, these criteria will no longer control the market, the competition will become unfair and this will undermine the free-market system. In this system, the utilitarian would claim bribery has no place. However, in countries with different economic systems which tend to depend on personal contracts, connections and barter, bribery is taken for granted and it's not considered immoral. In any case we do have to deal with countries which have different cultures and different ways of doing things. We have to choose between clean hands and international business activity. We cannot have both. The utilitarians would point out that our competitors, the Americans, the French and the British, all go along with bribery in countries where it is generally practised. If Canada wants to become a force in international trade, then it will have to play by international rules. This involves bribes and if we ignore this we will cease to be competitive as international traders.

The utilitarians would also point out that refusal to go along with another country's way of doing things displays a lack of moral tolerance and a surfeit of moral conceit. Surely it's morally wrong for us to impose our Canadian values on other cultures. If we take social differences into consideration, then all cultural values should be considered equally valid. Each culture is most likely to know what is in its own best interests and to be the best guardian of those interests. We expect foreign corporations to conform to our values; surely they would expect us to do the same when we do business in their country. The good corporate citizen should abide by that ancient adage 'When in Rome do as the Romans do.' To illustrate the utilitarian point, let's examine a different case in which cultural norms conflict.[11]

A manager is assigned to run a new overseas branch of a Canadian corporation in Moravia. Not long after his arrival he has to file the branch's first Moravian tax return. He is advised by the corporation's Moravian attorneys to file a tax return which greatly underestimates the real profits of the branch and the taxes it owes. It is explained to him that this is the standard practice in Moravia, and that it is merely the opening round in a bargaining process with the Moravian government to determine the branch's tax bill. The bargaining with the Moravian Revenue Service is actually carried out by tax agents who are hired by foreign corporations for the purpose. It is further explained that in the final stages of the process the government representative is made a personal payment to ensure a fair bargain for the corporation. This payment is added to the tax agent's fee, and is tax deductible. If the agent is skilful the bank will save a good deal of money and the corporation will enhance its profits. The Canadian manager, a religious fundamentalist, who comes from a small town in southern Ontario, is shocked by the suggestion that he should file a false income tax return. He thinks it is morally wrong to lie and filing false tax returns is not acceptable business practice in Canada. He feels he is representing his country in Moravia and so should be on his best moral behaviour. He is not going to demean himself by bringing his moral standards down to the Moravian level. It would simply be wrong to apply lower moral standards in a host country than one would use in one's own country. As a result the manager refuses to submit a false tax return. He refuses to hire a tax agent. He refuses to enter a bargaining process which involves bribing Moravian government officials. He submits what he considers an honest tax return, but as a result the corporation ends up paying a larger tax bill than it would have paid had he used the customary Moravian method. The corporation's relations with the Moravian Revenue Service deteriorate badly and the corporation loses a good deal of money. Eventually the parent corporation in Canada becomes so embarrassed with the situation that it replaces the manager who will not change his ways with someone who is more morally flexible and who will in future file the branch's tax returns in Moravian rather than Canadian style.

Approaching the manager's dilemma from the utilitarian perspective it is easy to see why the corporation thought, as it did in the real case, that filing a false income tax return was morally acceptable in this situation, even when it was not morally acceptable business practice in Canada. In the first place, doing so would be consistent with the principle of utility: it would produce the greatest amount of happiness for all those affected by the action. It would be more profitable for the corporation and its shareholders. It would pay less income tax and increase its profits and the shareholders' dividends. It would avoid embarrassment to the corporation, whose conduct would not be an insult to its Moravian hosts. Its relationship with the Moravian Revenue Service would improve and it would support a practice which provided useful employment to Moravians. The cost/benefit analysis is clearly on the side of doing business the Moravian way.

In the second place, the utilitarian would point out that to try to impose our way of doing business on a host country displays an incredible lack of moral tolerance and a surfeit of moral conceit. The principle of liberty applies to nations as well as individuals. Every culture, like every individual, has a right to moral self-determinism. Each culture, like each individual, is most likely to know what is in its own best interests and to be the best guardian of those interests. Adopting the Moravian system is consistent with the principle of cultural self-determination. Multinational corporations are primarily concerned with making a profit, and are not likely to be concerned about the interests of countries they do business with. And this is as it should be. To think that they ought to look after the interests of the host country would be to indulge in a form of false paternalism which has no place in international business practice.

It is clear then that the utilitarian perspective would tend to support the home corporation's decision to sack its Moravian manager and to replace him with one who was less morally squeamish. Intuitively most of us would agree with the utilitarians that the corporation did the right thing, while the manager did the wrong thing in rejecting Moravian mores and filing an honest tax return.[12] The good corporate citizen adapts his morals to the context of the host country. The AEC was simply following this practice in its attempts to sell its Candu nuclear reactors. Bribery in both cases is morally acceptable, and utilitarian theory explains our moral intuitions.

Finally, the utilitarians would argue that it's wrong for one country to impose its moral values on another. An example will make the utilitarian position clear. We in western cultures believe that monogamy, having only one spouse, is morally right, while polygamy, having more than one wife, and polyandry, having more than one husband, are morally wrong. However, in other cultures polygamy and polyandry are considered to be morally acceptable. Who is to say which form of marriage is morally better? Doesn't it make more sense to say simply that marriage customs differ from culture to culture, rather than to pronounce one type of marriage to be morally superior to those in other cultures? The utilitarians would argue that since moral values vary from culture to culture then morality must be culturally determined. For the utilitarian, morality only makes sense within the confines of a specific culture; hence the rightness or wrongness of acts will not be universal but relative to a particular social context. Our moralities reflect the values of the cultures in which we grow up. Hence it's not surprising that someone who grows up in Canada tends to acquire a Judaeo–Christian set of moral values. Moral diversity implies moral relativism, i.e. the rightness or wrongness of acts depends in fundamental ways on cultural norms.

The utilitarians would also point out that moral relativism supports the idea of moral tolerance. If the cultural context is crucial for establishing the rightness or wrongness of acts, then the values of all cultures are equally sound. Who is to determine whether the moral values of a Judaeo–Christian are superior to those of a Muslim or Buddhist? One culture should not judge another because all moral judgements are culturally biased. Since we cannot say one culture is better than another, we ought to be tolerant of each other's differences. Moral tolerance then implies acceptance of the idea of cultural autonomy, the view that each culture has a right to moral self-determination. The utilitarian would conclude that it is morally wrong to impose Canadian values on other cultures. Good corporate citizens abide by the laws and customs of the country with which they are doing business. If they use bribes, then we should do the same when doing business with them.

That was a utilitarian analysis, now let's look at a Kantian analysis. The line of reasoning to be outlined here is the one actually followed by the members of the Public Accounts Committee and other critics of the AEC's new marketing practices. They all used essentially Kantian approaches to what they perceived was a great moral scandal. So again we are dealing with real arguments used in the real case.[13] For the Kantians, it would be unethical to acquire international business contracts by bribery, because it is inconsistent with the principles of respect for persons, honesty and fairness.

In the first place, they would consider bribery to be intrinsically bad because it involves an intention to deceive. Bribes have to be distinguished from perks and tips. These are not considered immoral because they are open and above board, and there is no intention to deceive or corrupt. It's morally permissible to take a potential customer to dinner and pick up the tab but not to offer money directly. Bribes, especially to government officials, are given beneath the table. They are deliberately concealed from the competition and the country's citizens. It is true that all the competitors, and most citizens, suspect that bribery of some sort is going on. But this is still different from tipping because the amount and the people receiving them remain unknown. It is the intent to deceive other people which is wrong and not just the bad consequences which may arise from the practice. The false intent keeps corruption going at the expense of the people in the host country. It shows no proper respect for the citizens of the host country. Bribes are always dishonest, so it would be wrong to use them to secure international business contracts.

Second, bribery is unfair. The Kantian would agree with the utilitarian that fair competition is intrinsic to a market economy. If you have a market economy fair play must be one of its values. The rule is a constituent of the practice. But it is more than that for the Kantians. Fairness, like all obligations of justice, is a universal value. It is not just relative to a market economy. If you try to beat your competitors by dishonest means, you are not treating them as persons who are your equals. You cannot treat people equally if you accept or pay money under the table. This is especially so if the recipients are government officials who are required in any country to treat citizens equally. So bribery is wrong no matter what the circumstances. For the Kantian, bribery is not just bad business. It's morally wrong. The end never justifies the means.

Business practices which include bribery are not morally acceptable. The Kantian would point out that we frequently put moral restrictions on the way we do business. For example, Canadians wouldn't approve of our business people trading drugs to acquire international contracts. As a society, we do recognize that some things are wrong no matter what the cultural context. Moral tolerance at the international level cannot be absolute. We cannot tolerate evil. It needs to be opposed wherever it is found. Can we tolerate violations of fundamental human rights, torturing prisoners or racial discrimination? We cannot tolerate evil at the international level any more than we can tolerate it at the national level. Sometimes we have to pay an economic price for morality. Practices which display disrespect for persons cannot be tolerated in any society.

Besides, it is not clear that Canadian values differ that radically from those of the people in Argentina and South Korea. Do they really believe that bribery is a morally acceptable way of doing things, even if it was an accepted way of life under the military dictatorships? The governments of Argentina and South Korea at the time were quick to deny the accusations of corruption in their governments, which suggests that they knew that their own people and the world community at large thought bribery in business was not morally acceptable. Cultures have a lot more in common than relativists would have us think. Universal norms, which capture fundamental human values, often lie just beneath the surface profusion of cultural differences.

The Kantians would not be sympathetic to the Canadian corporation's decision to sack its Moravian manager for refusing to accept Moravian business mores. Approaching this dilemma from the Kantian perspective, it is easily seen why the manager thought that it would be immoral to file a false income tax return. To do so would be inconsistent with the principles of respect for persons, honesty and fairness. In the first place it is wrong to lie. To lie to people is to use them merely as a means to our ends and not as persons who possess intrinsic value. Lying, because it violates the principle of respect for persons, is always morally wrong. You should never take advantage of others even if they are stupid enough to ask you to do so. In the second place it would be unjust to apply one set of moral standards to ourselves and another to foreigners. Moral standards are universal and apply equally to all persons, to fellow citizens and strangers alike. Obligations of justice and fairness are universal values.

Finally, the Kantians would argue that we cannot tolerate evil. Can we allow evil to flourish so that good may prevail? From a Kantian perspective the answer is – never! To understand Kantian intolerance of evil, let's look at another example.[14] A Canadian civil engineer building a highway in a mountainous region in a third world country soon learns that safety standards are much lower than those used in road construction in Canada. Building the highway requires cutting through unstable rock formations and the danger of rock slides is very high. The engineer complains to both local officials and his home corporation. They ignore his criticisms of safety standards and several construction workers are killed by rock slides. When he goes public to prevent further deaths he is fired, and blacklisted by the corporation. Even the local work force turns against him because he appears to be disparaging their courage and threatening their jobs. Nevertheless Kantians would argue that the engineer does the right thing in blowing the whistle on both the corporation and the host country. Some things are just plain wrong wherever we find them. Appeals to cultural relativism are moral cop-outs. The engineer ought to blow the whistle, and the manager should not file a false income tax return, no matter what the consequences.

The Kantian would also argue that ethical relativism is inadequate and dangerous. The Kantians would point out that the relativists have not established their claim that morality is diverse. They maintain, as we saw, that moral universals do exist. They point to the fact that all societies recognize certain obligations towards their children, although they may express these requirements in different ways. They also point to the universal presence of the incest taboo in various forms in all societies. They would add that all communities have rules restricting violence within the society, although, again, these rules will differ from culture to culture.

Accordingly, to the Kantian, moral relativism implies that there could be no real moral disagreements between one culture and another. This is absurd. Countries run by military dictatorships advance a different view of human rights from democracies. In western societies, we take for granted the right to political dissent and the right to free association but these rights are consistently denied in dictatorships. We consider that denial to be morally wrong. We are not content to say merely that dictatorships have one set of values and we have another. That of course is true, but we feel compelled to make a moral judgement on those values. However, it is morally wrong to deny the rights of political dissent or free association to citizens of any country. Human rights are universal, and apply to all rational moral agents. The Kantian argues that some things are wrong no matter where they are found. Slavery or cannibalism are not made morally right simply because some culture practises them. All moral viewpoints are not equally valid. Finally, the Kantian would point out that the ideal of moral tolerance has its limits. It is sometimes our moral responsibility to try and impose our values on another society. No government has a right to torture or abuse prisoners, nor to discriminate against people on the basis of race or sex. This is why Canada was right in the 1980s in its attempts to coerce, through economic means, racist societies like South Africa to mend their moral ways. These practices should not to be tolerated no matter where they are found. The Kantian would conclude that it was morally wrong for the AEC to get an international contract by using bribery, even if this is common practice in international trade.

That finishes the examination of the Kantian response to the dilemma. Now let us sum up. In this dilemma we had a conflict between the utilitarian principle of expediency and the Kantian principles, honesty and fairness. The utilitarians would say that in some instances it's morally right to secure international contracts by bribery. They think that doing so would produce the greatest happiness for the greatest number. The utilitarians also think that bribery is not intrinsically wrong, it's just another way of doing business. Utilitarians don't think we should try to impose our values on another society. They believe that morality is largely determined by culture. Morality is not universal but diverse. The utilitarians favour cultural autonomy, and believe that each culture should be allowed to develop its own moral traditions without interference from others' cultures.

The Kantians, however, think it is morally wrong to secure international contracts by bribery. They believe that bribery is intrinsically wrong because it always involves dishonesty, unfairness and disrespect for persons. A bribe always involves the intention to influence someone improperly. The Kantian also holds that moral relativism is a mistaken and dangerous idea because it denies the objectivity and universality of morality. The Kantian believes that there are universal values that are not culturally determined. The values of all cultures are not equally moral. Bribery then is not an acceptable business practice for the Kantian.

In the Candu example the utilitarians abandon the principle of respect for persons as it is expressed in the values of honesty and fairness. The Kantians abandon the principle of social utility as it is expressed in our pursuit of material well-being and the satisfaction of basic human needs. In both cases important values are sacrificed, and each solution produces states of affairs which are less morally rich than we would desire. They are both deficient in important values. Nor do they in the end produce either happiness or justice, because these are conceived as alien to each other, as intrinsically incompatible.

In the Moravian tax example the utilitarian approach ranks respect for persons and its cognates, honesty and moral righteousness, lower than the principle of social utility and its cognates, material well-being and moral tolerance. The Kantian approach does exactly the opposite and reverses the ranking. But in both cases important values are sacrificed or diminished, and each solution reaches states of affairs which are less morally rich than we desire.

If we approach the Moravian dilemma from an idealist perspective, applying a principle of coherence which roughly stated says: any state of affairs X is morally better than any state of affairs Y, if X is morally richer, more highly integrated and more fecund than Y. This principle of coherence provides us with objective criteria, richness and integration, which can guide our attempts at solving complex moral dilemmas. Although we cannot derive an answer directly from it, we at least know what we are looking for, what we want to avoid, what an inadequate answer looks like, and what an adequate one would be like if and when we found one. What we should be looking for are more complex personal and social structures which would give adequate expression to the conflicting values. The idealist system I am recommending is thus not a system which has no intellectual framework; but it does require the development of a moral epistemology which is both richer and more coherent than either Kantianism or utilitarianism. Still, it is not relativistic in any serious sense.

In the income tax case Canadians surely want to hold on to and develop the honest business practices our society has nurtured and at the same time reap the profits gained by international trade. But how can we do both without sacrificing or seriously diminishing one of the values? Well, one thing we learned we cannot do is to simply impose our business morality on the host country. That doesn't work. We might then try to look at the problem from the perspective of the host country rather than from our own perspective, which is what we normally and naturally do. The Moravian method of tax collection is perceived by us as unjust, but is it really so? The bartering system they employ can reach a fair price between buyer and seller in other contexts, so why not between tax payer and government? And is our Canadian system of tax collection really that fair? The fact that some highly profitable Canadian corporations pay little or no income tax in Canada raises doubts about this claim. The same abuse is less likely to happen in a Moravian tax system. It might also humanize what is at present a very depersonalized and alienating bureaucratic system.

Besides, what is all this fuss about bribery? This is surely the height of hypocrisy since Revenue Canada allows Canadian corporations to deduct bribes and kick-backs in their income tax returns, much like the

Moravians do. Although the Canadian government was embarrassed when the opposition brought the policy to the attention of the public, and in 1992 proposed that it be changed, Revenue Canada seemed to treat the matter as a storm in a tea cup. It pointed out that when bribes are claimed as deductions, the corporation must identify who received them. If the recipient is a Canadian, then Revenue Canada can demand that taxes be paid on the bribe. The practice, according to Revenue Canada, is quite harmless because it does not involve a loss of revenue. What is lost on one side is gained on the other. A neat utilitarian solution to the problem.[15]

Kantian values can be expressed by different cultures in different ways, so they do not have to be monolithically imposed. A universal morality does not need to be a rigid set of inflexible rules or procedures, which takes no cognizance of the living communities which instantiate them. In cross cultural relationships we need to look at moral problems from the perspective of the host as well as the home country. The former may see the behaviour of the branch manager as just another expression of our stereotyped picture of the Moravians as naturally corrupt. Canadians would perceive Moravians as dishonest whether they were or not, and this offends them. It's insulting. It's a put down. Besides, Canadians, like everyone else, are in Moravia to exploit it and its people, if they can get away with it. The same is true of their dealings with the Argentinians and South Koreans.

Being good corporate citizens requires us to reverse our perspectives in order to increase our understanding of host countries, and being good hosts requires us to do the same thing with corporations doing business in Canada. Different states of affairs can express the same sets of values in different patterns of coherence. Once this is recognized, some problems involving conflicting cultural norms between a corporation's home and host countries might be resolved. We know that a successful resolution has been achieved when the moral agents or the social institutions involved have grown, or if the foundation for growth has been laid. In the Moravian case we would have developed a better understanding of the host country's and our own values, and this richer moral understanding will allow us to grow morally. We would become a more tolerant, less self-serving society, yet not sacrifice our proper attachment to our customary honest business practices. If the dialogue is successful, the host country should grow as well by realizing that some foreign corporations want to be good corporate citizens and are not simply out to exploit and humiliate their trading partners.

Some business people, like this Canadian manager, are genuinely concerned about combating corruption in a host country. Being a good corporate citizen goes beyond abiding by the letter of the law, or doing in Rome what the Romans do. The manager's worry about the apparent bribery involved in the Moravian tax system is as real and valid as the concern of the critics of the AEC's new marketing campaign which involved bribing government officials in both Argentina and South Korea. So the manager can go along with the system once his concern about the bribery has been taken seriously on both sides of the cultural barrier. There is some question as to whether the payment involved here should be called a bribe at all. Bribes are intended to influence government officials improperly and are usually large undercover payments.[16] In the Moravian case the payments were not large and were no secret. They looked more like tips or legitimate perks. If the negotiations between the corporation and the tax official took place over lunch, the agent representing the corporation could pick up the tab and the free lunch the tax agent received would normally not be considered a bribe or morally inappropriate.

In the Candu affair, however, the payments were very large, secretive and designed to influence government officials improperly, so they were clearly bribes. The Candu dilemma, or the dilemma faced by the Canadian civil engineer, cannot be solved simply by improving our understanding of the host country's values, although this understanding is probably a necessary prerequisite to reach any solution. We could perhaps solve the problem of unequal pay levels between the host and the home country of a corporation by appealing to economic circumstances.[17] A host country that permits a corporation to pay lower wages than it pays at home might justify the practice because of the low level of economic development in the host country. If we try to apply the principle of equal pay for equal work without considering the economic context we could produce more harm than good to the host country. It could freeze the country out of the international labour market. One of the main reasons a corporation may locate there is because of cheaper labour costs. If this enticement is lost, this may prevent the host country from becoming economically independent. This valid utilitarian consideration needs to be balanced by Kantian perspectives which suggest that this policy should be a temporary one that is part of an overall plan to push developing countries to reach economic equality.

Similarly with the Candu dilemma. Again, as Canadians we want to hold on to and develop the honest business practices our society has nurtured and also to reap the economic benefits of international trade. Both the Kantians and the utilitarians are partly right. But how can we do both without sacrificing one of the values? One suggestion, which came from the business and not the academic community, is to bring the problem to the attention of the Canadian public and the international community, so we can work towards developing better and more morally acceptable procedures in international trade. By completely undermining the clandestine element of international bribery, the public debate begins to transform the practice in the direction of perks and tips for services rendered, as in the Moravian tax case, practices which integrate conflicting utilitarian and Kantian values.

If we are going to identify the values that we want to integrate into a new order of international business relationships, then we must look at the problem from the perspective of the host country as well as from the competing ethical perspectives of the home country. This procedure may help us resolve some moral dilemmas in international trade but clearly not all. What, for example, does the civil engineer do when he or she confronts poor safety standards on construction sites? Here the situation is different, because it involves such a serious breach of the principle of respect for life that utilitarian and relativistic considerations have little relevance. In this case it looks like the only moral thing for the corporation to do is to take the side of its engineer, and refuse to participate in the construction project until the host country alters its safety standards.

It is obvious that to solve this dilemma we need to move towards a universal morality that applies equally to all cultures, one which is valid for the global and not just the local moral community. The notion that all moral values are equally valid is not one we can live with if we are to remain rational moral agents. We must of course show respect for all moral agents, even those we disagree with. We have to look at the problem of safety standards from different cultural perspectives; again, context might suggest different levels of risk which might be acceptable in different localities, but there will be a bottom line below which no one can go without compromising respect for human life.

No country has a right to have industrial safety standards which wantonly risk the lives of its workers. It is impossible consistently to tolerate every kind of conduct at the international level, as relativism recommends. The world cannot tolerate societies which discriminate against their citizens on racial grounds. Nor can it tolerate societies which torture political prisoners or use prisoners of war for political purposes and human shields, or which have unacceptably low safety standards in the work place. Nor can it tolerate societies which conduct experiments on human subjects without their informed consent. It cannot condone those which make bribery an intrinsic part of international trade. It cannot tolerate societies which use war and terrorism as their principal instruments for achieving political or economic goals.

The discovery that there are universal values is a natural and higher stage in our moral development. The idea of a global morality should not be sacrificed on the altar of absolute tolerance. This much we can grant to the Kantians. Global peace is what is required in the nuclear age. But there can be no real peace until a global morality exists. One of the great challenges of the modern world is to create a global morality which still respects the principle of cultural self-determinism. To achieve this we have to come to terms with the fact of moral diversity and understand the need for moral tolerance. Absolute intolerance is as unacceptable as absolute tolerance. This much we can grant to the utilitarians and the relativists. There is a sense in which morality will always be relative. Morality will always be ontologically relative to moral agents. There are no disembodied moralities. Morality does not exist in the abstract. It exists only in the members of concrete living cultures. It is always part of particular individuals living in historical societies, which are different from other individuals and societies. Morality will always be epistemologically relative, because human rationality can only function in terms of some intellectual frame of reference. There are no non-theoretical systems of ethics, nor can there be. To be anti-theoretical in ethics is intellectually and practically incoherent.

The universal morality we seek must be one which evolves out of the relativistic moralities of historical communities. It is not something which can be forced on living, growing societies by social engineers or moral experts, Kantian or utilitarian. There can be no abstract plan for realizing a global morality. Nor can we try to impose a set of abstract values, including an abstract theory of rights, on these living cultures. Liberal democracies like Canada rank political rights over economic rights, but socialist democracies like Sweden rank economic rights over political ones. One puts freedom first, the other puts health, food and full employment first. A universal morality requires that we give equal weight to both rights. A theory of human rights must evolve in step with the developing global morality. It cannot be forced on living communities, like manna from some abstract theoretical heaven.

Creating a universal morality will certainly be difficult, but nevertheless it needs to be achieved if we are to move towards a true global community and to achieve real security from nuclear and other wars. Shared morality is the stuff out of which communities are made. A global community needs a shared morality to develop both world government and world peace, and the international business community can have an important role to play in this project, as do the countries it represents.

Because a global morality cannot develop abstractly, each country must move towards this goal in its own way, in time with its own cultural drummer. To be viable it must grow out of the living relations between cultures. A society is not something which is created a priori out of the intellectual wombs of separate solitudes. It is created by the living web of relationships between individuals who are in part created by these relationships. We sometimes forget that cultures, like persons, become what they are through interaction with other cultures. The economic relations between the developed and the underdeveloped countries of the third world are, in part, a product of their historical colonial relationship with us. This relationship not only shaped their economies, it helped to shape ours as well. The global morality which, over time, emerges will be a product of the natural relations between cultures, and not something imposed by some privileged cultural elite or an abstract rational theory of ethics.

The doctrine of radical individualism, the view that individuals are ontologically independent of the social institutions which nurture them, when analogically transferred to interpret the relations between cultures, is as destructive to the development of a global morality as it is to developing adequate local moralities. To abandon the doctrine of radical nationalism, the view that cultures are ontologically independent of the international communities they interact with does not involve the rejection of the principle of cultural self-determinism. It does not lead to an unacceptable form of absolutism which denies any importance to the cultural context in which moral agents act. If it is to be viable, the principle must enshrine and integrate the values contained in both the principle of respect for persons and individual happiness.

The principle of cultural self-realization can be formulated, from an idealist perspective, as follows. Every culture has a right to moral self-determinism, so long as it does not interfere with the autonomous self-realization, or essential well-being, of other cultures, nor with the self-realization, or essential well-being, of the autonomous moral agents who are its citizens. The principle is fecund because it allows for the creative development of a global morality within concrete cultural contexts. All multinationals and their home countries then should try, in their own way, to create international relations which allow all moral agents, and the societies they dwell in, to flourish and grow. To fail to do so is to deny the ontological basis of any morality. What this project requires of us has yet to be discovered or invented, but we do have strong inklings of what must be involved. Our experience with international business clearly suggests that any society which wantonly risks the lives of its workers could not be tolerated in the global village. Neither could tolerance be extended to one which allows multinational corporations to exploit workers by paying them inadequate wages, or which makes bribery and corruption a way of life, or which discriminates against its citizens on the basis of race or gender. A society that uses war and terrorism as its principal instruments of international politics, or which conducts scientific experiments on human subjects without their informed consent, also cannot be condoned. Neither can one which displays wanton cruelty to animals, or which wantonly pollutes or destroys nature. This may only represent a small beginning on our journey towards a global morality, but it is a beginning nonetheless, and one which an idealist ethics is most likely to foster.

Chapter 10

The expanding moral universe

A young, idealistic university graduate from an Ontario School of Forestry takes a job with the Ontario Ministry of Natural Resources (OMNR) and is assigned a position in a small, northern Ontario town to manage the timber forests in the area. Not long after he moves north with his wife and four small children, he is asked by a senior official in the OMNR to issue tree-cutting licences to a local forestry baron who owns the town's sawmill, and who has close relations with the government and officials high up in the OMNR. The town depends heavily on the forest industry and its sawmill for its economic viability. If the sawmill closes down it will cause severe economic hardship for the whole community and put the forestry company into bankruptcy. The young forester conducts a survey of the area to get a reliable forest inventory because he believes the current OMNR estimates of the amount of trees available in the area are out of date and inaccurate. After completing the inventory he decides that the environmental balance of the forests in the area is too delicate to survive any new cutting. It would endanger the habitat of several rare species of birds and fish, as well as the forest itself. The young forester, who is a vegetarian and an animal rights activist, is very concerned about the fate of the animals which populate the forest. He informs the OMNR of the results of his survey but is ordered to issue tree-cutting licences anyway. If he refuses he knows he will lose his job and probably be unable to find another one in the forestry industry in Canada. If he stands up for his conservationist ideals he will bring immediate social and economic disaster to the town. If he acts in the interest of the town, he will destroy the forest and the wildlife that depends on it. What is the morally right thing for the young forester to do?

In the real case on which the dilemma is based, the forester decided to blow the whistle on the ministry and go public with his story to save the forest and the wildlife. As a result he was fired from his position and the community which up to this time had respected him turned against him. They did not share his radical environmentalist views. The ministry argued that he breached his oath of confidentiality which all civil servants are required to swear. His case was brought before a civil service review board which ruled that he had been wrongfully dismissed and they reinstated him in his position with the ministry. In any case the ravaging of the forest went ahead. He returned to his job but his career and his life were never the same. He was treated like a traitor who had betrayed both his co-workers and the people of the town.[1]

The way the forester resolves the dilemma will depend on the kind of environmental ethics he holds and this in turn will depend upon the general ethical tradition he is committed to. Let's contrast the attitudes our two main ethical traditions, utilitarianism and Kantianism, have towards animals and nature. If the forester's attitude towards nature is rooted in the Kantian tradition of respect for persons, he would choose people over animals and nature. However, if it is rooted in the utilitarian tradition of social utility he would choose animals over people. Let's look at the Kantianism position first.

The Kantian would argue that the forester should issue the cutting licences as he was ordered to do, because not to do so is inconsistent with the principle of respect for persons and professional ethics. Because humans are more important than animals or nature, the interests of the townspeople should take precedence over the interests of animals and nature. In a conflict between nature and people the Kantian would choose people because of their intrinsic value. Hence in this situation the Kantian would choose the interests of people over those of the forest and its animal and plant inhabitants.

Theories of environmental ethics can be roughly divided into two broad classes, those which are homo-centric or people-centred and those which are bio-centric or nature-centred. Kantianism is a homo-centric or people-centred theory which gives secular expression to the traditional Judaeo–Christian view of the moral relationship between people, animals and nature. Judaeo–Christian tradition teaches that God made people in his image. Humans are set apart from nature because they are spiritual beings possessing souls which are destined for eternal life. Animals and plants do not have souls, so they are of less importance. It is God's will that humankind exploit nature for its benefit. In the first chapter of Genesis the Bible says:

Then God said; 'Let us make man in our image and likeness to rule the fish in the sea, the birds of heaven, the cattle, all wild animals on earth, and all reptiles that crawl upon the earth'. So God created man in his own image; male and female he created them. God blessed them and said to them; 'be fruitful and increase, fill the earth and subdue it, rule over the fish in the sea, the birds of the heavens, and every living thing that moves upon the earth'.[2]

The Judaeo–Christian attitude towards nature is clearly homo-centric or people-centred. For the homo-centric, people possess intrinsic value and nature possesses only instrumental value. Nature has value because it sustains human life. Animals and trees are not ends in themselves. Hence we have no direct obligations towards them. They do not have moral standing and are not part of the moral universe.

Kantianism is also a homo-centric ethical theory. The principle of respect for persons implies a people-centred environmental ethics. Kantians hold that humans are fundamentally different from nature. Humans are different from nature because they are moral agents. Humans possess rationality, freedom of choice and moral respons-ibility. They are moral agents who possess dignity and intrinsic value. They cannot be used as mere means for the ends of others. Animals and plants do not possess the capacity to act morally, so they are not moral agents and hence don't possess intrinsic value. As Kant remarked:

> Beings whose existence depends, not on will, but on nature, have nonetheless, if they are non-rational beings, only relative value as means and are consequentially called things. Rational beings, on the other hand, are called persons because their nature already marks them out as ends-in-themselves.[3]

Animals, for example, cannot make promises, or enter into contracts, with humans or with each other. Just imagine someone treating his dog as if it could make moral contracts. Turning to his dog an owner says, 'Rover you must promise never to bite anyone again.' 'Wuff! Wuff!' replies Rover, sealing the promise, so to speak. Of course the moment his owner turns his back, Rover bites him on the ankle. His master is outraged and, wheeling round, says in a strict voice, 'But Rover you promised not to bite'! Since animals cannot enter into moral, or legal, contracts, and cannot accept the obligations and responsibilities involved in moral agency, they cannot be given moral, or legal, standing. They cannot be citizens, nor can they have a right to vote. To talk of giving animals rights, as some animal rights activists do, is to talk nonsense. Animals cannot have a right to life, because their lives cannot be forfeited if they take the life of another animal or even a human being. Capital punishment for animals is absurd. Can we hang the cat for killing the bird? Can we destroy the pit bull for attacking and killing a child? We certainly can, but we do not arrest it, read it its rights and put it on trial before a jury of its peers. We can protect animals from human cruelty by law, as we protect parks and monuments from vandalism. But do we give parks rights? It makes sense to treat animals with kindness but not with justice.

For the homo-centrics, only human beings can have rights, hence animals cannot have moral or legal standing. This does not mean that we can treat animals in any way we please. We may not have direct moral obligations towards animals but we do have indirect obligations. It may be morally permissible for us to use animals for our well-being, but not in ways which are dangerous to our material or spiritual well-being. Having the right moral attitude towards animals can benefit humans both materially and spiritually. Someone who pulls the wings off flies is likely to become inured to the suffering of other creatures and callous towards human suffering. The next thing the sadist will be doing is pulling the arms of humans. As Kant contended we have a duty to ourselves not to be cruel to animals. Kant said:

> Even more intimately opposed to man's duty to himself is a savage and at the same time cruel treatment of the part of creation which is living, though lacking reason (animals). For thus is compassion for their suffering dulled in man, and thereby a natural predisposition, very serviceable to morality in one's relations with other men is weakened and gradually obliterated.[4]

For the Kantian, there should be no wanton cruelty to animals. Using animals for food would be morally permissible and possibly required, provided that humane slaughtering techniques were used. The failure to use animals for food could involve a neglect of our duties to the poor and starving. As long as the animals were killed as painlessly as possible this would be acceptable to the Kantians. For the Kantian, animals have no right to life as people do, because they do not possess intrinsic value. The Kantian position is very close to that developed by the Canadian Council on Animal Care, which represents the Canadian status quo with respect to our treatment of animals.[5]

Kantians also believe that it is morally permissible to use animals for scientific research. But they would be against any experimental use of animals which involved unnecessary pain or distress. As Kant said: 'physical experiments involving excruciating pain for animals and conducted merely for the sake of speculative inquiry (when the end might also be achieved without such experiments) are to be abhorred.'[6]

To fail to use animals for medical research could involve the neglect of our duties to the sick, the diseased and the disabled. When Doctors Banting and Best discovered insulin in their research into a cure for diabetes, they used dogs, many of whom died or were put painlessly to death once they were no longer experimentally useful. Animals are also used to test new drugs before they are used on humans. In fact animal testing is required by law in many countries before drugs and other products can be used on or sold to the public. If we want safe drugs we have to test them on animals. Animals are also required in the training of doctors, medical researchers and other scientists. Not to use animals for teaching purposes would also be a breach of our duties to others. So there is no question of eliminating the experimental or teaching use of animals as some animal rights activists advocate.

The Kantian position here is similar to that developed by the Canadian Council on Animal Care.[7] The Kantians point out that much of the research done with animals also benefits them. It is therapeutic research which helps to control and eliminate disease in animals as well as in human beings. If the research is non-therapeutic then the researcher should use alternative research techniques which do not involve animals when this is possible and practical. They should of course minimize pain and stress as much as possible. They should use lower animals, where possible, before higher animals: worms before rabbits, dogs and apes. When the protocol of an experiment requires crippling or induced disease the animal should be put to a quick and painless death.

For the Kantian, it would also be morally permissible to use animals for labour and for clothing, although the use of leg-traps, or battering baby seals to death with clubs, would not. It would also be morally permissible to use animals for sport, amusement, in circuses, in rodeos or for edification in zoos, provided these activities did not involve wanton cruelty.

To talk of animal rights is silly enough but to talk of the rights of trees, roses, cabbages and rocks as some environmentalists do is madness.[8] How would we go about assigning rights to rocks, for example? Don't smash that rock; it has as much right to existence as you have! Precious stones have value only because humans think them beautiful or rare. Perhaps the moon or planets like Mars have rights, as some have argued.[9] We might want to keep the moon free from human contamination, at least until we know it is biologically dead. The Americans did this when they landed on the moon not because they thought the moon had rights but because it was in humankind's interest to do so. The concepts of moral and legal rights have no meaningful application to things other than humans.

For the Kantian, we have an indirect duty to nature not to destroy it wantonly. Someone who loves the beauty of nature learns to value things independent of their immediate utility. As Kant wrote:

> A propensity to the bare destruction of beautiful though lifeless things in nature is contrary to man's duty to himself. For such a propensity weakens or destroys that feeling in man which is indeed not of itself already moral, but which still does much to promote a state of sensibility favourable to morals – namely, pleasure in loving something without any intention of using it.[10]

The Kantians believe we have no direct obligations to nature. However, having the right moral attitude towards nature can again benefit humankind, both materially and spiritually. Wanton destruction of nature undermines human virtue. Someone who never learns the intrinsic value of nature and appreciates it only for its utility, will not be likely to learn to value other human beings for their own sake. They will value others only when it is in their interest to do so. Failure to appreciate nature encourages selfishness. Kantians would argue that we have a right to exploit nature but not to do so in ways which are dangerous to our physical or spiritual well-being.

Kantians aren't convinced that we need a complete change of attitude to solve the environmental crisis. Kantians don't think we need to abandon western traditions to solve this crisis, as some environmentalists believe. Kantians point out that the idea of domination of nature is not the only attitude Judaeo–Christians can have towards nature. Many Judaeo–Christians have argued that the idea of stewardship of nature is just as important as the idea of dominion over nature in western culture. Adopting an attitude of stewardship develops an environmental ethics which would stress conservation. It would imply no wanton destruction of nature. Like anything left in trust, nature should be properly cared for. Kantians believe we do have an indirect obligation to future generations of humankind, to future moral agents, if not to all sentient existence. Nature does not belong simply to the present generation, but to our children and our children's children. Our obligations to future generations require us to adopt a prudent attitude towards nature.

These obligations may, however, be outweighed by our duties towards ourselves.

Like Judaeo–Christians, Kantians do recognize that we have a duty to protect the environment because of the benefits nature provides to humankind. As far as we know there is only one naturally habitable environment in the solar system, the planet Earth. The planet provides non-renewable resources which need to be properly managed if they are to continue to benefit us. The homo-centric argues that if we take a long range viewpoint the interests of humankind and nature are normally the same. Wholesale cutting of the forest in our dilemma might be bad for everyone in the long run. It's imprudent to squander our resources. If the lumber baron gets his licence and the lumber mill keeps running, people may not suffer in the short term but they will suffer in the long term. They might well run out of lumber for the mill, and that will spell disaster both for the town as well as the animals and the forest. It's possible that we can't solve any ecological problems without doing damage to persons either in the short term or the long term. But in any immediate conflict between nature and people the Kantian believes that we must choose people because of their intrinsic value.

In this situation the Kantians would argue that the interests of the town should take precedence over the interests of animals and nature. In this conflict animals and nature cannot even stand the short ravages of a more prudent cutting policy. So whether we appeal to the short or the long run, the forest seems doomed unless cutting is completely stopped. It's either no cutting or no forest. It's either short range benefits for the town or no benefits at all. For the Kantian, we would be failing in our duty to the present generation if we did not proceed with at least prudent short term cutting. The present generation takes precedence over future generations. We are not required to sacrifice ourselves for the sake of potential moral agents, or for the sake of animals and nature.

The young forester then should choose people over animals and nature. He should issue the cutting licences as he was directed to do. He certainly should not go public with his dispute with ministry officials, as the forester in the real case did.[11] To do so would involve a breach of his duty as a professional civil servant. In Ontario civil servants take an oath of confidentiality which is only lifted if they resign. The forester should of course make all possible efforts to resolve his differences with ministry officials, but once he has tried this his duty is to obey or resign. Blowing the whistle in this case would be morally wrong.

That was a Kantian analysis of the dilemma, now let's look at a utilitarian analysis. The utilitarian would argue that the forester did the right thing in not issuing the cutting licences as he was ordered to do and in blowing the whistle on the ONMR. The morally right thing to do in this case was to choose the forest and the animals which depended on it over the townspeople. The principle of utility includes the whole of sentient existence and not merely human existence. The interests of animals must be given equal consideration with the interests of humans.

The utilitarian attitude towards nature is not homo-centric. If it is not fully bio-centric, it is at least zoo-centric or animal-centred.[12] For the utilitarian the only intrinsic value is happiness, and the only intrinsic evil is suffering. Since animals can suffer and be happy they must be given standing in the moral universe. Animals possess intrinsic value. They are ends in themselves, just like humans. For the utilitarian the moral community must logically be expanded, as Mill noted, to include the whole of sentient existence.[13] Animals would have moral and legal standing. It should not surprise us then that utilitarians have been leaders in the animal rights movement.

The utilitarian argues that a zoo-centric ethics must replace our current homo-centric ethics if we are to develop a proper moral relationship with animals and nature. As Peter Singer has argued, a homo-centric ethics appears inconsistent.[14] Animals are discriminated against because they do not possess sufficient reason to be classified as moral agents, hence they are denied moral standing. Yet our homo-centric culture recognizes that children, the mentally disabled, and the senile have moral and legal rights. They are accepted as part of the moral community even if they do not meet the standards of mental competence required to be classified as moral agents. Diminished intellectual capacity is not a relevant difference which would justify denying children or the mentally disabled or the senile moral or legal standing, or justify denying them their basic rights. It is no more relevant with respect to fundamental rights than race or gender are. The only reason we discriminate against animals is because they do not belong to our species. Singer concludes that speciesism is as bad morally as racism and sexism.[15] It is a form of unjust discrimination.

We are prejudiced in the way we define moral agency. Animals are surely moral creatures. They feel love towards each other and humans. They are capable of courage and self-sacrifice. They can display spite, selfishness and cowardice. They feel shame when they are caught doing something wrong. They are much more intelligent than we give them credit for. They are as sensitive as humans are to pain and death. There are serious questions concerning the Kantian notion of humane slaughtering techniques. Is there such a thing? We know that prisoners on death row suffer greatly simply because they know that they are going to die. But do not sheep and cattle going to slaughter suffer the same agony? Animals can deliberately bring about good and bad consequences. They are capable of complex social relationships which clearly have moral dimensions.[16]

Adopting a zoo-centric ethics implies that we have direct moral obligations to animals. First, we have a duty to maximize animal welfare and minimize animal suffering. We have duties of both non-maleficence and beneficence towards animals. Not only must we not be cruel to animals, as the homo-centric holds, but we must also be positively concerned about their welfare. We must not be cruel to chickens certainly, but we must also see that they have enough space and freedom to establish a pecking order, something which modern factory chicken farming often denies them.

Second, animals must be treated not only with benevolence, as Hume argued, but with justice as well.[17] Animals ought to be treated with equality because they are sufficiently like us in the relevant respects. Utilitarians must give equal treatment to the interests of any sentient creature affected by their actions and not simply to the humans affected. Animals, like humans, have moral and legal rights because rights are based on needs as well as the capacity to make contracts.

A zoo-centric ethics which recognizes direct obligations of benevolence and justice towards animals has two important implications. If we take zoo-centrism seriously there must be, as Peter Singer argues, no experimental use of animals and no killing of animals for food. We ought all to become vegetarians.[18] The slaughter of animals in experiments is a monument to people's cruelty to animals. Some 80 million animals are used as subjects of scientific research in the USA alone in a year.[19] Most animal experiments are non-therapeutic and are not related to the animal's well-being or even to the general well-being of the species, but are conducted to further human well-being. But surely one might object that animals are necessary for medical and scientific research. Even so, most animal experiments are not used for medical research or to advance science. The majority are used, and frequently killed, to test the safety of luxury products, such as cosmetics. We certainly want safe products for human use but does it require this magnitude of animal suffering? If it does, should we choose our cosmetics over animal suffering?

Take the infamous Draize test for example.[20] John Draize invented this test to determine whether a chemical is likely to irritate or harm human eyes. The substance was sprayed into the eyes of guinea pigs or rabbits, who had their eyelids surgically removed and were restrained in stocks so they could not move their heads. The results recorded ranged from mild reddening of the eyes, to severe ulceration of the eyes, to blindness. In some cases the eyes simply dropped out of their sockets. Revlon, for example, used the test routinely until it was stopped by the protests of animal rights crusader Henry Spira.[21] We could well ask if cosmetic testing of this kind is necessary. Certainly we all want to look attractive and most of us require some sort of cosmetics to appear so. But is our legitimate desire to be attractive a sufficient justification for such severe animal suffering? Surely not. We certainly want safe cosmetic products, and the testing of drugs and sprays is required by law. But, again, do we really need these products? Perhaps we do not need cosmetics, but what of medicines, which are also required by law to be tested? And what of medical research in general? Was it immoral for Banting and Best to use dogs in their research which led to the discovery of insulin? This is a tougher decision, but again we cannot choose our well-being at the expense of the well-being of animals. As Singer has argued, our present practice is inconsistent.[22]

If it is morally permissible to sacrifice animals for the greater good of humankind, then it is morally permissible to sacrifice children, foetuses and the mentally handicapped. These groups should not be given preferential treatment over higher animals. Foetuses, babies and people reduced to the state of human vegetables are no longer persons, rational animals, while some higher animals like monkeys, apes and dolphins are sufficiently intelligent to be classified as persons. This does not imply that we ought to experiment on foetuses or babies. It does suggest that if we are to be fair we must either abolish the experimental use of animals or make use of babies as well as animals. The utilitarians clearly prefer the former option, because that minimizes both animal and human suffering. The utilitarians would certainly not be happy with the generally conservative approach of institutions like the Canadian Council on Animal Care. The snail's pace of reform which the status quo supports betrays an unacknowledged speciesism.

A zoo-centric ethics also implies that we should all become vegetarians because it would be immoral to kill animals for food. Human carnivorism involves the needless enslavement and slaughter of animals. If cannibalism is wrong so is carnivorism. It's irrelevant to argue that we have always been flesh eaters. The point is we do not need meat to get a balanced diet. We can live perfectly healthy lives on a vegetarian diet. Hunting and herding have always involved cruelty to animals – for example, the use of leg-hold traps in hunting and factory farming in herding. In order to produce succulent meat, veal calves are forced to live lives of terrible suffering. Rachels gives the following horrific description of their predicament:

> Veal calves, for example, spend their lives in pens too small to allow them to turn around or even lie down comfortably – but from the producer's point of view, that is good, because exercise toughens the muscles, which reduces the 'quality' of the meat; and besides allowing the animals adequate living space would be prohibitively expensive. In these pens the calves cannot perform such basic actions as grooming themselves, which they naturally desire to do, because there is not enough room for them to twist their heads around. It is clear that the calves miss their mothers, and like human infants they want something to suck: they can be seen trying to suck the sides of their stalls. In order to keep their meat pale and tasty, they are fed a liquid diet deficient in both iron and roughage. Naturally they develop cravings for these things. The calf's craving for iron becomes so strong that if allowed to turn around, it will lick its own urine, although calves normally find this repugnant. The tiny stall which prevents them from turning solves this 'problem'. The craving for roughage is especially strong, since without it the animal cannot form a cud to chew. It cannot be given any straw for bedding, since the animal would be driven to eat it, and that would affect the meat. So for these animals, the slaughterhouse is not an unpleasant end to an otherwise contented existence. As terrifying as the process of slaughter is, for them it is a merciful release.[23]

Although a zoo-centric ethics implies direct obligations to animals, it does not imply direct obligations to everything in the natural world. The utilitarian moral universe directly includes birds, reptiles and fish. Oysters, insects, bacteria, viruses, trees, plants or rocks, are only indirectly included. Nevertheless, since all sentient existence depends on nature, nature ought to be treated as if it were an end in itself. In any event, it's difficult to establish a strong case for animals and nature based on human needs. When the crunch comes our homo-centric bias will always make us choose people over animals and nature. What if the best thing for the forest and the animals who depend on it is not to cut it at all? Even prudent cutting could destroy the ecological system the forest supports.

Zoo-centrics believe we have an obligation to future generations of all sentient creatures, and not just humans. These obligations are of two kinds, positive and negative. First, there's the negative obligation to avoid doing things which would harm future generations. Zoo-centrics give logical priority to negative obligations because it's easier to agree on what will harm sentient creatures than it is to agree on what will benefit them. Second, there is the positive obligation to enhance the environment for the future. We then have a duty to leave the environment in better shape than it was in when we inherited it. It is not enough simply to leave it in as good a condition as we found it. The utilitarians conclude that only a radical change in our attitude towards animals and nature will resolve the problems of speciesism and our present environmental difficulties.

In any case the utilitarians are less likely to ignore nature than the homo-centrics, and in this dilemma they would think that the right thing to do was to try to protect the forest and its denizens against the encroachments of the town.

That was a utilitarian response to the dilemma. Now let's sum up. In this dilemma we have a conflict between the utilitarian principle of zoo-centrism and the Kantian principle of homo-centrism, i.e. a conflict between animal-centred and people-centred moralities. If we adopt the utilitarian's zoo-centric attitude, the needs of animals and nature would take precedence over the special needs of humankind. The utilitarian would also support the animal rights movement, would be against the use of animals in scientific research and most likely would be a vegetarian.

If we adopt the Kantian homo-centric attitude towards nature, which is prevalent in our Judaeo–Christian culture, the needs of humankind would always take precedence over animals and nature. The Kantian believes that animals do not have rights and that it is morally permissible to use them for our benefit. Once again we see that if we adopt a purely conservative Kantian approach or a purely liberal utilitarian approach to the dilemma we will arrive at solutions which are less rich and satisfactory than we would want. The conservatives do not give animals and nature the consideration they deserve, and the liberals appear committed to sacrificing the needs of humans for the sake of animals. In order to solve the environmental crisis which this dilemma illustrates, we need to go beyond the limitations set by both conservative Kantianism and liberal utilitarianism.

We certainly need to recognize, as the utilitarians do, that our moral universe needs to be expanded to include the whole of sentient existence. Animals, as well as humans, possess intrinsic value. They must be assigned moral and some sort of legal standing. They are ends in themselves and hence cannot be treated as mere means to human well-being. This much we can grant to the utilitarians. But this may not be enough to save the earth's ecosystem. Many environmentalists believe that utilitarianism, like Kantianism with its human bias, cannot cope with the environmental crisis, theoretically or practically.[24]

First, they point out that utilitarianism may include animals under its moral umbrella but it excludes, except indirectly, all the rest of nature. It is biased against the lower species and against other living things, like trees and plants. Environmentalists believe that we need to expand our moral universe further to include not only sentient existence but all living things. Trees indeed must be given moral and legal standing. The case of the furbish louse wort, a rare relative of the snapdragon, illustrates the concerns of the environmentalists.[25]

American environmentalists tried in the late 1970s to halt the construction of a dam in Maine to save the furbish louse wort. The supporters of the dam appealed to the need for electric power, jobs, future recreational space and increased property values. All that the environmentalists could argue was that the furbish louse wort was a rare plant which might become extinct if the dam were built. But they couldn't demonstrate that its extinction would produce any negative long range effect on the well-being of humankind. The environmentalists were easily ridiculed for caring more about a stupid plant than they did for their fellow humans or some animal species which the dam would help, and so they lost their case. The only way to make real progress with environmental problems is to begin to treat nature as if it were an end in itself.

The environmentalists point out that sentient existence, which includes both humans and animals, is part of a wider interdependent ecological system which includes the lower organisms and plants, hence the ecosystem possesses intrinsic value and should be given moral and legal standing. We must become true bio-centrics and recognize that all living things possess intrinsic value and our moral universe must be expanded to include them. The principle of sanctity of life includes more than human life and even all of sentient creation.

Bio-centrics believe we will never be able to alter our moral attitudes towards animals unless we discard our traditional homo-centric belief that God gave people dominion over nature.[26] They believe that unless we rid ourselves of this exploitative attitude towards nature, the solution to speciesism and the current environmental crisis will elude us. The bio-centrics think we need a whole new moral attitude towards nature to solve the crisis. It must be recognized that nature possesses intrinsic value. We must protect nature for its own sake.

Bio-centrics also point out that western culture is essentially homo-centric. Animals and plants have no moral standing in western culture because they are not seen as part of the moral community. But not all cultures are homo-centric. Canadian native cultures, for example, are essentially bio-centric.[27] These cultures recognize that people are part of a larger spiritual community that includes all living things. It's this complex interdependent system of nature which needs to be considered, not just humans. The bio-centrics argue that western peoples should learn from other cultures that humankind is not the only life form in nature which possesses intrinsic value. In any choice between people and animals on one side and nature on the other, nature must be given precedence because it supports all forms of sentient existence – animals, birds, fish, as well as humans.

The bio-centrics hold that even utilitarianism, which is a move in the right direction, is part of the problem rather than part of the solution. In the end the principle of expediency will allow humans to prevail even over animals. Because people are rational pleasure seekers when the crunch comes utilitarians will choose their interests first. In practice it is impossible to protect wildlife by appealing to long range human interests. The case of the snail darter illustrates the concern of the bio-centric.[28]

In the late 1970s environmentalists in the USA tried to halt the Tellico Dam Project on the Tennessee River in order to save the snail darter, a rare member of the perch family, which was on the endangered species list. They failed to stop the project as there was no way they could show that the loss of this rare species of perch would equal the human loss if the dam was not built. The snail darter went the way of the furbish louse wort.

If we are to cope with the environmental crisis our moral universe needs to be expanded to include the whole of nature. A tree may not be sentient but it does have interests. We can talk sensibly about the good of trees as well as the good of people and animals. Trees have needs, just as we do. They need the sun and rain in order to flourish. Trees and plants are ends in themselves and so must be given both moral and legal standing. This much we can grant to the bio-centric. But again this might not be enough. Idealists would certainly be sympathetic to bio-centrism, but even this more embracing attitude is not sufficient for an idealist ethics.

First there is the problem of conflicting claims which arise when more and more entities are recognized as having moral standing. This certainly leads to a richer but also a more incoherent world. Because they are committed to giving equal consideration to every living thing, the bio-centrics have no more adequate way of dealing with conflicts than the zoo-centrics do. Consider the following example.

An environmentalist is walking through a tropical jungle when he encounters a pregnant female tiger who is about to attack a baby who has wandered away from a local village. The environmentalist is carrying a loaded high powered rifle which he has used before to scare off poachers and protect this rare species of tiger. He recognizes that this is the sole remaining female white tiger. If he shoots the tiger to save the baby there will be no more white tigers. If he allows the tiger to kill the baby, there will be one less human being in an already overpopulated world. There are billions of babies but only one pregnant white tiger. What is the environmentalist to do?[29]

It is clear that the bio-centric, like the zoo-centric, must let the tiger devour the baby. But this is counter-intuitive. Most would agree that it is morally right to save the baby because it is innocent. Protecting the innocent is consistent with the principle of sanctity of life. This suggests that the bio-centric attack on homo-centrism is partially misconceived, and that the doctrine needs to be reexamined.

Kantian homo-centrism contains three propositions:

1 People have a special place in the universe because they are moral agents.
2 People are the only truly valuable entities in the universe – only humankind possesses intrinsic value.
3 Animals and nature have value only when they benefit humankind. Animals and nature possess only instrumental value.

Proposition 1 is thought to imply propositions 2 and 3. The homo-centrics are essentially correct. Only humankind, so far as we know, is capable of creating systems of moral values. Only people can take charge of their moral universe. They have the capacity to be creative in morality and to take responsibility for their conduct: things animals cannot do. The Kantian homo-centrics do, however, exaggerate the difference between people and animals. Higher animals do possess many of the characteristics which mark the moral agent. They can feel shame and guilt, and they display affection towards each other and to members of other species. They are also capable of courage and self-sacrifice, and they can display spite, selfishness and cowardice. They are intelligent, at least at adapting means to ends. But they are not full moral agents, because they cannot create a system of morality by assenting to prescriptions about intrinsic value. The difference may ultimately be a matter of degree rather than of kind, but it is still fundamental. Proposition 1, human beings have a special place in the universe, when properly understood, is true. Human beings are the most complex agents in the universe (so far as we know). But does proposition 2, i.e. only humankind has intrinsic value, follow from this? The answer is no. What follows is that a human being is a centre of moral creativity. People can create systems of morality and act in accordance with them. This is what is wrong with the homo-centric. They don't see that it is not inconsistent to hold both that people are unique in being moral agents, and that animals and nature possess intrinsic value. We have direct obligations to animals and nature as well as to humans. Nature in its own way is as unique as humanity.

What is wrong with the bio-centrics is that they believe it is necessary to deny people their special place in the universe in order to develop an adequate environmental ethics. The truth appears to be just the opposite. If we denied people's moral creativity we would be unable to talk about developing a proper moral attitude towards nature. So accepting proposition 1 concerning humankind's uniqueness in the universe does not lead to moral solipsism, i.e. the view that only humankind can have standing in the moral universe. Nor does it follow if we recognize that people are self-centred in other ways. It is probably true that people can only interpret nature from a human perspective. This follows because all moral reasoning presupposes a theoretical frame of reference. But would this not also imply that our perception of nature would necessarily be biased? It's true that people invent the theories of value through which they interpret nature and themselves. Homo-centrism, zoo-centrism and bio-centrism are products of human thought. They are theories invented by humans. The question of whether to be a utilitarian or a Kantian does not arise for the tiger. If this is so, can we ever escape from our bias and judge nature impartially? The answer is yes.

It doesn't follow from the fact that our perspectives must always be personal that they have to be biased. I have already argued that moral reasoning is hypothetical, and that there is a dialectical relationship between assenting to principles and living in accordance with them.

Ethical systems have ultimately to be tested against experience. Hence our perspectives may be personal, created by the systems of thought we invent to interpret our worlds, but not biased. Assenting to intellectual frameworks does not disbar us from objectivity. In fact the opposite appears to be true: without some frame of reference, no moral wisdom could be achieved.

A homo-centric viewpoint in this sense is unavoidable, but it is not biased against nature. We are free to adopt moral viewpoints which assign intrinsic value to animals and nature, or which assign intrinsic value to people only, or which assign intrinsic value to people and animals and to nature as a whole. Proposition 2 does not follow from proposition 1. The fact that human beings are full moral agents does confer on them an intrinsic value which they do not have to earn. It gives them a special place in the moral universe. But humanity cannot take pride in itself unless it uses its moral agency to promote virtue and goodness, and this would surely include recognizing that animals and nature, as well as people, possess intrinsic value. Proposition 3, animals and nature possess only instrumental value does not follow from proposition 1. Homo-centrism, properly understood, means that humanity must take on more responsibility rather than less. In the dilemma we are discussing this would mean managing the forest in a way that takes in the long range interests of both the animals and the people involved. This might even involve a gradual phasing out of the forest industry in this particular area and the bringing in of new industries or alternatively the relocation of the townspeople.

Second, there are emerging problems on the fringes of our moral universe which bio-centrism cannot handle, theoretically or practically. Humankind has already ventured into space. We have landed on the moon. Orbiting the earth has become routine. We are planning to land on Mars. People in space present us with new moral problems. Ought we to transform planets like Mars, create Earth-like atmospheres to make them habitable for humans? Or ought we to create new bio-spheres and ecosystems on apparently inert planets like Mars? Or does Mars have a right to be left in its natural state?

Space scientists, like Bob Haynes and Christopher McKay, have pointed out that all current ethical theories have a common characteristic which makes them incapable of dealing with the moral problems of space.[30] They are all geo-centric, Earth-centred theories which automatically exclude Mars, the solar system and the universe as a whole from the moral universe. Space projects may be easily shown to be morally permissible from our Earth-based perspectives. Homo-centrism, zoo-centrism and bio-centrism all exclude inanimate objects, like Mars, from the moral universe. But if we adopt a cosmo-centric perspective, moral permissibility for humans in space would require further justification. From a cosmic perspective inanimate objects like Mars would have to be assigned some sort of intrinsic value. Every object in the universe must be viewed as unique. Rocks indeed would have moral standing. An idealist ethics would necessarily be cosmic.

A cosmic ethics would require a commitment to the principle of sanctity of existence, i.e. existence is more valuable than non-existence. Everything which exists would possess intrinsic value. With the adoption of this principle our moral universe has expanded to include the whole of creation. The moral universe is now co-extensive with the natural universe. They are both parts of an integrated ontological system. When we talk of giving moral standing to inanimate objects we have reached the outer edge of the moral universe, beyond which lies religion, metaphysics and mysticism. Here we must stop because we have reached the limits of moral understanding.

Appendix: The Open College dilemmas

1. THE BATHHOUSE STUDIES

A social scientist wanting to study public and police attitudes towards homosexuals who have casual sexual encounters in bathhouses disguises himself as a homosexual voyeur in order to observe and interview homosexuals. Unknown to his subjects, he also records their automobile licence plate numbers so he can do follow-up studies.

Later, in the disguise of a public health official, he goes to their homes and acquires very personal information about their families, marriages, jobs, religion, children, etc. The results of the study show beyond reasonable doubt that public authorities, especially the police, hold unjustifiable negative stereotypes of the people who frequent bathhouses.

The scientific community thinks the results are extremely valuable since they help to reveal the stereotyping of and bias against minority groups. And, consequently, some police forces are persuaded that it is a waste of time to spend public resources in order to arrest the people involved in this victimless crime.

Question

Is the social scientist doing the morally right thing in obtaining his information in this manner?

(See Chapter 4: Experimental ethics.)

2. THE IDEALISTIC FORESTER

A young, idealistic university graduate from an Ontario school of forestry takes a job with the Ontario Ministry of Natural Resources

(OMNR) and is assigned a position in a small, northern Ontario town to manage the timber forests in the area. Not long after he moves north with his wife and four small children, he is asked by a senior official in the OMNR to issue tree-cutting licences to a local forestry baron who owns the town's sawmill and who has close relations with the government and the OMNR. The town depends heavily on the forest industry and its sawmill for its economic viability. If the sawmill closes down it will cause severe economic hardship for the whole community and put the forestry company into bankruptcy.

The young forester conducts a survey of the area to get a reliable forest inventory, because he believes the current OMNR estimates of the amount of trees available in the area are out of date and inaccurate. After completing the inventory he decides that the environmental balance of the forests in the area is too delicate to survive any new cutting. He informs the OMNR of the results of his survey but is ordered to issue tree-cutting licences anyway. If he refuses he knows he will lose his job and probably be unable to find another one in the forestry industry in Canada.

Question

What is the morally right thing for the young forester to do?
(See Chapter 10: The expanding moral universe.)

3. THE CASE OF ASSISTED SUICIDE

Three friends of assorted ages serve as volunteers in a nursing home and a chronic care facility in a hospital. They are very concerned about the suffering of aged, bed-ridden patients who are no longer able to function in any normal fashion or relate to anyone in a meaningful way. Each of them has also lived through trying months and years watching her own aged parents suffer a great deal of pain and frustration as they gradually lost their hearing, their eyesight, use of their limbs and mental powers.

The three friends talk a great deal about the dangers of living too long and each decides that at an appropriate time she will commit suicide so as not to get caught in a nursing home or terminal care facility.

When the oldest of the three reaches 82 she decides the time has come and asks for the assistance of one of her friends. She plans to run her car engine in her garage with the door closed. The only problem is that the door can only be closed from the outside. She tells her grown-up family, who check daily on her, that she is going away for a week and arranges with her friend to come along at the agreed time to close the garage door. The friend, who has great respect for the older woman, does as requested.

Question

Did the friend perform a morally right act?
(See Chapter 6: Gentle exits.)

4.   THE POLICE AND THE OHIP OFFICIAL

The police have been trying for a long time to find the mastermind behind a criminal ring that recruits teenagers into drug peddling and prostitution. They finally have one lead. They learn that the head of the operation broke his ankle sometime in August 1981 and had it attended to in a certain small town hospital.

They go to the appropriate Ontario Health Insurance Plan (OHIP) official and ask to see the patient treatment records for the month of August. The official refuses on the grounds that revealing medical records violates patients' privacy. The police are unable to pursue their only lead and the ring carries on.

Question

Was the decision of the OHIP official morally right?
(See Chapter 1: Private spaces.)

5.   THE TEACHER AND THE FAILING STUDENT

A brilliant high school student in Grade 13, who has consistently headed his class every year, fails in his final exam. He is in line for an important scholarship which he urgently needs if he is to go on to university. The rules of the scholarship require that 50 per cent of the final marks be based on the assignments turned in during the year, and 50 per cent be based on the marks from the final examination.

At the time of writing the examination, the boy's mother is critically ill and dying. The teacher knows this. No other student qualified for the scholarship.

Question

Is it morally right for the teacher to upgrade the exam?

(See Chapter 3: Academic honesty. In order to establish a student perspective on academic honesty, this dilemma was changed from a case of upgrading an examination result to one of plagiarizing an essay.)

6.   THE CASE OF THE DOWN'S SYNDROME CHILD

A baby is born with Down's Syndrome. Doctors tell the parents that the child is likely to be severely retarded and have a poor quality of life. The baby also has a hole in its heart and an intestinal blockage which, if not removed, would lead to the baby's death within a very short time. The parents request the doctor not to operate so the baby may be allowed to die.

Question

Did the parents do the morally right thing?

(See Chapter 6: Gentle exits.)

7.   AFFIRMATIVE ACTION IN THE WORK PLACE

Anne-Marie, a 28-year-old black woman, and Helen, a 32-year-old white woman, both apply for a waitressing job with a particular outlet of a large restaurant chain. Both women have approximately five years' waitressing experience behind them and both are willing to work weekends. Anne-Marie is married but has no children, while Helen, recently widowed, is the mother of two young boys. The chain management, in response to recent government pressure, has instituted an affirmative action policy. At present, at the outlet where Anne-Marie and Helen have applied there are about 10 per cent minority employees. The goal of the affirmative action programme is to have 20 per cent minority employees.

The branch manager decides to comply with management's strong affirmative action policy and hires Anne-Marie. Helen, who is unable to find employment, is forced to apply for public assistance in order to support herself and her two small children.

Question

Did the restaurant manager do the morally right thing?

(See Chapter 8: Women's voices.)

8.   THE CANDU AFFAIR

During the late 1960s and early 1970s Canada was having difficulty in selling its Candu nuclear reactors. It became obvious to the Atomic Energy Commission that a more aggressive marketing campaign would be needed to improve its position in this highly competitive international market. The most effective way to do this was to use commercial agents who knew the foreign countries in which sales could be made. The survival of the industry was at stake, as were many jobs. In addition, there was concern about the already large financial investment Canada had made in the nuclear power industry.

The senior manager responsible for this new marketing campaign soon learned that the commercial agents who had been engaged needed to use AEC money to bribe government officials in certain foreign countries if a sale was to be made. Bribery was widespread in these countries and Canada's NATO competitors appeared willing to use bribery to gain sales.

Question

What is the morally right thing for the manager to do?
   (See Chapter 9: Global ethics.)

9.   THE FROZEN EMBRYOS

Two geneticists offer to arrange an in vitro conception for a couple they know who wish to have a child but are unable to do so in the normal way. Even if the wife could conceive she would be unable to carry the foetus to full term.

Since a surgical procedure is necessary to remove an ovum from the wife, doctors arrange to take three in case their first attempt does not work. They fertilize three ova, find a surrogate mother for one of the embryos and freeze the others in case the first does not develop. The first embryo does develop and the couple are presented nine months later with a beautiful child. They don't want any more children and are quite uninterested in what becomes of the frozen embryos. The geneticists would like to use the embryos for research.

Question

What is the morally right action for the geneticists to take?
   (The discussion in Chapter 4: Experimental ethics, can be used as a guide to the analysis of this dilemma.)

10.   THE CASE OF THE BOMB AND THE BABYSITTER

John's best friend, Bill, is a member of an anti-nuclear organization. John is not himself a member of the group but shares a concern about the need to work for peace and does all he can to support his friend in his peace activities. The group has become completely frustrated at the lack of progress the disarmament movement has made in Canada. Canada is still not a nuclear-free zone and the cruise missile is being tested there. Everyone in the organization agrees that the non-violent approach has got nowhere. None of the authorities seems willing to take the group's disarmament initiatives seriously. They decide that a planned campaign of some kind of violent disruption is necessary to get the authorities to listen. But they want to be certain that no one will be physically injured in the process.

A plant which manufactures parts for the cruise missile is selected as the first target. A bomb will be set off near the front entrance of the plant and the organization will take credit for it in the hope that its pleas will be heard. The time chosen is in the small hours of the morning when no one employed in the plant will be working. The agreement is struck and the plans laid. John's friend, Bill, is one of the team chosen to hide the bomb and set it to go off at the agreed time. Bill is a single parent and asks John to babysit his child while he carries out his assignment. John sympathizes with the group's frustration but seriously questions whether any violent act is the way to bring about peace. He also fears that despite precautions someone might be killed or hurt.

Question

What is the morally right thing for John to do?
(See Chapter 5: Urban terrorists, for a variation in this dilemma.)

11.   MORALITY IN A CRISIS

A passenger-cargo ship foundered and sank off the coast of Newfoundland in a storm. Two large life boats managed to get clear before the ship sank. One of the life boats was overloaded and soon began to take on water. The first mate in charge thought the boat would sink unless its load was lightened. He decided that the only way to do this was to throw a number of its passengers overboard. He reasoned that the three members of the crew were needed to man the large life boat, that women and children should be saved, and that married couples should not be split up. The rest were expendable. The mate and the crew threw 13 passengers overboard. The boat stopped taking on water, and in a few hours its occupants were rescued. The mate was later tried and convicted for multiple homicide and sentenced to life imprisonment.

Question

Did the first mate do the morally right thing?
   (See Chapter 7: Moral quandary.)

MORAL DILEMMA ANALYSIS QUESTIONS

1. Is this a real dilemma?
2. What is the morally right thing to do in this situation? Why?
3. What moral values, principles or rules, if any, support your answer?
4. Are the values, principles or rules which support your answer utilitarian, Kantian, others? Specify. (See Chapter 2 for an outline of these theories.)
5. How would a utilitarian respond to the dilemma?
6. How would a Kantian respond to the dilemma?
7. What moral values are involved in the dilemma?
8. Does your answer to the dilemma enable you to express these values properly? Fully?
9. Can you imagine social or personal states of affairs which would express all these values harmoniously and fully?
10. Are these values important and/or essential to the community? To the community's institutions or social practices (e.g. religion, marriage)? To yourself?
11. In what way would the community, and its institutions, have to develop to express these values fully and harmoniously?
12. In what way would you have to develop personally to express these values fully and harmoniously in your conduct?
13. In what way would utilitarianism have to develop fully to integrate these values theoretically?
14. In what way would Kantianism have to develop fully to integrate these values theoretically?
15. In what way would other approaches to morality (e.g. religious) have to develop fully to integrate these values?

Notes

Introduction

1 'Making a Moral Choice', Open College/CJRT FM, 10 February 1985.
2 Ibid.
3 M. Norquay and Don MacNiven, *Making A Moral Choice/Discussion Guide*, Open College/Ryerson, Toronto, 1985, p. 4.
4 'Making a Moral Choice', 10 February 1985.
5 See above, Appendix: The Open College dilemmas, pp. 205–211.
6 Robert Nozick, *Anarchy, State and Utopia*, Basic Books, New York, 1974, p. 42. See also ibid., pp. 43–45.
7 Jonathan Glover, *What Sort of People Should There Be?* Penguin Books, Harmondsworth, 1984, p. 17. Glover maintains that his thought experiments cannot directly substantiate moral claims because unlike scientific experiments they are subjective rather than objective. Nevertheless they can be used indirectly to establish moral claims, like whether we ought to create experience and thought machines and how we should use them. This is possible because they help us discover shared values or common preferences which we can use for determining social policy. See *What Sort of People Should There Be?*, pp. 130–136. Glover's methodology has much in common with that of R.M. Hare, developed in *Freedom and Reason*, Clarendon Press, Oxford, 1963. Of course there may be a marginal few who will differ from the vast majority of us, but perhaps this doesn't matter for Glover. However, they would be similar to Hare's 'fanatics', who present a major problem for the theory. See my 'Hare's Universal Prescriptivism', *Dialogue*, Vol. 3, 1964, pp. 191–198. Subjectivity, even in Hare's and Glover's sophisticated forms, cannot be easily defended.
8 Glover, *What Sort of People Should There Be?*, p. 60.
9 John T. Noonan Jr, *How to Argue about Abortion*, The Ad Hoc Committee in Defense of Life, New York, 1974, p. 2.
10 Michael Tooley, 'Abortion and Infanticide', *Philosophy and Public Affairs*, Vol. 2, No. 1, 1972, pp. 60–62.
11 See my article, 'Towards a Unified System of Ethics', in Douglas Odegard (ed.), *Ethics and Justification*, Academic Printing and Publishing, Edmonton, Alberta, 1987, pp. 167–177.
12 See my *F.H. Bradley's Moral Psychology*, Edwin Mellen Press, Lewiston, New York, 1987, especially Ch. 5. A similar use was made of dilemmas in

Kohlberg's system of moral education. See, for example, Lawrence Kohlberg, *The Philosophy of Moral Development*, Harper & Row, New York, 1981.

1 Private spaces

1 In the real life example the RCMP were actually looking for a deep cover agent of a foreign power, not the leader of a narcotics ring. Deep cover agents enter Canada illegally under an assumed identity and are assigned various intelligence gathering and espionage roles. They are the most difficult foreign agents to detect and pose the greatest potential threat to national security. The RCMP had learned from other sources that a deep cover agent existed in Canada and was probably living somewhere in southern Ontario. They did not have a name, but they knew the agent was a 50-year-old male who had been recently treated for a sprained ankle in a public hospital in the Niagara area. They needed to act with despatch, so RCMP investigators were sent directly to the Toronto district of OHIP. They informed senior OHIP officials there that they were seeking an agent of a foreign power and that the matter involved national security. They requested permission to look at confidential claims files to locate the names and recent addresses of all males of the appropriate age who had been treated for a sprained ankle in the Niagara area at the relevant time. The OHIP officials, unlike the one in the hypothetical example, granted the RCMP access to the confidential claims files. In order to receive payment for their medical services, Ontario physicians are required to make an official claim with OHIP. Some 100,000 of these confidential files were reviewed by the officers and 82 were photo-copied and sent to Ottawa, where they remain in the possession of the RCMP. Whether the information led to the location or arrest of the deep cover agent was never made known. Apparently OHIP officials routinely released confidential health information to the RCMP and other Canadian police forces as a matter of policy, even though this was illegal. It was a breach of section 44 of the Ontario Health Disciplines Act, which imposed a general legal obligation of confidentiality on all OHIP employees. There were explicit exceptions to the rule but these did not permit disclosure to the police; indeed this was specifically prohibited by the act. See The Hon. Justice Horace Krever, *The Report of The Commission of Enquiry into the Confidentiality of Health Information*, Queen's Printer for Ontario, Toronto, 1980, Vol. II, Ch. 16, 'The Police and Law Enforcement', pp. 1–9. I changed the case from spying to drug dealing because the original case in which the OHIP official actually released information to the RCMP would not, I thought, strike the public audience I first tested this dilemma on as a real moral dilemma.

2 Cf. my article 'Towards a Unified System of Ethics', in Douglas Odegard (ed.), *Ethics and Justification*, Academic Printing & Publishing, Edmonton, Alberta, 1988, pp. 167–177.

3 Cf. S.E. Toulmin, *An Examination of the Place of Reason in Ethics*, Cambridge University Press, Cambridge, 1950; H.A. Pritchard, *Moral Obligation*, Oxford, 1949; and R.M. Hare, *Moral Thinking*, Clarendon Press, Oxford, 1981.

4 Romans 3:7–9, *The New English Bible*, Oxford University Press/Cambridge University Press, London, 1970, pp. 193–194.
5 See Chapter 2, pp. 29–52, above.
6 See Don Johnson, 'Privacy of Computer Files in Question', *Globe and Mail*, 27 December 1990, p. A9.
7 See Jonathan Glover's useful discussion in *What Sort of People Should There Be?*, Penguin Books, Harmondsworth, 1984, pp. 59–71.
8 See *Privacy and Computers, A Report by the Canadian Department of Communications and Justice*, Ottawa, 1974.
9 For a utilitarian perspective see J.S. Mill, *On Liberty* (1859), Bobbs Merrill, New York, 1956.
10 See Gilbert Sharpe, *The Law and Medicine in Canada*, Butterworths, Toronto, 1987, p. 188.
11 See *Key Legislative Issues relating to Child Abuse*, Department of Health and Welfare, Ottawa, February 1980, pp. 44ff.
12 'AIDS: Failure to Warn Woman Sparks an Ethical Dilemma', *Toronto Star*, 16 September 1987.
13 Sharpe, *The Law and Medicine in Canada*, p. 191.
14 See Neil L. Chayet, 'Confidentiality and Privileged Communication', *The New England Journal of Medicine*, Vol. 275, No. 18, pp. 1009–1010, 3 Nov. 1966, reprinted in Samuel Gorovitz, Ruth Macklin, Andrew L. Jameton, John M. O'Connor and Susan Sherwin (eds), *Moral Problems in Medicine*, 2nd edn, Prentice-Hall, Englewood Cliffs, New Jersey, 1983, pp. 233–234.
15 Ibid., pp. 233–234.
16 See L.E. Rosovsky, *The Canadian Patient's Book of Rights*, Doubleday Canada, Toronto, 1980, pp. 28–50, and *Patients' Rights in Ontario*, The Patients' Rights Association, Toronto, 1982. These rights do not include the right to know the status of one's medical condition, but patients ought to have that right if we take the principle of respect for persons seriously.
17 Krever, *Confidentiality of Health Information*, Vol. III, pp. 3–5. Not only did OHIP routinely release confidential information to the police, it also released confidential information to private detectives working for insurance companies. The Ontario public was rightly shocked at these practices, which clearly threatened patients' rights to privacy.
18 Kantians are actually divided on the solution to the problem of conflict of rules. Kant himself did not provide a clear answer. Sometimes they allow exceptions to moral rules, but at other times they deny this and prefer to redescribe the actions so that the conflict disappears. See Chapter 2, pp. 31–32, above.
19 Justice Krever recommended that this situation be changed and that patients should be given proper access to their medical records on request. So far the Ontario government has failed to implement the recommendation, but the Liberal administration appeared to be ready to do so before it was defeated in 1990. See Krever, *Confidentiality of Health Information*, Vol. I, Recommendation 39, p. 21. See also 'Ontario Plans to Let Patients See their Files', *Toronto Star*, 3 November 1989, p. A19.
20 Krever, *Confidentiality of Health Information*, pp. 1–122.
21 'Towards a Unified System of Ethics', pp. 167–177.
22 See Robert E. Butts, 'Mr. Mill's Logic', *William Whewell's Theory of Scientific Method*, University of Pittsburgh Press, Pittsburgh 1968, pp. 265–310.

23 Cf. 'Towards a Unified System of Ethics', p. 174, and my 'Business Ethics in the Global Village', in Douglas Odegard and Carole Stewart (eds), *Perspectives on Moral Relativism*, Agathon Books, Toronto, 1991, pp. 133–147.
24 See Krever, *Confidentiality of Health Information*, Vol. I, Recommendation 21, pp. 16–17.
25 Justice Krever found that the OHIP official's conduct was wrong, because it involved a clear breach of law which could not be condoned, even on the grounds of national security or the public good. However, he thought the conduct of the OHIP official was understandable given that OHIP's de facto policy was one of full co-operation with law enforcement agencies in the execution of their legitimate duties. When asked why they encouraged their employees to break the law, senior OHIP officials replied that they had never really thought about it. After all, both they and the police were merely acting in the public interest, and there is nothing wrong with that. Justice Krever recommended that the names of the OHIP officials be kept confidential and that no charges be laid. He was also sympathetic to the policy of co-operation with the police. He recognized the public interest in allowing the police the right to information relevant to their legitimate duties. He even thought that they should have more OHIP information than they were now legally entitled to, especially with respect to enrolment data. See Krever, *Confidentiality of Health Information*, Vol. 1, p. 45. Nevertheless he still recommended that there should be no release of confidential medical information to law enforcement agencies without a warrant.
26 See *Privacy and Computers*, p. 11.
27 See my *Bradley's Moral Psychology*, Edwin Mellen Press, Lewiston, New York, 1987, pp. 200–246.

2 Western moral traditions

1 Alasdair MacIntyre, *After Virtue*, University of Notre Dame Press, Notre Dame, Indiana, Second Edition, 1984, pp. 36–78. Jonathan Glover identifies these dominant Western traditions as utilitarian and natural law, see P. Thompson, *The Moral Question*, TV Ontario, Toronto, 1982, p. 4. Donagan identifies the Kantian with the natural law tradition; see Alan Donagan, *The Theory of Morality*, University of Chicago Press, Chicago, 1977, pp. 6–9.
2 Kantians, however, tend to see their systems in terms of deductive logic, while utilitarians tend to see their systems in terms of inductive logic. See my *Bradley's Moral Psychology*, Edwin Mellen Press, Lewiston, New York, pp. 1–42, for a fuller discussion of the fact/value problem.
3 Both Alasdair MacIntyre, *A Short History of Ethics*, Macmillan, New York, 1966, pp. 110–120, and Donagan, *The Theory of Morality*, p. 6, give excellent accounts of this development. For a fuller philosophical discussion of the divine command theory see my *The Moral Question: Ethical Theory*, TV Ontario, Toronto, 1982, pp. 30–31.
4 See Thomas Hobbes, *Leviathan*, edited with an introduction by C.B. MacPherson, Penguin Books, London, 1968; John Rawls, *A Theory of*

Justice, Harvard University Press, Cambridge, Massachusetts, 1971; John Plamanatz, *The English Utilitarians*, Blackwell, Oxford, 1958.

5 Technically, for Kant, an action is morally right if it conforms to a morally acceptable rule, and wrong if it is inconsistent with such a rule. Donagan has argued that this implies that motives and intentions are not relevant for determining right and wrong in Kantian ethics; see *The Theory of Morality*, pp. 37–52. But this appears to be mistaken. For Kant, at least, an action is also right if it is performed from the motive of duty. Conscientious persons do their duty for duty's sake. Since they act on principle, their actions will be right if they conform to morally acceptable rules. So the two criteria are essentially the same. See Immanuel Kant, *The Groundwork of the Metaphysics of Morals* (ed. H.J. Paton), Harper & Row, New York, 1964, Chs 1 and 2.

6 Cf. Donagan, *The Theory of Morality*, pp. 6ff, for an adequate account of the relationship between Kantian-type ethical theories and the correspondence theory of truth.

7 R.M. Hare, *Freedom and Reason*, Clarendon Press, Oxford, 1963, pp. 67–85.

8 Cf. Immanuel Kant, 'On a Supposed Right to Lie from Altruistic Motives' (1797), in L.W. Beck (ed.), *Kant's Critique of Practical Reason*, Chicago, 1949, pp. 346–350.

9 Immanuel Kant, 'The Metaphysics of Morals', in *Kant's Ethical Philosophy*, Hackett, Indianapolis, 1983, pp. 84ff, and my discussion of the topic in *Bradley's Moral Psychology*, pp. 94–96.

10 See A. Donagan, *The Theory of Morality*, pp. 143–209. Donagan uses both the Pauline principle and the principle of the lesser evil to resolve moral dilemmas. The latter, however, is ad hoc for Kantian ethics in a way which the Pauline principle is not.

11 See my *Ethical Theory*, pp. 18–55. The early forms of the theory tended to be subjectivist/emotivist – e.g. David Hume, 'An Enquiry into the Principles of Morals' (1777), in Alasdair MacIntyre (ed.), *Hume's Ethical Writings*, Collier Books, New York, 1965 – then they became objectivist – e.g. J.S. Mill, *Utilitarianism* (1863), Bobbs Merrill, New York, 1957. Currently both forms of the theory share the philosophical spotlight. Cf. A.J. Ayer, *Language, Truth & Logic*, Gollancz, London, 1936, Second Edition 1946, for a subjectivist/emotivist version of the theory, and Peter Singer, *Practical Ethics*, Cambridge University Press, Cambridge/New York, 1979 for an objectivist version of the theory.

12 MacIntyre, *After Virtue*.

13 See René Descartes, *Discourse on Method and the Meditations*, Penguin Books, London, 1968.

14 See, J.F. Bennett, *Locke, Berkeley, and Hume*, Clarendon Press, Oxford, 1971.

15 MacIntyre, *After Virtue*, Ch. 4.

16 Cf. J.S. Mill, *On Liberty* (1859), Bobbs Merrill, New York, 1956, Ch. 5, and G.E. Moore, *Principia Ethica*, Cambridge University Press, Cambridge, 1903, pp. 171–180. Hume, 'An Enquiry into the Principles of Morals' pp. 23–156, appears to be an exception here, as he is with most things philosophical. He is the only major utilitarian who develops the theory in terms of the concept of virtue rather than the concept of right actions. However, he does understand the virtues in terms of dispositions to act rather than as complex traits of character. His theory of virtue is designed to answer the question of what our duty is, i.e. what actions are right and

ought to be done, and what actions are wrong and ought to be eschewed. So his priorities are ultimately the same as other utilitarians.

17 Hume for example distinguished between natural and artificial virtues. He considered benevolence a natural virtue and justice an artificial one. See, for example, his 'An Enquiry into the Principles of Morals', Chs 2 and 3.

18 Cf. Hobbes, *Leviathan*, p. 188, and Kant, *The Groundwork of the Metaphysics of Morals*, p. 89.

19 See my *Bradley's Moral Psychology* for a fuller account of some of these assumptions.

20 Donagan, *The Theory of Morality*, Ch. 2, pp. 32–74.

21 See C.B. MacPherson (ed.), Hobbes' *Leviathan*, pp. 9–64, and my review of *John Stuart Mill: The Collected Works*, Vols IX and XI, University of Toronto Press, Toronto, 1978/79, in *Canadian Journal of Political Science*, 1982.

22 Hume, 'An Enquiry into the Principles of Morals', Ch. 1.

23 Ibid., Ch. 2ff.

24 See for example Kant, *The Groundwork of the Metaphysics of Morals*, p. 61. There he says: 'It is impossible to conceive anything at all in the world or even out of it, which can be taken as good without qualification, except a good will.' Also see Mill, *Utilitarianism*, p. 51: 'Will is the child of desire . . .'

25 Hobbes, *Leviathan*, p. 126: 'For, that any man should take pleasure in other mens great harmes, without other end of his own, I do not conceive it possible.'

26 Mill, *Utilitarianism*, Ch. 2, pp. 27–32, and Joseph Fletcher, *Situation Ethics*, Westminster Press, Philadelphia, 1966.

27 Donagan, *The Theory of Morality*, pp. 65ff, argues that the Kantian principle of respect for persons captures the essence of Christian morality. This would seem to cast doubt on MacIntyre's claim in *After Virtue* that Kantianism is merely an offshoot of Protestant Christianity and is not continuous with the Christian Middle Ages. On the other hand, the fact that Protestant Christianity tends to be more reformist than Catholic or Orthodox Christianity would tend to support MacIntyre's thesis that Kantianism represents a radical break with our Christian past.

28 Cf. Hobbes, *Leviathan*, Ch. 6, and Kant, *The Groundwork of the Metaphysics of Morals*, Ch. 3, pp. 97ff.

29 Cf. Mill, *Utilitarianism*, pp. 30–33, and Kant, *The Groundwork of the Metaphysics of Morals*, Ch. 2, pp. 89–91. See also Donagan, *The Theory of Morality*, p. 7. There he defines a theory of morality: 'it is a theory of a system of laws or precepts, binding upon rational creatures as such, the content of which is ascertainable by human reason'.

30 Cf. Hume, 'On Suicide', in MacIntyre (ed.), *Hume's Ethical Writings*, pp. 297–308, and Kant, *The Groundwork of the Metaphysics of Morals*, p. 89. Hobbes is an exception within the utilitarian tradition. He thought that suicide was inconsistent with our natural law of survival. See *Leviathan*, p. 189. I treat this as a relic left from the natural law system Hobbes was in the process of restructuring. Donagan, *The Theory of Morality*, pp. 76–79, is an exception within the Kantian tradition because he thought suicide was a rational choice in certain specific situations, hence consistent with self-respect. I treat this as an attempt to import into Kantianism modern liberal views on death and dying with dignity. Whether they really square

with Kantianism is a moot point. The exception to the rule against suicide involves accepting the principle of the lesser evil as implicit in respect for persons, and this is suspect.

31 Cf. G.E.M. Anscombe, 'War and Murder', in James Rachels (ed.), *Moral Problems*, Third Edition, Harper & Row, New York, 1979, pp. 393–407.

32 Donagan, *The Theory of Morality*, pp. 154–155.

33 Cf. Kant, *The Groundwork of the Metaphysics of Morals*, pp. 65–67. Mill, *Utilitarianism*, Ch. 5, pp. 52–79, tries to derive obligations of justice from obligations of non-malevolence. See also my *Moral Theory*, pp. 23–36.

34 See Carol Gilligan, *In a Different Voice*, Harvard University Press, Cambridge, Massachusetts, 1982. Generally, feminist ethics seems to identify Kantian ethical theory, including Rawlsean contract theory, as clearly possessing a male bias, but is less clear about the status of utilitarianism because of its contextual and emotive tendencies. Utilitarian theories which emphasize rational systems of justice and individual rights (e.g. J.S. Mill) are thought to be more male-biased than those which stress benevolence and emotion (e.g. Hume). The most radical view holds that all traditions in western moral philosophy are gender-biased, but this position is difficult to maintain. See Annette Baier, 'Hume, the Women's Moral Theorist?', in E.F. Kittay and D. Meyers (eds), *Women and Moral Theory*, Rowman & Littlefield, Totowa, New Jersey, 1987, pp. 37–54.

35 See R.S. Downie, 'The Justification of Punishment', in Rachels (ed.), *Moral Problems*, pp. 321–331.

36 See MacIntyre, *After Virtue*, pp. 36–61, and *A Short History Of Ethics*, pp. 121–269. For an interesting attempt to unify the two versions of the principle see Tom L. Beauchamp and James F. Childress, *The Principles of Biomedical Ethics*, Oxford University Press, New York, 1979, pp. 59–105.

37 Peter Singer, *Animal Liberation*, Avon Books, New York, 1977. I owe the term 'zoo-centric' to my colleague Peter Penz, Faculty of Environmental Studies, York University, Toronto. I originally called the utilitarian position 'bio-centric', but this more aptly describes an idealist system of environmental ethics. Utilitarians are certainly non-human centred, but they are not fully nature-centred as idealists are.

38 Kant, *The Metaphysics of Morals*, pp. 105–106.

39 MacIntyre, *After Virtue*, pp. 1–21.

40 Ibid., pp. 56–58.

41 John R. Searle, 'How to Derive an "Ought" from an "Is"', in W.D. Hudson (ed.), *The Is/Ought Question*, Macmillan, London, 1969, pp. 120–134.

42 Ludwig Wittgenstein, *Philosophical Investigations*, Blackwell, Oxford, 1958.

43 R.M. Hare, 'The Promising Game', in Hudson (ed.), *The Is/Ought Question*, pp. 144–156. But see Searle's reply to Hare, pp. 263–264. None of Searle's rebuttals is convincing. Searle argues that his moral tautology 'Keep Promises' does not categorically entail moral obligations because tautologies are hypothetical. He says: 'no one is claiming that tautologies "prescribe" behaviour categorically but only conditionally on some institutional fact.' This certainly makes his dispute with Hare less fundamental, but is not a sound reason for interpreting moral rules, which are constituents of practices, as tautologies rather than synthetic prescriptions.

44 Cf. my 'The Idea of a Moral Expert', *Moral Expertise*, Routledge, London, 1990, pp. 1–10. And cf. my *Moral Theory*, Ch. 1.
45 D. MacNiven, P. MacEwen and C. Paiva, 'A Code of Ethics for Canadian Philosophers: A Working Paper', *Dialogue*, XXV, 1986, pp. 179–189; M. McDonald, M.H. Parizeau and D. Pullman, *Towards a Canadian Research Strategy for Applied Ethics*, Social Sciences and Humanities Research Council, Ottawa, May 1989. The motion to establish a code of ethics for Canadian philosophers was narrowly defeated – 19 for, 22 against, 3 abstentions – at the 1987 annual meeting of the Canadian Philosophical Association. See the *Fall Newsletter*, 1987, Canadian Society for the Study of Practical Ethics.
46 See the dilemma on the police and privacy in Chapter 1 above.
47 Ron Wideman, *Personal and Societal Values: a Resource Guide for the Primary and Junior Division*, Ministry of Education, Ontario, 1983, p. 6.
48 See my 'Moral Education', in W. Hare and J.P. Portelli (eds), *Philosophy of Education*, Detselig, Calgary, Alberta, 1988, pp. 285–291.
49 See Arthur Kaplan, 'Mechanics on Duty: The Limitations of a Technical Definition of Moral Expertise for Work in Applied Ethics', *Canadian Journal of Philosophy*, Supplementary Vol. VIII, 1982, pp. 1–18; Cheryl N. Noble, 'Ethics and Experts', *The Hastings Centre Report*, June 1982, pp. 7–9.
50 Peter Miller, *Journal of Moral Education*, 1975.
51 Donagan, *The Theory of Morality*, pp. 66–74.
52 See, for example, D. Gauthier, *Morals by Agreement*, Clarendon Press, Oxford, 1986, and Jan Narveson, 'Justifying a Morality', in Douglas Odegard (ed.), *Ethics and Justification*, Academic Printing & Publishing, Edmonton, Alberta, 1987, pp. 257–276. Rawls, *A Theory of Justice*, may be an exception to this, because his method of 'wide reflective equilibrium' bears a strong resemblance to the idealist methodology I outlined in Chapter 1 above. See also Kai Nielsen, 'In Defense of Wide Reflective Equilibrium', in Odegard (ed.), *Ethics and Justification*, pp. 19–38.
53 G.E. Moore, *Ethics*, William & Norgate, Oxford, 1912.
54 Rawls, *A System of Justice*.
55 Hare, *Freedom and Reason*.
56 Mill, *Utilitarianism*.
57 Kant, *The Groundwork of the Metaphysics of Morals*; W.D. Ross, *The Right and the Good*, Clarendon Press, Oxford, 1930; Donagan, *The Theory of Morality*.
58 Bradley, *Ethical Studies*.
59 MacIntyre, *After Virtue*. Whether MacIntyre will remain an idealist is moot.
60 Cf. my 'The Idea of a Moral Expert', in *Moral Expertise*, Routledge, London, 1989, pp. 2–11.

3 Academic honesty

1 See Chapter 2, pp. 50–52, above.
2 Ibid, p. 32.
3 See Chapters 1 and 2.
4 See Sissela Bok, *Lying*, Pantheon Books, New York, 1978.
5 See Jerry Carrol, 'Plagiarism: Publish or Perish', *Globe and Mail*, 10 August 1991.

6 See my *The Moral Question: Ethical Theory*, TV Ontario, Toronto, 1982, p. 10.
7 See my 'Moral Education', *Canadian Forum*, May 1984, pp. 16–17.
8 *York University Faculty of Arts Newsletter*, Vol. 2, Issue 1, September 1989, pp. 5–6. See also Mary Gooderham, 'How Cheaters Prosper – and Why it's Tough to Stop Them', *Globe and Mail*, 30 November 1992, cover story pp. A1, and A6.
9 See my *Ethical Theory*, pp. 10–11.
10 Clive Beck, 'Relativism and Moral Education', in Douglas Odegard and Carole Stewart (eds), *Perspectives on Moral Relativism*, Agathon Books, Toronto, 1991, pp. 103–112, argues for a similar form of moral education based on objective values but resting on the essentially utilitarian value of individual well-being: 'Moral actions are good and right only because and in so far as they promote human well-being' (p. 107). He also correctly recognizes that utilitarianism does not really solve the problem of subjectivism in moral education. It does not address the fact that different teachers and students have different views about the nature of morality and hence different approaches to the issue of moral relativism (p. 109). Nor that it is practically impossible for teachers, parents, governments or interest groups in society to remain morally neutral with respect to moral education in the schools (p. 110). Since there is no unified theory of ethics and no general moral consensus within the society, moral values remain essentially a matter of individual opinion for Beck.
11 Cf. Alan Donagan, *The Theory of Morality*, University of Chicago Press, Chicago, 1977, pp. 154–155: 'A fundamental principle which categorically forbids violating the respect owed to human beings as rational must condemn any plan for promoting human well-being by which respect would be violated.'
12 R.M. Hare, *Freedom and Reason*, Clarendon Press, Oxford, 1963.
13 Cf. my *Ethical Theory*, 1982, p. 4.
14 See *Teaching and Learning at York: A Guide for Teaching Assistants and Course Directors*, York University, Toronto, 1990, p. 100.
15 Idid., p. 70.
16 Ibid., p. 99.
17 Cf. S. Katz, 'Academic Offenses: An Update', *York University Faculty of Arts Newsletter*, September 1989, p. 5.
18 See V.B. Carter, *Authors by Profession*, Vol. I, Society of Authors, London, 1978, for the evolution of authorship as a business between 1500 and 1800.
19 York University, *Faculty of Arts Calendar, 1992–93*, pp. 342–344.
20 *Teaching and Learning at York*, p. 71.
21 Thomas Hobbes, *Leviathan*, Penguin Books, London, 1968, p. 139.
22 Alasdair MacIntyre, *After Virtue*, University of Notre Dame Press, Notre Dame, Indiana, Second Edition, 1984, pp. 6–78. See also H.A. Bassford, 'Medical Ethics', in Don MacNiven, *Moral Expertise*, pp. 128–143, who distinguishes between 'role-specific' and 'general' moral norms. He argues that in some circumstances general moral norms should take precedence over role-specific ones, i.e. a patient's rights over the patient's health in cases of conflict. Bassford's general norms, although external to the practice of medicine, clearly possess intrinsic value; hence they count morally.
23 See Chapter 2, p. 42, above.

24 Cf. J.S. Mill, *On Liberty* (1859), Bobbs Merrill, New York, 1956, Ch. 1, which identifies the same question as basic for any objective theory of morality.
25 *Teaching and Learning at York*, pp. 102, 72–74.
26 MacIntyre, *After Virtue*, Chs 10–14.
27 F.H. Bradley, *Ethical Studies*, Second Edition, Oxford University Press, London, 1959: Essay 5, 'My Station and Its Duties' pp. 160ff.
28 F.H. Bradley, *Ethical Studies*, Essay 2, 'Why Should I Be Moral?' See also my *Ethical Theory*, pp. 9ff.
29 See Chapter 2, p. 47, above.

4 Experimental ethics

1 The dilemma is based on a famous study in sociology by Laud Humphreys, *The Tea Room Trade*, Aldine Publishing Company, Chicago, 1975, which is now commonly used as a case study in bio-medical ethics. Cf. Tom L. Beauchamp and James F. Childress, *Principles Of Biomedical Ethics*, Second Edition, Oxford University Press, New York, 1983, pp. 285–287. The real studies were less well received than the hypothetical studies in this dilemma and were the centre of a contentious and divisive debate, both about their scientific value and the ethics of the research, in the sociology department in the university in which they took place. See Beauchamp and Childress, p. 287. The hypothetical dilemma was modified to fit a Canadian context. Bathhouses were substituted for public washrooms, which were the centre of police attention at the time the dilemma was first presented during my CJRT FM/Ryerson Open College radio series, 'Making a Moral Choice', Toronto, 1985.
2 Medical Research Council of Canada (MRC), *Ethics In Human Experimentation (Guidelines)*, Ottawa, 1978, p. 23.
3 Stanley Milgram, *Obedience to Authority*, Harper & Row, New York, 1974.
4 Ibid., p. 3.
5 Ibid.
6 Ibid., p. 189.
7 Ibid., pp. 1, 179.
8 Ibid., pp. 7–8.
9 See Diana Baumrind, 'Some Thoughts on Ethics of Research', *American Psychologist*, No. 19, 1964, pp. 421–413.
10 MRC *Guidelines*, 1978, pp. 16–24.
11 Milgram, *Obedience to Authority*, 'Problems in Ethics', pp. 193–202.
12 J.S. Mill, *Utilitarianism* (1863), Bobbs Merrill, New York, 1957, p. 20.
13 Humphreys, *Tearoom Trade*, Aldine Publishing Co, Chicago, 1957: 'Problems in Ethics'.
14 MRC, *Guidelines on Research Involving Human Subjects*, 1987, p. 27.
15 Ibid., pp. 3–4.
16 The example is based on one used by James Rachels, *The Elements of Moral Philosophy*, Random House, New York, 1986, pp. 95–96. Rachels argues, I think correctly, that the utilitarian would have to say that the Peeping Tom did no wrong because no harm was done.
17 See R.M. Hare, *Freedom and Reason*, Oxford, 1963, pp. 10–21; Rachels, *The Elements of Moral Philosophy*, pp. 7–11.

18 MRC *Guidelines*, 1978, p. 8.
19 MRC *Guidelines*, 1987, p. 9.
20 See John Mendelsohn, *Medical Experiments on Jewish Inmates of Concentration Camps: The Holocaust*, Vol. 9, Garland, New York, 1982.
21 See 'Doctor's Dilemma: Can Mankind Profit from Nazis' Human Experiments?', *Gazette*, Montreal, 6 November 1988, p. B9.
22 MRC *Guidelines*, 1978, p. 10, and MRC *Guidelines*, 1987, p. 3.
23 MRC *Guidelines*, 1987, p. 3.
24 See MRC *Guidelines*, 1978, p. 59.
25 Milgram, *Obedience to Authority*.
26 MRC *Guidelines*, 1978, pp. 27–34, and MRC *Guidelines*, 1987, pp. 27–35.
27 MRC *Guidelines*, 1987, p. 3.
28 Ibid., p. 28.
29 See the useful discussions of these problems in ibid., pp. 27–36. See also the discussion of the Nuremberg code in the Law Reform Commission of Canada, *Working Paper 61*, on Bio-medical experimentation involving human subjects.
30 MRC *Guidelines*, 1978, p. 24.
31 See David Wiesenthal's useful analysis, 'Recent Developments in Social Psychology in Response to Ethical Concerns', in my *Moral Expertise*, Routledge, London, 1990, pp. 11–25.
32 See my *The Moral Question: Ethical Theory*, TV Ontario, Toronto, 1982, pp. 16–17.
33 Alan Donagan, *The Theory of Morality*, University of Chicago Press, 1977, pp. 143–171. Donagan uses the principle of the lesser evil as well as the Pauline principle to establish a consistent Kantianism. He argues that both principles are implicit in an ethics based on the principle of respect for persons. This may make good ethical sense, but the principle of the lesser evil is a utilitarian rather than a Kantian principle.

5 Urban terrorists

1 The dilemma is based on the activities of the so-called Squamish Five, who, in 1981 and 1982, conducted a series of terrorist attacks against the government of British Columbia, and industries they viewed as polluters and distributors of pornography, in the name of peace and social improvement. This culminated in the 14 October 1982 Toronto bombing of Litton Systems Canada Limited, manufacturers of parts for the guidance system of the cruise missile, which the Americans were testing in western Canada. See 'The Squamish Five', by Ken Glass, with Paul McKenna, CBC Television, 6 November 1988. The group, who called themselves 'Direct Action', wanted to aim their acts of violence against the property of the arms manufacturers rather than people. They believed that drawing a clear distinction between violence against property and violence against people made terrorism ethically acceptable for the peace movement. Whether they were sincere or not is a moot point, because they had carried out armed robbery to finance their terrorist campaign. In the Litton bombing there were personal injuries, some serious, to several Litton employees and two Toronto policemen, but no one was killed. The

group exploded the bomb in the early hours of the morning even though there was a night shift at work then. When they originally planned the bombing earlier in the year, there was no night shift working. They also arranged for a telephone warning to the plant which would enable the plant to be evacuated before the bomb exploded. The phone call was made but the bomb exploded prematurely. The Squamish Five were caught by the RCMP in January 1983 and brought to justice. All five were found guilty of various crimes and sentenced to prison terms ranging from six years to life.

One of the group has completed a doctoral degree at Queen's University at Kingston, Ontario, through that university's prisoners' academic programme. He has apparently repented, and now believes that the use of violence against property or people to advance peace is morally unacceptable.

2 Jan Narveson, 'Pacifism: A Philosophical Analysis', in James Rachels, *Moral Problems*, Third Edition, Harper & Row, New York, 1979, pp. 408–441. Narveson argues that pacifism is inconsistent as such, but Paul Thompson has argued correctly that it is not inconsistent for all ethical systems. See *The Moral Question: Ethical Theory*, pp. 11–12. It is, however, inconsistent for utilitarianism because it is inconsistent with the principle of minimizing harm.

3 This example is based on the famous Charles Whitman case, a man who slaughtered 15 people with sniper fire from a university tower in Austin, Texas. See above, Chapter 1, p. 15.

4 Narveson, 'Pacifism', pp. 414–415.

5 For a discussion of the distinction between moderate and extreme pacifists see Paul Thompson, *The Moral Question*, pp. 11–12.

6 Jacques P. Thiroux, *Ethics, Theory and Practice*, Third Edition, Macmillan, New York, 1986, p. 156.

7 See J. McKenna, 'The Just War', in Rachels (ed.), *Moral Problems*, pp. 382–392. McKenna lists seven characteristics which define the just war: (1) it must be declared by a legitimate authority; (2) the threat or injury must be real; (3) the good achieved must outweigh the evil; (4) there must be a reasonable hope of victory; (5) war must be the last resort after all reasonable diplomacy has failed; (6) there must be no ulterior motives; (7) the methods must be moral. This definition would clearly rule out nuclear war.

8 See G.E.M. Anscombe, 'War and Murder', in Rachels (ed.), *Moral Problems*, p. 393.

9 Rachels (ed.), *Moral Problems*, p. 378.

10 Edward W. Keyserlingk, *Sanctity of Life or Quality of Life in the Context of Ethics, Medicine and Law*, Law Reform Commission of Canada, Ottawa, 1979, for a useful discussion of the principle.

11 Narveson, 'Pacifism', pp. 408–425.

12 Thiroux, *Ethics, Theory and Practice*, pp. 155–156.

13 G.E. Moore, *Ethics*, Williams & Norgate, Oxford, 1912, pp. 72–83, and J.S. Mill, *Utilitarianism*, Bobbs Merrill, New York, 1957, Ch. 2, pp. 23–24. There Mill says:

It is more unjust to utilitarianism that this particular misapprehension should be made a ground of objection to it, in as much as utilitarian moralists have gone beyond almost all others in affirming that the motive has nothing to do with the morality of the action, although much with the worth of the agent. (pp. 17–18)

14 Alan Donagan, *The Theory of Morality*, University of Chicago Press, Chicago, 1977, pp. 157–164.

15 Ibid., p. 164.

16 Cf. my *Bradley's Moral Psychology*, Edwin Mellen Press, Lewiston, New York, 1987, pp. 140–143, where this idealist theory of virtue was first developed.

6 Gentle exits

1 Law Reform Commission of Canada, *Euthanasia, Aiding Suicide, and Cessation of Treatment*, Working Paper No. 28, Ottawa, 1982, p. 52. See also *Milligan's Correlated Criminal Code & Selected Federal Statutes*, Butterworths, Toronto, 1979, Section 224; and *You and the Law*, Third. Edition, Reader's Digest Association, Westmount, Quebec, 1985, p. 814.

2 Law Reform Commission of Canada, *Euthanasia, Aiding Suicide and Cessation of Treatment*, Report No. 20, Ottawa, 1983, p. 31. This final position was much stronger than that recommended in the Commission's Working Paper No. 28. In that paper the Commission had recommended that the offence of aiding suicide should be retained, but because of the morally extenuating factors of compassion and altruism which are often involved, in practice it should be rarely invoked.

3 See Chapter 5, p. 98, above.

4 Ibid., pp. 95–97.

5 This example is similar to the famous Baby Jane Doe case in the United States:

> In late 1983 there was a great public controversy over an infant known to the public only as Baby Jane Doe. This unfortunate baby, born in New York State, suffered from multiple defects including spina bifida (a broken and protruding spine), hydrocephaly (excess fluid on the brain), and perhaps worst of all, microencephaly (an abnormally small brain). Immediate surgery was needed, but the parents chose not to authorize it, even though they knew that without surgery the baby could not live longer than two years. (James Rachels, *The Elements of Moral Philosophy*, Random House, New York, 1986, pp. 1–2)

Dr Koop, then the surgeon general of the United States, and certain right to life groups, tried to have the courts overrule the parents' decision, but the courts eventually sided with the parents and the surgery was never performed. In this case the Kantian would side with Dr Koop and the right to life groups, who argued that not to perform the surgery, even in this most difficult case, was a violation of Baby Jane Doe's right to life and her right not to be discriminated against because of her handicaps.

6 E.W. Keyserlingk, *Sanctity of Life or Quality of Life in the Context of Ethics, Medicine and Law*, Law Reform Commission of Canada, Ottawa, 1979, pp. 9–18.

7 Law Reform Commission of Canada, Working Paper No. 28, p. 8.

8 See Joseph and Julia Quinlan, *Karen Ann. The Quinlans Tell Their Story*, Bantam Books, New York, 1977.

9 Law Reform Commission of Canada, Working Paper No. 20, pp. 18, 21, 27–28.

10 See Arthur Schafer, 'A Question of Life or Death', *Globe and Mail*, 4 March 1992, p. A16.

11 Law Reform Commission of Canada, *Criteria for Determination of Death*, Report No. 15, Ottawa, 1981.

12 Alan Donagan, *The Theory of Morality*, University of Chicago Press, Chicago, 1977, p. 171.

13 It is currently suggested that the word 'handicapped' be replaced by the word 'challenged' because the former expresses a bias against this minority group. There is some merit in this claim but the recommended term, although less pejorative, does not capture the problem which the dilemma raises. In the end it is probably best to let the people involved decide for themselves what they wish to be called, and the dominant groups should normally accept their wishes.

14 See *Milligan's Correlated Criminal Code*, p. 197, and *You and The Law*, p. 471.

15 See Diane Frances, 'Banking on Artificial Blood', *Maclean's*, 17 December 1979, and Tom Harpur, 'Jehovah's Witnesses Split over Transfusions', *Toronto Star*, 20 January 1982, p. A27.

16 Immanuel Kant, *The Metaphysical Principles of Virtue*, translated by James Ellington, Liberal Arts, The Library of Indianapolis/Bobbs Merrill, New York, 1964, p. 83.

17 Ibid., pp. 84–85.

18 Donagan, *The Theory of Morality*, p. 78. Donagan also argues, p. 79, that suicide is morally permissible 'To obtain release from a life that had become, not merely hard to bear, but utterly dehumanized'.

19 See above Chapter 5.

20 Law Reform Commission of Canada, Report No. 20, pp. 21, 31.

21 See, for example, Derek Humphry, *The Right to Die* (1980) and *Final Exit* (1991), Hemlock Society, Eugene, Oregon. See also Jo Roman, *Exit House*, Seaview Books, New York, 1980.

22 Law Reform Commission of Canada, Working Paper No. 28, p. 52.

23 David Hume, 'On Suicide', in A. MacIntyre, *Hume's Ethical Writings*, Macmillan, 1965, pp. 297–308.

24 Cf. Richard Brandt, 'The Morality and Rationality of Suicide', in James Rachels (ed.), *Moral Problems*, Third Edition, Harper & Row, New York, 1979, p. 460. Brandt claims that this definition is morally neutral because it does not exclude so called 'heroic' or 'altruistic' suicides, but this claim seems moot.

25 Hume, 'On Suicide', p. 300.

26 Ibid., pp. 304–305.

27 Ibid., pp. 305–306.

28 Cf. J.S. Mill, *Utilitarianism* (1863), Bobbs Merrill, New York, 1957, pp. 59–61.

29 Cf. Kant, *The Metaphysical Principles of Virtue*, pp. 77ff.

30 For an insightful utilitarian analysis see Thomas Nagel, 'On Death', in Rachels (ed.), *Moral Problems*, pp. 449–459.

31 See Joseph and Julia Quinlan, *Karen Ann*.
32 Law Reform Commission of Canada, Working Paper No. 28 and Report No. 28.
33 Rachels, *The Elements of Moral Philosophy*, pp. 6–7.
34 Kant, *Metaphysical Principles of Virtue*, pp. 78–79.
35 J.S. Mill, *On Liberty* (1859), Bobbs Merrill, New York, 1956, Ch. 1.
36 E.g. Donagan argues in *The Theory of Morality* that suicide in certain cases is consistent with the principle of respect for persons.
37 'Do Not Go Gentle into that Good Night', in Dylan Thomas, *Collected Poems*, Dent, London, 1952, p. 116.

7 Moral quandary

1 The dilemma is based on a real incident which occurred in the nineteenth century. The USS *William Brown* foundered in rough seas and sank off Newfoundland in 1841. Life boats were manned. One boat, the long boat which had room for 60 passengers and crew, had been overloaded. There were 74 passengers and crew in the boat. The long boat was taking on water and the first mate thought it would soon sink in the rough seas. He ordered a sailor, seaman Holmes, to throw 14 people out of the boat. Thirteen men were tossed overboard, and one young woman leapt over to be with her lover who had been ejected. A few hours later the long boat and its passengers were rescued and taken to safety on another ship. Seaman Holmes was later arrested and charged with unlawful homicide. He was found guilty in a Philadelphia court and sentenced to life imprisonment. During the trial the criteria used to decide who should be sacrificed and who saved emerged. The first mate and the rowing team, all members of the crew of the *William Brown*, were spared, presumably so they could row the boat. Children were spared, as were married women, single women and married men. Bachelors, however, were deemed expendable. The selection criteria clearly represented the prevailing mores of the day. If the ship goes down, you save the women and children first, the men and the crew last, unless they are needed for the rescue operations. The defence generally used utilitarian arguments to make its case. The prosecution generally used Kantian arguments to make its case. Why the first mate was never charged with counselling or ordering unlawful homicide was not made clear, even when he appeared to define the criteria that cost the 13 bachelors their lives. See James F. Childress, 'Who Shall Live When Not All Can Live?', *Soundings*, Vol. 43, No. 4, Winter 1970.
2 James Rachels, *The Elements of Moral Philosophy*, Random House, New York, 1986, p. 7.
3 See Childress, 'Who Shall Live?'
4 See Shana Alexander, 'They Decide: Who Lives, Who Dies', *Life*, No. 53, 9 November 1962.
5 Peter Singer, 'Famine, Affluence, and Morality', in James Rachels (ed.), *Moral Problems*, Third Edition, Harper & Row, New York, 1979, pp. 263–278.
6 Ibid., p. 266.
7 James Rachels, 'Active and Passive Euthanasia', in his *Moral Problems*, pp. 493–494.

8 See Alexander, 'They Decide'.
9 The example is based on a real case involving a Pittsburgh asbestos worker named Robert McFall and his cousin, David Shimp, in 1978, discussed in Tom L. Beauchamp and James F. Childress, *Principles of Biomedical Ethics*, Second Edition, Oxford University Press, New York, 1983, pp. 315–317. I changed the relationship between the patient and the potential donor from cousins to brothers to make the case more difficult. For the same reason, I changed the donation from bone marrow to a kidney. Beauchamp and Childress provide useful discussions of the case, pp. 108 and 154. They agree that David Shimp had neither a duty of non-maleficence nor beneficence towards his cousin Robert McFall.
10 Garrett Harding, 'Lifeboat Ethics: the Case Against Helping the Poor', in Rachels (ed.), *Moral Problems*, pp. 279–292.
11 See Paul Thompson in my *The Moral Question: Ethical Theory*, TV Ontario, Toronto, 1982, pp. 40–41, for a useful rebuttal of Harding on these solutions.

8 Women's voices

1 *Getting Human Rights Enforced*, Ontario Human Rights Review Task Force, Toronto, 1992, p. 2.
2 Both equal rights and affirmative action programmes are protected by the Canadian Charter of Rights and Freedoms; see section 15.
3 See Richard Wasserstrom, 'Rights, Human Rights, and Racial Discrimination', in James Rachels (ed.), *Moral Problems*, Third Edition, Harper & Row, New York, 1979, pp. 7–11.
4 See *Personal and Societal Values*, Ontario Ministry of Education, Toronto, 1983, and *Teaching and Learning at York University*, Toronto, 1990, pp. 10–12.
5 See, United States Supreme Court, 'University of California v. Bakke (1978)', in Rachels (ed.), *Moral Problems*, pp. 60–82.
6 See Betty Rozack, 'Women's Liberation', in Rachels (ed.), *Moral Problems*, pp. 25–35.
7 Carol Gilligan, *In a Different Voice*, Harvard University Press, Cambridge, Massachusetts, 1982.
8 Lawrence Kohlberg, *The Philosophy of Moral Development*, Harper & Row, New York, 1981.
9 Ibid., pp. 409–412. Kolhberg subdivides each of his three main stages into two, giving him a total of six stages. This complexity in his theory is not important to the debate between him and Gilligan.
10 Gilligan, *In a Different Voice*, p. 30.
11 Ibid., p. 31.
12 See Annette C. Baier, 'Hume, the Woman's Moral Theorist?', in E.F. Kittay and D. Meyers (eds), *Women and Moral Theory*, Rowman & Littlefield, Totowa, New Jersey, 1987, pp. 37–55, for a very useful discussion of the relations between utilitarianism and feminist ethics. Feminists tend to reject utilitarianism because its methodology is masculine, even if its basic moral principles are feminine. Baier demonstrates that the affinities between feminism and utilitarianism are much greater than this.

13 Gilligan, *In a Different Voice*, pp. 71ff.

14 See E.W. Pelrine, *Abortion in Canada*, New Press, Toronto, 1972, for a generally liberal utilitarian defence of the pro-choice position.

15 See United States Supreme Court, 'Roe v. Wade', in Rachels (ed.), *Moral Problems*, pp. 109–117.

16 See Pelrine, *Abortion in Canada*, and 'Law, Politics Feel Impact of Charter', *Toronto Star*, 11 April 1992, p. A12.

17 *Milligan's Correlated Criminal Code*, Butterworths, Toronto, 1979, pp. 205–209.

18 See L.E. Rosovsky, *The Canadian Patient's Book of Rights*, Doubleday Canada, Toronto, 1980, and *Patients' Rights in Ontario*, The Ontario Patients' Rights Association, Toronto, 1980.

19 Judith Jarvis Thompson, 'A Defense of Abortion', in Rachels (ed.), *Moral Problems*, pp. 130–150. Thompson argues with considerable ingenuity that an abortion can be morally permissible even if the foetus is a human being with a right to life. Women are not necessarily obligated to give their bodies over to others to keep them alive, especially without informed consent, i.e. rape and incest.

20 See *Milligan's Correlated Criminal Code*, pp. 34–38.

21 See Paul Thompson in my *The Moral Question: Ethical Theory*, TV Ontario, Toronto, 1982, pp. 34–36, for an insightful defence of the self-defence argument in the context of abortion.

22 See, for example, ibid., pp. 32–34.

23 Michael Tooley, 'Abortion and Infanticide', *Philosophy and Public Affairs*, Vol. 2, No. 1, 1972, pp. 37–65.

24 See, for example, Wayne Sumner, *Abortion and Moral Theory*, Princeton University Press, Princeton, New Jersey, 1981.

25 R.M. Hare, 'Abortion and the Golden Rule', in Rachels (ed.), *Moral Problems*, pp. 151–173.

26 See Wasserstrom, 'Rights, Human Rights, and Racial Discrimination', pp. 7–24.

27 *Canadian Charter of Rights and Freedoms*, section 15, Carswell, Toronto, 1989.

28 See, for example, F. Weizmann, N. Wiener, D. Wiesenthal and M. Ziegler, *Scientific Racism*, Dept. of Psychology, York University, Toronto, Report No. 180, March 1988.

29 See my *Ethical Theory*, p. 37, for a discussion of positive and negative rights.

30 *Canadian Charter of Rights and Freedoms*, section 15.

31 See United States Supreme Court, 'University of California v. Bakke', in Rachels (ed.), *Moral Problems*, pp. 60–82.

32 See 'Case of Reverse Discrimination Polarized Groups over Rights Issues', *Globe and Mail*, 7 February 1989, p. A2.

33 Ann Dummet, 'Racism and Sexism, a False Analogy', in Rachels (ed.), *Moral Problems*, pp. 36–47.

34 Kolhberg, *The Philosophy of Moral Development*, p. 354. Kohlberg accepted the need to modify his stage theory in the light of Gilligan's research but he still holds that his Rawlsean/Kantian-type theory is fundamental. He believes that a morality of Agape or love presupposes a morality of justice.

35 Gilligan, *In a Different Voice*, pp. 5–23.

36 See John T. Noonan, *How to Argue about Abortion*, Ad Hoc Defense of Life Committee, New York, 1974, for a generally conservative Kantian-type defence of the pro-life position.

37 See Rosovsky, *The Patient's Book of Rights*.

38 In Canada the legal status of the foetus is unclear but there has been some effort to protect the unborn legally as a result of the abortion debate. See *You and The Law*, Third Edition, Reader's Digest Association, Westmount, Quebec, 1985: 'The Rights of the Unborn', pp. 464–465.

39 See for example, Alan Donagan, *The Theory of Morality*, University of Chicago Press, Chicago, 1977, p. 83.

40 See Thompson, *The Moral Question*, pp. 32–34.

41 Ibid., p. 33.

42 See Donagan, *The Theory of Morality*, pp. 157–171, for a useful discussion of the morality of abortion and contraception from a Kantian perspective.

9 Global ethics

1 Cf. my article 'Towards a Unified System of Ethics', in Douglas Odegard (ed.), *Ethics and Justification*, Academic Printing & Publishing, Edmonton, Alberta, 1988, pp. 168–69. Nuclear technology raises many other moral problems. The more fundamental moral problem might be nuclear technology itself rather than the international sale of nuclear technology.

2 The dilemma is based on real problems surrounding the sale of Candu nuclear reactors in the late 1960s and 1970s. The main source for the example was programmes broadcast on 8 and 15 November 1977 by the Canadian Broadcasting Corporation (CBC), in the current affairs series 'The Fifth Estate', hosted by Eric Mallin. 'The Fifth Estate' programmes grew out of an investigation by the Public Accounts Committee of the Canadian Parliament into the financial affairs relating to the sale of Candu nuclear reactors by Atomic Energy of Canada, the crown corporation that developed and markets Candus. Chaired by Allan Lawrence (Progressive Conservative MP, Toronto), the Public Accounts Committee raised serious questions concerning the manner and the morality of the sale of Candus to Argentina and South Korea. The auditor general of Canada had reported the previous year that some C$25 million of AEC expenditures were unaccounted for. There were no receipts and no record of where the money had gone. Under questioning by the committee, AEC officials explained that the money had been used to pay fees to foreign commercial agents who were hired to help market the Candus during the period 1972–74. These explanations were still not acceptable to the committee because they left unexplained how the money was actually spent. The committee thought that the AEC had displayed poor business practice if not something worse. The CBC's 'Fifth Estate' investigation established firmly that some of the missing money was used for bribing Argentinian government officials and armed forces officers. They discovered that the AEC had entered into partnership with an Italian corporation, whose managing director knew the Argentinian market well. They also learned that at least C$1.5 million went to high ranking officers in the Argentinian Air Force. They were not able to identify the government

officials involved but a later investigation by the Argentinian government revealed that José Galbard, the minister of economics, had received a C\$4 million bribe, which was instrumental in tipping the scales in favour of Canada and against the USA, our closest competitor. See Peter Moon, 'Disputes, Scandals Plague Candu Sales', *Globe and Mail*, 28 December 1990. The 'Fifth Estate' also established with high probability that some of the C\$18.5 million fee paid to Saul Isenberg, an Israeli entrepreneur hired to facilitate the South Korean sale, was used to bribe South Korean government officials.

3 See Chapter 2, p. 32, above.
4 See my *Moral Theory*, TV Ontario, Toronto, 1982, pp. 11–12.
5 J.S. Mill, *Utilitarianism* (1863), Bobbs Merrill, New York, 1957, pp. 27–28. There Mill argues that utilitarianism, although not derived from or dependent on Christian ethics, is compatible with the ethics propounded by Jesus in the New Testament.
6 Joseph Fletcher, *Situation Ethics*, Westminster Press, Philadelphia, 1966.
7 See my *Moral Theory*, pp. 12–13.
8 May and Abraham Edel, *Anthropology and Ethics*, Thomas, Illinois, 1959, pp. 34–43.
9 Ibid., pp. 44–67.
10 The use of commercial agents certainly helped the AEC sell Candu reactors. After the scandal it apparently stopped the practice and sales fell off once more. The AEC did not sell any more Candus until 1981, when it made sales to Romania, which was still under the control of Nicolae Ceausescu. The Romanian sale, however, remained under a different moral cloud because of the dreadful living conditions of workers who were building Candu power stations. See 'Romanian Candu Poses a Dilemma', *Toronto Star*, 5 January 1990, p. A24. A second reactor was sold to South Korea in 1990 in what seem less controversial moral circumstances. See Moon, 'Disputes, Scandals Plague Candu Sales'.
11 This example, adapted to a Canadian context, is taken from a widely used example in business ethics. Cf. T. Donaldson and P.H. Werhane, *Ethical Issues in Business*, Prentice-Hall, Englewood Cliffs, New Jersey, 1983, pp. 84–86. See my 'Business Ethics in the Global Village', in Douglas Odegard and Carole Stewart (eds), *Perspectives on Moral Relativism*, Agathon Books, Toronto, 1991, pp. 103–112, on which much of this chapter is based.
12 Cf. T. Donaldson, 'Multi-national Decision Making: Reconciling International Norms', in Anthony Ellis (ed.), *Ethics and International Relations*, Manchester University Press, Manchester, 1986, p. 29.
13 In the real case, as the CBC 'Fifth Estate' programmes demonstrated, Kantian arguments were generally put forward by critics of the AEC, while those who defended the AEC, including the management, used mostly utilitarian arguments. Allan Lawrence, the chair of the Public Accounts Committee, was among those who morally chastised the AEC for its use of bribery to sell Candu reactors. Lorne Grey, then the managing director of the AEC, denied any knowledge of bribes or other wrongdoings on the part of the commercial agents the AEC had hired to market Candus. He said that he did not know what had happened to the money and frankly he didn't care. The agents were hired because the AEC thought them competent and responsible. Besides, they were successful and this was what

both the Canadian government and the Canadian people expected of a crown corporation.

14 Adapted to a Canadian context from Donaldson, 'Multi-national Decision Making', pp. 128–129.
15 See *Globe and Mail*, 20 April 1989.
16 Cf. J.T. Noonan Jr, *Bribes*, Macmillan, New York, 1984.
17 Hugh Lehman, 'Equal Pay for Equal Work in Third World', in Ellis (ed.), *Ethics and International Relations*, pp. 155–162, gives an excellent analysis of the problem. Lehman is not entirely utilitarian as his analysis recognizes the Kantian dimensions of the problem.

10 The expanding moral universe

1 The dilemma is derived from the now famous Donald MacAlpine case. See Jamie Swift, 'Cut and Run, the MacAlpine Case: Power vs. Ethics in the Forest', *Harrowsmith*, Vol. 8, No. 3, October/November, 1983, pp. 38–54 and *Cut and Run*, Between the Lines, Toronto, 1983, Ch. 8, pp. 231–265. Donald MacAlpine was fired by the Ontario Ministry of Natural Resources (OMNR) in 1982 for publicly criticizing OMNR's forest management policy. The OMNR claimed that MacAlpine had acted unprofessionally by breaking the oath of confidentiality which all Ontario public servants are required to take and by violating the whistle blowing procedures laid down in the code of ethics of the Ontario Professional Foresters Association (OPFA) by not discussing the matter with the minister before going public.
   MacAlpine, a recent graduate in forestry from Lakehead University, Thunder Bay, Ontario, had been asked by the OMNR to grant a licence to Buchanan Forest Product Limited to cut timber on Black Bay Peninsula on Lake Superior. He refused to do so on the grounds of good forest management. His department insisted he issue the licence in any case. MacAlpine refused once more and appealed to the Ontario Professional Foresters Association for help, but they dismissed his appeal. He then released the story to the local papers and when the news broke he was fired by the OMNR for unprofessional conduct. He took his case to the Ontario Civil Service Review Board and was reinstated.
2 *The New English Bible*, Oxford University Press/Cambridge University Press, London, 1970, p. 2.
3 Immanuel Kant, *The Groundwork of the Metaphysics of Morals* (ed. H.J. Paton), Harper & Row, New York, 1964, p. 96.
4 Immanuel Kant, *The Metaphysical Principles of Virtue*, Bobbs Merrill, New York, 1964, p. 106.
5 See for example the pamphlet by H.C. Rowsell and A.A. McWilliam, 'The Animal in Research; Domination or Stewardship', Canadian Council on Animal Welfare, Ottawa, 1979.
6 Kant, *The Metaphysical Principles of Virtue*, p. 106.
7 See for example the pamphlet 'Surveillance over the Care and Use of Experimental Animals in Canada', Canadian Council on Animal Care, Ottawa, 1979.
8 See for example C.D. Stone, *Should Trees Have Standing?* Avon Books, New York, 1975.

9   Christopher P. McKay, 'Does Mars Have Rights?', in my *Moral Expertise*, Routledge, London, 1990.

10 Kant, *The Metaphysical Principles of Virtue*, p. 106.

11 See Laura Westra, 'Public Steward or Government Servant?', *Philosophy in Context*, Vol. 17, 1987, pp. 26–39. Westra grants that MacAlpine ought to have contacted Allan Pope, the then minister in charge of the OMNR, but still makes a very strong case for saying that he acted in conformity with the codes of ethics of both the OPFA and the OMNR. Her basic argument is that both codes place an obligation on foresters and civil servants to act in the public good. Since MacAlpine was acting in the public interest his whistle blowing was not unprofessional. His duty to the public took precedence over his duty to the government and this justified his breach of the confidentiality oath. Westra admits that her defence of MacAlpine depends on interpreting the ambiguities of the codes, especially the concept of 'the public good' which is vague in both codes, in his favour. Her defence then is problematic if she argues that MacAlpine did not break the letter of the codes but perhaps very strong if she argues that he acted in the spirit of the codes.

12 The term 'zoo-centric' was suggested to me by my colleague Peter Penz of the Faculty of Environmental Studies, York University, Toronto.

13 J.S. Mill, *Utilitarianism*, Bobbs Merrill, New York, 1957, p. 16.

14 Peter Singer, 'Animal Liberation', in James Rachels (ed.), *Moral Problems*, Third Edition, Harper & Row, New York, 1979, pp. 93–94.

15 Ibid., pp. 83–100.

16 See for example Mary Midgley, *Animals and Why They Matter*, Penguin Books, Harmondsworth, 1983.

17 See A. MacIntyre, *Hume's Ethical Writings*, Macmillan, 1965, pp. 41–42.

18 For a fuller discussion of the concept of speciesism, see Peter Singer, *Animal Liberation*, Avon Books, New York, 1975.

19 See Singer, 'Animal Liberation', p. 91.

20 See James Gorman, 'The Burden of the Beasts', *Discover*, February 1981, pp. 22ff.

21 Ibid.

22 Peter Singer, *Practical Ethics*, Cambridge University Press, Cambridge, 1979, especially pp. 93–105. Singer argues that some animals, like apes, dolphins, dogs and cats, can be classified as 'persons' in the Kantian sense, and so ought to be treated with equality, like other moral agents.

23 James Rachels, *The Elements of Moral Philosophy*, Random House, New York, 1986, pp. 88–89.

24 See for example John A. Livingston, *The Fallacy of Wildlife Conservation*, McLelland & Stewart, Toronto, 1982, and Arne Naess, 'The Shallow and Deep Long Range Ecology Movement: A Summary', *Inquiry*, Vol. 16, 1973, pp. 95–100.

25 B.G. Norton, 'Environmental Ethics and Non-Human Rights', *Environmental Ethics*, Vol. 14, Spring 1982. I have expanded the example to include animals. In the real case some animal species would also have suffered.

26 See Lynn White, 'The Historic Roots of Our Ecological Crises', *Science*, March 1967.

27 See Swift, *Cut and Run*, Ch. 2, pp. 28–49.

28 See B.G. Norton, 'Environmental Ethics and Non-Human Rights', pp. 18–19.
29 I owe this example to Peter Timmerman of the Institute of Environmental Studies, University of Toronto.
30 See Robert H. Haynes and Christopher McKay, 'Ethics and Planetary Engineering', in my *Moral Expertise*, Routledge, London, 1990, pp. 161–197.

Index